SHIPWRECK TALES

OF

THE GREAT LAKES

"....Wrecks, explosions, beachings, collisions, and founderings without number have marked the short, but eventful history of navigation on the Great Lakes. It is an awful death list, 400 and 500 in a single season, that the beautiful Great Lakes have claimed as their prey. Is it any wonder that they have gained for themselves the reputation of being the most perilous bodies of water in the world?...."

> --- from an article titled "Tragic Mysteries of the Great Lakes" by J. Edgar Lyons, published in the *Vermilion* (Ohio) *News* on March 8, 1906.

"....strange things happen on the Inland Seas, as on the oceans."

> --- from the book *The Great Lakes and The Vessels That Plough Them* by James Oliver Curwood (1909).

BOOKS BY CRIS KOHL:

Dive Southwestern Ontario! (1985)

Shipwreck Tales: The St. Clair River (to 1900) (1987)

DIVE ONTARIO! The Guide to Shipwrecks and Scuba Diving (1990)

DIVE ONTARIO TWO! More Ontario Shipwreck Stories (1994)

Treacherous Waters: Kingston's Shipwrecks (1997)

The 100 Best Great Lakes Shipwrecks, Volume I (1998)

The 100 Best Great Lakes Shipwrecks, Volume II (1998)

TITANIC, The Great Lakes Connections (2000)

The Great Lakes Diving Guide (2001)

Shipwreck Tales of the Great Lakes (2004)

SHIPWRECK TALES

OF THE

GREAT LAKES

CRIS KOHL

SEAWOLF
Communications

Seawolf Communications, Inc.
PO Box 66
West Chicago, IL 60186
USA

ISBN 0-9679976-7-4 (cloth)

First Edition
1   3   5   7   9   10   8   6   4   2

Printed and bound in the United States of America on acid-free paper

ISBN 0-9679976-4-X (paper)

Library of Congress Control Number: 2003103326

FRONT COVER PHOTO, INSET: The first ship to sail the waters of the upper Great Lakes in 1679 had to be pulled through the fast-flowing St. Clair River into Lake Huron. The *Griffon's* first trip was also her last, establishing the inland seas' greatest mystery. Artist Stan Norris of Sarnia, Ontario, painted this scene in the 1970's; it is displayed at the Moore Museum in Mooretown, Ontario. The *Griffon's* story begins on page 9. ART COURTESY OF, AND COPYRIGHT © BY, STAN NORRIS

FRONT COVER PHOTO, BACKGROUND (AND TITLE PAGE BLACK-AND-WHITE BACKGROUND PHOTO): In May, 1986, a scuba diver located this pristine shipwreck of an 1870's schooner in 185 feet of water. The story of the *Cornelia B. Windiate* begins on page 101. PHOTO BY CRIS KOHL

BACK COVER PHOTOS: 1. *Griffon* shipwreck timber? PHOTO BY CRIS KOHL. 2. Archival postcard of the steamer *Tashmoo*. CRIS KOHL COLLECTION. 3. Diver/historian Doug Pettingill on the wreck of the *George A. Marsh* wreck. PHOTO BY CRIS KOHL. 4. The raising of the "mystery ship" schooner from Green Bay in 1969. PHOTO BY AND © BY DR. RICHARD BOYD. 5. Birdseye view of Chicago's Streeterville area. PHOTO BY CRIS KOHL. 6. Archival postcard of the Convict Ship *Success*. CRIS KOHL COLLECTION. BACKGROUND: Maritime historian Cris Kohl on a tugboat at Duluth. PHOTO BY AND © BY CHET CHILDS.

INTRODUCTION

The Great Lakes are the largest collective body of fresh water in the world. The inland seas are also a waterway system which opened up the center of the continent, allowing people and goods to be transported deep inside the heart of North America.

An incredibly active maritime presence over the past 300 years spurred the development of the Great Lakes. Large, lively shoreline cities such as Toronto, Buffalo, Cleveland, Detroit, Milwaukee -- and the largest and liveliest of them all, Chicago -- along with numerous other cities and towns, owe their positions and status today to yesterday's Great Lakes maritime bustle when thousands of sail and steam ships energetically ventured in commerce and construction, and helped put the cities of the inland seas on the map. These were the ships -- the schooners and the steamers and the sidewheel paddlewheelers -- and the men and the women -- the sailors and the cooks and the passengers -- in an age when the blue waters of the Great Lakes propelled the golden hue of measurable, magnificent progress -- that made the North American continent the impressive force it is today.

Most Americans and Canadians today are unaware of the extent of the maritime influence which carried the torch of development and growth to the far corners of the Great Lakes and beyond. They are not aware that over 20,000 different commercial ships have sliced across these freshwater seas in the past 300 years, and that a third of them became shipwrecks here, often under amazingly dramatic and/or utterly tragic circumstances. They are unaware that the cold, fresh waters of the Great Lakes have provided us with the best preserved shipwrecks in the world, and that scuba divers today have a vast choice of exploration opportunities from among more than 1,000 shipwrecks -- ice water museums -- which have been located to date. Most people are unaware that the magnitude of Great Lakes maritime history easily matches that of more traditional nautical areas like New England or Florida.

Here are dramatic stories, told in chronological order, about Great Lakes shipwrecks and which put human faces onto those tragedies -- tales laced with murder and mystery, deception and mayhem, humor and honor, dignity and glory. Read about the many quests for the fabled *Griffon*, the first ship (and the first shipwreck!) on the upper Great Lakes, lost with all hands in 1679; discover the sheriff's horrible secrets about the wrecked schooner, *Explorer*; learn how a shipwrecked steamer and its eccentric captain literally helped build Chicago; discover how one captain kept his shipwreck survival a secret; uncover the lesson we failed to learn when a well-meaning bartender raised an entire shipwreck from the Great Lakes in 1969.

Truth is stranger than fiction. Stay warm and dry in your armchair as this book transports you through cold waters and into incredible Great Lakes maritime history.

Cris Kohl
High Lake, Illinois
Summer, 2004

ACKNOWLEDGEMENTS

No book is the product of a single writer, without access to human resources and research facilities, no matter how highly that writer regards himself. In all aspects of life, things become easier when we get a little help from our friends (a familiar notion).

In these economic times, when museums and archives are experiencing financial challenges, several fountainheads of affordable source information still flow.

This author's sincere *Thank You* goes out to the following individuals and organizations (with their staffs) for their contributions and assistance in the undertaking of this book:

Henry Barkhausen, C. Patrick Labadie, Ralph Roberts, Rev. Peter Van der Linden, the late Dr. Richard Wright, the late Herman Runge, Clive Cussler, Joyce Hayward, Darryl Ertel, Steve Whitman, Dean Ziegler, Doug Pettingill, James Taylor, Susan Yankoo, George Wheeler, Jim Jarecki, Pete Chval, Keith Pearson, Chet Childs, Joe Oliver, Howard Openlander, Valerie Olson van Heest, Mary G. Creasey, Judy Liddle, Dr. Richard Boyd, Dr. John Halsey, Dr. Charles & Jeri Feltner, Peter Engelbert, John Steele, Paul Ehorn, Steve Radovan, Dave Trotter and Undersea Research Associates, Mark Kismer, Richard Palmer, Linda Parrish, Gwen Wilson Zwick, Tom Farnquist, Bob Geno, Sean Moore, James A. Andrews, Robert McGreevy, Stan Norris, the late Paul LaPointe, and the late Don Edwards.

The former Institute for Great Lakes Research, Bowling Green State University (OH) (absorbed into the Archival Collections of Bowling Green State University, which I also thank wholeheartedly, particularly Robert Graham and his assistants), the National Archives (Great Lakes branch), the Great Lakes Marine Collection of the Milwaukee Public Library/ Wisconsin Marine Historical Society, the Great Lakes Historical Society, Vermilion (OH), the Manitowoc (WI) Maritime Museum, Manitowoc (WI) Public Library, the West Chicago Public Library, the Oswego (NY) Public Library, the Door County Public Library at Sturgeon Bay (WI), the St. Clair County Public Library in Port Huron (MI), the Michigan State Historical Library in Lansing, the Boston (MA) Public Library, the Harrah (OK) Historical Society, the Harrah (OK) Public Library, the Oklahoma State Historical Library, the Oklahoma Grand Lodge, Don Cochran (Venango Museum of Art, Science & Industry, Oil City, PA), the Rutherford B. Hayes Presidential Center in Fremont (OH), the Chicago Public Library, the Chicago Maritime Society and the Underwater Archaeological Society of Chicago.

I thank the following Canadian organizations, all in Ontario: the Gore Bay Museum, the Mississagi Straits Lighthouse Museum and Park (particularly Peggy Mullen and Helen Van Every), the Net Shed Museum in Meldrum Bay, the Public Archives of Canada in Ottawa, the Chatham Public Library, the Chatham-Kent Museum (particularly curator Tanya Neave), the Goderich Public Library (in particular, Karen Blackwell), the Sarnia Public Library (particularly Jeffrey Allan Beeler), Canada Steamship Lines in Montréal (particularly Communications Co-ordinator Jane Chong), the Marine Museum of the Great Lakes at Kingston, the Metropolitan Toronto Public Library, and Save Ontario Shipwrecks.

An intensely heartfelt *Thank You* to Jim and Pat Stayer for assistance ranging from their boating generosity (and skills) to computer training sessions, with much in between.

My apologies to anyone I may have inadvertently overlooked.

The largest *Thank You* goes to my patient wife, Joan Forsberg, who worked enthusiastically as my proofreader, insightful editor, research assistant, underwater model, travel buddy, personal trainer and unflinching believer. She is absolutely the best.

CONTENTS

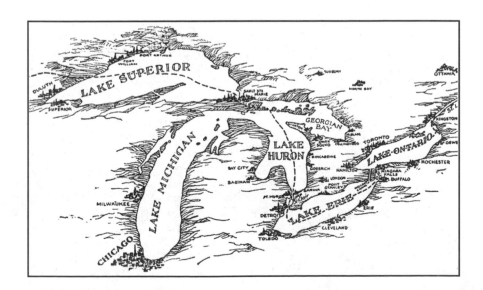

DEDICATION:

To all those who preserve and disseminate

Great Lakes Maritime History,

particularly

Henry Barkhausen, C. Patrick Labadie,

Ralph Roberts, Rev. Peter Van der Linden,

and the late Herman Runge and Dr. Richard Wright,

whose work

must not be lost or forgotten

THE GREAT LAKES'
SECOND-OLDEST SHIPWRECK

O ne of the smallest of the commercial ships ever to ply Great Lakes waters has the largest reputation of them all. And what a reputation it is! Born of one man's desperate need for money, laced with an overwhelming desire for empire, literally hacked out of a northern wilderness in winter, launched with backward glances in life-threatening circumstances, sailed across rock-and-reef-flecked lakes, pulled up swiftwater rivers, jubilantly loaded with a fortune in furs and mysteriously lost at an undetermined location while undermanned by a grumbling crew, the dramatic tale of the barque *Griffon* has not diminished in its impact during an enigmatic history spanning more than 325 years. Often wrongly dubbed "First Ship on the Great Lakes" or "The Great Lakes' First Shipwreck," the commanding distinction of the *Griffon* in Great Lakes maritime history does not need to be complemented by such incorrect claims to fame.

Numerous expeditions have been launched to locate this fabled and elusive historic shipwreck in hopes of solving the greatest mystery of the Great Lakes. All have failed, but optimism remains and searches continue, prompting this writer, in one of his earlier books, to describe the *Griffon* as "the dream of maritime archaeologists" and the "holy grail of freshwater shipwrecks."

Profile of the barque Le Griffon.
CRIS KOHL COLLECTION

The story of this long-lost ship, the *Griffon*, begins with the arrival of a robust 22-year-old French explorer/adventurer/fortune-seeker named Réné Robert Cavelier, better known in history by his title, Sieur de la Salle, or simply, La Salle, in Montréal in the year 1666. Much has been written about this notable character, detailing his well-documented life, so only some of the significant points of his history, key to an understanding of the *Griffon* story, will here be related.

Born in Rouen, France, on November 21, 1643, La Salle, after receiving a Jesuit (the religious order of the Society of Jesus) education, offered to devote his life to that Roman Catholic branch. Specifically, La Salle wished very much to be sent to work at the Jesuit mission in China, which at that time could be reached only by means of a long and perilous journey departing from Portugal and sailing around Africa's Cape of Good Hope, then eastward past India. The proud and stubborn La Salle even offered the Society of Jesus a monetary bribe, 8,000 French *livres* to be contributed to the Chinese Mission by his pecunious parents. The Jesuit authorities, however, viewed this merely as La Salle's yearning for the glory which might become his for the work he would do in such a remote and exotic location, and, suspecting that La Salle's ambitious personal character traits did not mix well with the selfless Jesuits' spiritual goals, they denied his request.

La Salle.

This drawing suggests that he led a dandy's existence in civilization, but this rugged explorer spent much of his life facing the hardships of the wilderness.

CRIS KOHL COLLECTION

La Salle's restless, domineering nature eventually forced him to petition the Society of Jesus for release from the religious vows he had taken. The Jesuits agreed that his temperament made him a poor candidate for the priesthood, and released him. Although La Salle remained unquestioningly faithful to his religion for the rest of his life, his relationship with the Jesuits likewise stayed strained.

La Salle had received inviting accounts of life in the "New World" from his missionary brother in Canada and also from a cousin who had become a successful businessman in Montréal. These quickly paved the way for his journey across the Atlantic Ocean to New France, the French colonial possessions in Canada (basically the present-day provinces of Québec, New Brunswick and Nova Scotia).

In 1667, the colony of New France consisted of a series of villages randomly dappling both sides of the mighty St. Lawrence River. The largest towns were Montréal, with a population of 625, Trois Riviéres with 455, and Québec (today named Québec City to differentiate it from the Canadian province of Québec), with 550 people living in 70 closely constructed houses, the most developed community in terms of buildings in the entire colony.

In Montréal, a religious connection from his brother's Sulpician order offered La Salle a seigneury, that is, a long strip of land to which he would have feudal rights, at a nearby strategic but wild area bordering the St. Lawrence River. La Salle named his lands La Chine, French for "China"-- with obvious optimism about the close proximity of Asia. Since the time of Christopher Columbus 200 years earlier, explorers of the North American continent sought a route to the Orient which they, the French included, thought surely existed. Today, the name of La Salle's large tract of land outside Montréal retains a close spelling: Lachine.

At La Chine, La Salle established a palisaded fort and a trading post, while also subletting his new land to farmers. He himself studied Indian dialects and whatever vague maps he could find of the lands to the west and south of him. His imagination convinced him that the Great Lakes, sprinkled portions of which had just begun to be explored, mainly by Jesuit missionaries in the preceding 50 years, somehow had to lead to the shores of the

For centuries, the birchbark canoe was the sole mode of transportation used on the Great Lakes and beyond by Indians and, later, fur trading French-Canadian voyageurs, or coureurs de bois, *the "runners of the woods." This illustration shows the positioning of the crew, the goods, and, in this case, the non-paddling passengers.*
ORIGINAL PAINTING BY MRS. HOPKINS. PUBLIC ARCHIVES MUSEUM, OTTAWA

Orient. Such was the limited extent of geographical knowledge in the late 1600's, and so strong was La Salle's lifelong goal of reaching China.

La Salle, determined to fill in many of the blanks comprising the *terra incognito* in the interior of North America, felt concern that the Dutch, the English and the Spanish would seek to expand their own territorial and trade relation horizons in the New World. The Dutch were established in New Amsterdam (New York), the English in numerous east coast colonies speckled from Massachusetts to Virginia and Carolina, and the Spanish controlled Florida, California and Mexico, not to mention vast portions of Central and South America.

The Spanish, however, were lured only by the immense mineral wealth (gold and silver) so noticeably present in the southern lands, content to leave the northern portion of the New World to other Europeans. French attention from the very beginning focused on the treasure of the rich fur trade in the St. Lawrence River watershed's northern portion, a system which pierced the heart of the continent and conveniently provided transportation access, via the ubiquitous canoe, upon its seemingly limitless and interconnected highways of lakes and rivers. Rumors of the potentially lucrative trade in animal pelts in the unexplored Mississippi River system also aroused interest among the Montréal merchants.

In a massive threat to French colonial expansion in 1670, the English court granted a charter to a new fur trading company for rights to expand and do business, specifically the commerce of fur trading, in all the lands of North America whose waters drained into Hudson Bay. This formidable stretch of real estate, soon to be dotted with British outposts, would effectively block French expansion to the west and north of New France. To this day, that company, the Hudson's Bay Company, has a large commercial presence in Canada.

La Salle, eager to assert a strong French presence on the largely unexplored Great Lakes and Mississippi River, sought financial backing from the government of New France. With perfect tunnel vision, it refused him any assistance, believing his plan to be mainly a personal commercial scheme which should be backed by private capital instead of government funds.

French authority over business policies had difficulty extending control over the so-called "free traders," merchants and their freebooting workers involved in illicit trade, including the fur trade, for whom any means of making money was legitimate, including selling their furs and other products to the Dutch and to the English. Montréal was full of free traders, both open and clandestine.

La Salle, with his honesty, lofty ideals and ambitious plans, often interfered with the free traders' underhanded means of keeping business from others and making fast money for themselves. Understandably, the ambitious explorer soon met with stubborn resistance from Montréal's wolves of commerce. La Salle's ensnarement in a tangle of debts owed to his enemies would be his downfall.

La Salle put his personal fortune on the line in his efforts to expand his country's sphere of influence, but his repeated application for government funding indicates his concern over the use of his own limited and dwindling supply of money.

Count Frontenac, the new governor of New France, whose independent nature quickly earned him the nickname "The Fighting Governor," and La Salle formed strong bonds of friendship, but even so, government money eluded La Salle's projects.

At the recommendation of Count Frontenac, La Salle returned to France in 1674 and presented himself to the French court with his ideas for French expansion. The court gave La Salle, with certain stipulations on how to manage it, the valuable and strategic seigneury of Fort Frontenac (where today the city of Kingston, Ontario, stands) on the shores of Lake Ontario.

Homeward bound in 1675, La Salle met a young (about a year older than himself) friar on board the ship carrying them to New France. Father Louis Hennepin's eyes blazed as he regaled La Salle with stories he had overheard when he hid himself behind the doors of disreputable taverns in French ports just to hear the sailors' thrilling stories of their exciting experiences across the seas. Hennepin animatedly told La Salle about his hopes for exciting experiences in the new land. Three years later, La Salle would remember this man's energetic enthusiasm and lust for adventure.

Upon La Salle's return to New France, he reconstructed and enlarged the fort at his seigneury on the eastern end of Lake Ontario. From that location, he would base his future explorations.

Not everyone in New France, even among the influential business class, wished La Salle success. Montréal's merchants viewed La Salle's new location as a business threat, even more so when they learned that he planned to expand his commercial concerns towards the unexplored southwest. Even the pious black-robed Jesuits, put off by Count Frontenac's aloofness towards them, spread the story that Frontenac's friend, La Salle, was conspiring to engage in illicit trade through his position at Fort Frontenac.

The fort prospered under La Salle's guiding hand, and in 1677, with the strongest recommendations from an impressed Count Frontenac, La Salle returned to France with more experience, a more impressive resumé and solid plans for more explorations and the establishment of commercial centers in the lands which would be newly claimed for France. Count

Frontenac, eager for commercial expansion beyond New France, had been repeatedly frustrated by the Great Lakes Jesuit missions which opposed the fur trade (because, they claimed, it supplied the Indians with brandy, and commerce generally hindered the main Jesuit purpose of converting the natives to Christianity), set up La Salle with numerous supporters in the royal court who were known to oppose the Jesuits.

La Salle spent many months in Paris awaiting the King's decision about his proposals. Meanwhile, the man from New France found little appeal in the glamorous and civilized aspects of life in the French capital. Physically, the vast labyrinth of narrow, winding streets made him feel claustrophobic, while the clamor and noise confused him. He longed for the quiet, wilderness panoramas of the New World. La Salle once wrote to a colleague, "I have chosen a life suited to my solitary nature."

Finally, permission was granted to La Salle to develop navigation and shipping on the Great Lakes and to construct an additional ship to explore thoroughly that mysterious river called the Mississippi.

The precise wording of the French King, Louis XIV's, proclamation, issued on May 12, 1678, included these words, in which the capitalized first-person-plural pronouns (as was the habit of European monarchs of that era) refer to the King who is doing the proclaiming:

> *To Our dear and well beloved...Sieur de la Salle, GREETING: We have favorably received the most humble petition presented to Us in your name, to permit you to discover the Western part of New France; and We have more willingly assented to that proposal as there is nothing We have more at heart than the Discovery of the Country, where there is a prospect of finding a way to penetrate as far as Mexico...signed by Our hand, [We] do permit you to labor in the Discovery...and to construct forts in the places you may think necessary...on condition...that you complete your enterprise within five years...and that you perform the whole at your own expense and that of your associates, to whom We have granted as a privilege, the trade in furs of the region....*

A few other conditions, forbidding trade with certain tribes such as the Ottawas, for example, were also outlined. However, the King granted La Salle a monopoly of the valuable trade in buffalo hides, which, due to the buffalo's geographic range, strengthened his plans to construct a large ship on the Mississippi River so that these hides could reach French markets faster once the mouth of that mighty river was determined.

La Salle had requested 20 years to fulfill his proposals, but the French

Crown reduced the time limit to five years. Losing no time in Paris, La Salle immediately engaged skilled labor (shipwrights, blacksmiths, woodworkers) and purchased ship supplies (iron rods, anchors, rigging) to take to New France. While in Paris, La Salle drew up plans to build one large vessel on Lake Erie, and another to be built later on the Mississippi River once he located and traversed the watershed between the Great Lakes basin and that of the Mississippi-Missouri-Ohio rivers.

Again, government funding was totally lacking. La Salle used his personal fortune, plus funds which he could borrow from family and friends, but he still lacked the required amount. In light of the poor economic conditions in France at that time, interest rates were quite high. La Salle was compelled to accept one loan at a 40% rate of interest -- and that came from one of his cousins! Back in Montréal, La Salle was forced to borrow from merchants who relished the idea of being in a position to ruin him. Needless to say, La Salle had great difficulty in escaping these financial clutches.

In Paris, La Salle also met and became good friends with Henri de Tonty, a distinguished adventurer eager to join La Salle in these projects. Tonty, at 28, seven years younger than La Salle, tall, handsome, distinguished, honorable, a military Neapolitan with a record of heroism, had a hand blown off by an exploding grenade in the Sicilian Wars. Cutting away the torn flesh and jagged bone with his other hand, Tonty bandaged his

Henri de Tonty, the man with the iron hand and La Salle's most trusted and faithful officer. Cris Kohl Collection

wound and continued to lead his soldiers into battle. This injury ended his military career, but it did little to impede his actions. Indeed, the imaginative Tonty had had an iron claw fashioned and strapped onto the stump of his arm to replace the lost hand, and although he wore a glove much of the time over the artificial appendage, he could perform hard labor as well as the next man and he had no difficulty with conventional weapons. Once, when a hulking giant of a *coureur de bois* attacked him, Tonty left him unconscious with one blow to his head with his metallic hand. Other times he subdued rebellious workers or Indians, leaving them with broken teeth and bleeding mouths. Word of this man with the iron hand spread among Great Lakes Indians, keeping them at a distance in a cautious state of bewildered awe. They called him "Silver Hand."

Tonty quickly became La Salle's faithful lieutenant and best friend. Many of La Salle's successes were helped in large part by his true friendship with this man.

In September, 1678, La Salle, Tonty and their entourage of skilled workers and supplies arrived at Québec on board the bark *Saint-Honoré*, which had departed France on July 14th. Greeting them enthusiastically was an eager 36-year-old appointee to the mission at La Salle's Fort Frontenac. The Recollect Father Louis Hennepin, excited about joining the upcoming expedition, undertook the difficult journey to Québec to welcome La Salle back from Paris. Father Hennepin, observant friar and keeper of the journal, provided the most complete written account of La Salle's travels for the reading pleasures of the outside and the future worlds. A pious priest with an adventurous heart, Father Hennepin did have problems with humility, and although his later "recollections" of participation in La Salle's expeditions incorrectly painted this wilderness Friar Tuck as the hero in numerous dramatic instances, the colorful descriptions he provided of other aspects of these explorations are of considerable value.

From Québec, the party and their supplies traveled in canoes and bateaux to Montréal and then on to Fort Frontenac. La Salle and Tonty remained for a time in Montréal to raise additional funds.

La Salle gave orders for a party of 15 fur traders from Fort Frontenac to fill several canoes and head to the Lac des Illinois (Lake Michigan), obtain there as many furs in trade with the Indians, and await the arrival of the ship which La Salle had yet to construct. These fur traders took a large consignment of trade goods with them, all paid for by La Salle.

Experience had taught La Salle what goods the Indians wished to own: for a single beaver pelt, they would receive either one axe, one pound of glass beads, one pound of tobacco, six knives, four pounds of shot, or one-half pound of gunpowder. Two beaver skins purchased one comb and a looking-glass. Five beaver pelts bought one laced female dress, while six beaver furs would acquire a laced coat. One gun cost ten beaver belts. The controversial trading of alcohol to the Indians was a bartered transaction, the price dependent upon the type and quality of the liquor and the degree of the purchaser's desperation.

While in Québec, La Salle was persuaded by Count Frontenac to take an active part in what became known as the "Brandy Parliament of 1678." Bishop Laval and a number of leading traders opposed the trafficking of alcohol with the Indians, and hoped to receive a majority vote at a meeting called specifically for that purpose with 20 leading merchants, one of whom was La Salle. The explorer argued that it was impossible to keep liquor from the Indians because the Dutch and the British would provide it for them if the French refused, at the same time winning over the allegiance of their tribes. La Salle cited the case of 300 Indians who headed to Montréal with their furs, but turned instead to Albany (and the Dutch) when they heard that they would be traded no alcohol by the French.

Fifteen of the 20 merchants voted to continue the trade of alcohol to the Indians, Bishop Laval stormed off immediately for Paris to request intercession from the King, and La Salle continued his exploration preparations, albeit now with yet another reason for being the target of Jesuit enmity.

By November 8, 1678, most of the participants and components had assembled or been assembled at Fort Frontenac to prepare for the first leg of La Salle's expedition. Excitement ran high, and there was no talk of turning back at this point.

*   *   *

Between 1673 and 1677, La Salle ordered four sailing ships to be constructed for coastal trading and cargo carrying around Lake Ontario and down the St. Lawrence River as far as Ogdensburg, New York. These vessels proved to be wise business investments for La Salle, who reported a cost saving of 33% in freight expenses between Fort Frontenac and Montréal after these ships replaced canoes. The participants and supplies of his major expedition, upon arrival at Fort Frontenac, could be transported via these water taxis from the fort at the eastern end of Lake Ontario to the mouth of the Niagara River at the western end. Each of these four ships was a small, two-masted barque, or bark, as the English spelled it, of approximately 40, 30, 25 and 25 tons respectively. The length of these vessels was from 35 to 45 feet, with a beam of 10 to 13 feet and a depth (from deck to keel inside the hold) of five to six feet. It was unlikely that any of these small ships carried a bowsprit or any of the ornamentation usually carved onto a vessel's bow or stern. A small cabin under each quarterdeck, lit by candles or small oil lamps, provided sleeping space. The minimum number of crewmembers required for such small vessels was from three to five. A small iron stove in the cabin allowed for cooking, with smoke funneling through an iron stovepipe emerging from a deck opening.

Two of La Salle's four small ships at Fort Frontenac were designated for use in his transport of men, supplies and ship's equipment from one end of Lake Ontario to the other. The first one, unidentified by name and perhaps never given one, would carry Father Hennepin and 16 others, plus

17

The FRONTENAC *being outfitted by La Salle at Fort Frontenac, Lake Ontario, 1678.* DRAWING BY GEORGE CUTHBERTSON, COURTESY OF THE CANADA STEAMSHIP LINES

considerable supplies and equipment to build the large ship on Lake Erie.

The second vessel, called the *Frontenac*, a name bestowed upon the ship by La Salle after his political ally (and possibly the second of La Salle's four Lake Ontario ships given that name), would depart later with La Salle, Tonty and the remainder of the men, supplies and equipment. The *Frontenac*, at 40 tonneaux, or tons, was the largest of La Salle's fleet so far.

Spirits soared during the departure of the first vessel, as indicated by Father Hennepin's entry in his journal: "I took leave of our monks [two other priests stationed there] at Fort Frontenac, and after mutual embraces and expressions of brotherly love and Christian charity, I embarked." Reality rapidly replaced this initial exuberance with serious concerns.

The first stage of this expedition sailed away on November 18, 1678, despite threatening weather, and thus commenced the first recorded voyage of a ship on the Great Lakes, sailing right into the eye of what future generations on the Great Lakes would knowingly refer to as "the gales of November." Following the north shore of Lake Ontario heading west, Hennepin recorded that the weather remained stormy, and on November 26th, the men being quite uneasy, they sailed the ship into the mouth of what we now call the Humber River, close to the Indian village of Taiaigon, near present-day Toronto. Temperatures dropped, and the vessel soon froze in place. The crew expended considerable labor to chop a channel through the ice to the open waters of Lake Ontario.

18

After several more miserable days being tossed about on the cold, unfriendly freshwater sea, the human cargo thankfully reached the mouth of the Niagara River on December 6, 1678, where they quickly unloaded the supplies and pulled the small brigantine up on shore to avoid damage from the upcoming winter ice. They hoped the December weather would not worsen for the voyage of the second ship, the _Frontenac._

This initial contingent daringly erected a stockaded fort across the Indians' traditional trading routes on the east side of the Niagara River several miles upstream of its mouth, knowing full well that who controlled Niagara, controlled the commerce in furs with the Indians of the interior. La Salle's crew also commenced the clearing of a road towards Lake Erie. The Senecas were incensed by these activities.

The Senecas were one of the five tribes (along with the Cayugas, the Mohawks, the Oneidas and the Onondagas) comprising the Five Nations of the Iroquois Confederation, natives who had joined forces in the 1570's and who had allied themselves with the English in the New England colonies in hostile conflict with the French and their Indian allies. Because Lake Erie lies deep inside Iroquois domains, because English settlements clung close to the seaboard and because the French avoided this enemy territory like the proverbial plague, Erie was the last of the five Great Lakes to be seen by European explorers. The Huron Indians had been all but wiped out by the warring Iroquois at the French Jesuit missions along Georgian Bay in the late 1640's; those tragic events, including the martyrdom of several Jesuit priests like Fathers Brébeuf and Lalemont, are well-documented in the Jesuit Relations. Other Indian tribes were also seriously decimated by ruthless waves of Iroquois violence. In 1678, 30 years later, the Iroquois tribes, still supreme over a vast geographical area, were seemingly warming to the idea of keeping peace with the French, a move wholly encouraged by the French in their eagerness to expand their influence.

La Salle, still at Fort Frontenac, heard rumors of the Senecas' hostility to the fort erected at Niagara, and he knew that his entire expedition was in jeopardy. Gambling with the weather, La Salle, Tonty and more men and supplies braved a lake crossing in late December. La Salle eagerly wanted to evaluate the situation with the Senecas for himself.

The _Frontenac_ departed Fort Frontenac on Christmas Eve day, 1678, sailing into the ice-flecked gray waters of Lake Ontario. La Salle, well aware of the dangers of being on Great Lakes waters in winter, warned the new pilot whom he had brought back with him from France, a giant of a man named Lucas, that the piece of land named the Quinte Peninsula jutted dangerously far out into the lake and had to be avoided at all costs. La Salle suggested that the pilot steer the _Frontenac_ due south after leaving Fort

Frontenac, until they sighted the southern shoreline, before turning westward. With his expertise given, La Salle went below deck for some sleep.

Several hours later, alarmed shouts from the crew made La Salle jump to the deck. Through the pitch darkness, they heard crashing waves, and La Salle knew that they had blundered precariously close to the rocks along the Bay of Quinte. Taking the tiller, turning to port and cursing the pilot for his stupidity, La Salle personally took over and headed the vessel south into the wind, beating a zigzag course into open waters. Through the pilot's carelessness, the ship had nearly been wrecked on Christmas Eve.

This was the first of several experiences which would give La Salle cause for concern about either the loyalty or the competence of his pilot. History has not left us much evidence about this man , and even his name is suspect. He was either a Frenchman named Lucas Dare (or Lucas Daré), or a Scandinavian referred to by historians as "Lucas the Dane." The name "Dare" could have been misread by early chroniclers of history as "Dane," with a jump being made to conclude incorrectly that Lucas was a Dane. La Salle himself, in his letters, referred to him only as "Lucas."

The next day, Christmas Day, the *Frontenac* dropped anchor at the mouth of the Genesee River (near present-day Rochester, New York), where La Salle and Tonty went ashore in a canoe, as planned, to make contact with the Senecas for the purchase of a supply of corn and to try to reconcile them to La Salle's plans and to the fact that the establishment of trade with the French would be to their advantage.

The diplomatic La Salle was satisfied in achieving successful results with the Seneca Indians, receiving permission from them to proceed with his fort and shipbuilding plans (to construct the "Big Canoe," as the Indians called it) at Niagara. After purchasing the corn, La Salle and Tonty returned to the *Frontenac* and continued their journey towards Niagara.

Nine leagues from Niagara (a league is generally considered to be a distance of three miles, but a French league is 2.7 miles), the wind died and the *Frontenac* sat dead in the water. With no change after a reasoned wait, and frustrated by their halted progress, La Salle and Tonty went ashore to finish their journey on foot. La Salle gave orders for Lucas to steer the *Frontenac* towards the Niagara River once the wind picked up again, with explicit instructions on how to sail the boat if the wind came from certain directions.

La Salle and Tonty proceeded to the new fort, where, much to La Salle's chagrin, he found 16 of his workers huddled in fear. He was furious upon being told that work on the new ship had not yet started, and he became further enraged when he found out that Hennepin and another of La Salle's lieutenants, La Motte, were not with the men. The two of them, hearing rumors of restlessness among the Senecas due to the white men's presence, formed a two-person, gift-bearing embassy to the local natives. Upon their return, La Salle learned that they had accomplished less than he himself had with the Indians, and Hennepin and La Motte had given away a small fortune in presents.

The barrage of bad news for La Salle did not end before one more serious episode reached him. With the *Frontenac* becalmed, La Salle had told Lucas, the ship's pilot, that if the wind arose from the northwest, he should proceed with the ship to Niagara, but if the wind emerged from the west, he should retreat to the shelter of the Genesee River and wait for the weather to change.

On the night of January 8, 1679, Lucas and the shivering men on board the anchored *Frontenac* decided to go ashore and build a bonfire on the beach for warmth. Rather than return to the clammy ship, they succumbed to the tempting warmth of the bonfire and slept there next to the flames. As it turned out, the wind picked up while they slept, the unmanned *Frontenac's* two anchor rodes (lines) chafed through, the barque snapped free and pounded to pieces on the shoreline near Lake Ontario's Thirty Mile Point, a place which the French called Cap Enragée, or "Mad-Cape". Years later, Hennepin gave a different (and somewhat inaccurate) account of the *Frontenac's* loss in his *A New Discovery* book:

> ...that Barque was unfortunately cast away on the Southern Coast of the Lake Ontario, by the fault of two Pilots, who could not agree about the Course they were to steer, tho' they were then only within two Leagues of Niagara. The Anchors and Cables were sav'd, but several Canows made of Barks of Trees with Goods and Commodities were lost....

La Salle was enraged, particularly at the pilot, Lucas the Dane. No lives were lost, but all of the crucial hardware for the new ship, with the exception of anchors and some cables which could be salvaged, was gone. A considerable quantity of supplies vital to the success of the expedition had been lost.

Thus the sailing ship, La Salle's barque *Frontenac,* entered the history books as the first shipwreck in the Great Lakes. Most historians since that time, however, have kept the loss of this vessel locked away in undeserved obscurity or swept under the historical carpet, preferring to regale a drama-hungry public with the more tragic and mysterious tale of La Salle's next ship. The exact location of Cap Enragée has also eluded modern historians.

The loss of the *Frontenac* was just the beginning of La Salle's long series of calamities in his explorations, among which counted three more increasingly important shipwrecks.

Dismayed yet determined to carry on, he ordered his men over to the Lake Erie side of the portage to begin cutting wood for the construction of the great ship he had planned.

*   *   *

By January, 1679, winter had fallen in earnest upon the Niagara peninsula, yet work, as uncomfortable as it was at this time of the year, progressed on the great ship. La Salle himself is said to have helped lay the keel and to have driven the first bolt into the new ship. The crew, however, grew to grumbling, and numerous excuses found their way to La Salle's ears for why some of the men no longer wished to work. However, those ears were deaf, and La Salle and Tonty, amidst the arguings and whisperings, clearly promised punishment for any acts of violence, while those considering desertion were offered a choice of staying where they were and working on the ship, or hiking back to Fort Frontenac in the middle of winter through wilderness and rough terrain populated by un-friendly Indians. The rebellions ceased and the men returned to vessel construction.

By late January, a small house was constructed so the men could have living quarters, and a blacksmith's shop, complete with forge, was also ready. The new ship, being built near the waters of Cayuga Creek between today's communities of Niagara Falls and Black Rock, New York, already had its launching ways in place.

The local Seneca tribe, however, having thought twice about their promise to cooperate with La Salle's plans, occasionally swooped down upon the construction site and alarmed the workers by running past them brandishing their tomahawks, causing great consternation among La Salle's men. At night, the wolflike howlings and other manmade animal calls kept the men on edge. On one occasion, an Indian, feigning drunkenness, almost killed the blacksmith, who saved himself only by holding a hot iron bar in a set of tongs between himself and the intruder. Not even La Salle's negotiations could prevail upon the Indians to sell him corn or meat for his men, even though much of their food supply had been lost in the sinking of the *Frontenac*. Eventually, however, a few Indians who believed in the French acted as hunters and suppliers of food for them.

Leaving the discipline of the camp to Tonty and the vessel's construction to another seemingly trustworthy man, master-builder Moise (or Moses) Hillaret, La Salle and a few men returned to the mouth of the Niagara River and built two blockhouses at the site of the old fort. This newer, larger fort

The Griffon *on the wilderness stocks. The smithy is on the extreme left.*
Drawing by George Cuthbertson, courtesy of the Canada Steamship Lines

La Salle named Fort Conti, after one of his supporters at the Royal Court in Paris.

However, La Salle knew that he would need replacement parts for the ones lost in the sinking of the *Frontenac* before the new ship under construction could be completed. With ice on the lake and thick along its shoreline, water transportation was out of the question. He decided to undertake the monumental task of hiking along Lake Ontario's north shore from Niagara to Fort Frontenac in the middle of winter. He took two men with him. The trio finished the 250-mile journey in two weeks, traveling

This unknown artist's 1697 rendition of Father Hennepin's recollection of the construction of the bark GRIFFON near Niagara Falls nearly 20 years earlier may not be totally accurate, particularly the palm trees and the jagged mountain peaks in the background.   CRIS KOHL COLLECTION

exclusively on snow and lake ice.

Thus La Salle was not at Niagara to see the completion of the great ship in late spring or early summer of 1679. In light of the cold winter construction season, the mutinous workers, the Indian interruptions and the low supplies, it seems a miracle that this heavily-built vessel was completed in such short time. Several days prior to the launching, guards were posted, having heard inklings of an attack planned by the Senecas to destroy their new ship.

This new vessel, rigged as a barque (or bark, in English), displaced 45 tons in her keel length of about 50 feet and her overall length of about 70. While the hull and most of the planking was local white oak, the iron work would have been forged at the construction site, excluding the nuts and bolts, which were likely brought prefabricated from France. After a brace of sawyers laboriously cut logs into flat, thin boards, these planks were bent into a hull-curved shape by either steaming them or immersing them in boiling water for several hours. The hull design was that of the popular style for trading ships, the Dutch galleot, with its low draft for access to

Detail of the GRIFFON'S *construction at Niagara in 1679, based upon Father Hennepin's recollections in 1697.*   CRIS KOHL COLLECTION

shallow bays and harbors, a high poop deck, a nearly rounded stern, and the square upper bow.

On the important launch day, date unknown because even Father Hennepin failed to note it in his journal, but estimated to have been in late May, 1679, the friar gave the ship his blessing and all the men sang the *Te Deum Laudamus* (a hymn both thanking and asking God for good fortune).

Wooden supports were knocked out of the way and the ship slid down the wilderness ramp into the cold, clear waters of the creek. The impressive site of this floating fort filled the Indians with wonder. One of the two small, brass cannons, or carriage guns, on board the great ship fired a salute in celebration; the thunderous noise terrified the natives. The *Griffon* also carried three iron, swivel-mounted arquebuses, large bell-mouthed muskets used as small cannon, for a total of five weapons; Hennepin's second book inexplicably increased the ship's number of arms from five to seven, and he upped her tonnage from 45 to 60 -- confusing discrepancies for later historians.

All of the ship's builders, after securely anchoring their new vessel in the river's current a safe distance off shore, set up their swinging hammocks below deck and enjoyed a peaceful night, free from concerns about marauding natives wielding torches and tomahawks, the first night free of fear since they had left Fort Frontenac half a year earlier.

When it came time to christen the new ship, Tonty ventured to name it.

The griffin creature of ancient mythology was half lion and half eagle.   CRIS KOHL COLLECTION

He recalled a remark he had heard from La Salle: "I will make the griffon fly above the ravens." A pair of griffons (also spelled griffins and gryphons), a mythological animal with the body and legs of a lion but the wings and beak of an eagle, was emblazoned on the family coat-of-arms of La Salle's friend and sponsor, Count Frontenac. The ravens, or crows, symbolized the blackrobed Jesuits. The significance of this sarcastic challenge was obvious, so Tonty named the ship *le Griffon.* Two carved griffons graced the *Griffon,* one as a figurehead beneath (not above, as indicated in some drawings) the bowsprit, and the other etched in relief on the transom, or the entablature of the stern. These added considerably to the formidable appearance of the ship.

Within a few more weeks, the finishing touches of rigging the vessel and completing her interior were accomplished. It was glorious summertime, and the bored men slowly ventured to spend their nights sleeping ashore again. The idle ship and her restless crew were ready to sail. The only thing missing was La Salle.

*   *   *

U pon returning to Fort Frontenac, La Salle was shocked to find that all of his holdings had been placed under seal. He found out why when he heard the rumors circulating among his creditors: that the loss of the *Frontenac* had ruined him; that he never intended to return from the wilderness, planning instead to flee to Mexico; that he planned to sell his furs to the Dutch and the English; that Indians had massacred most of his men. But La Salle stood his ground and refused to give his commercial opponents any victory. He became more determined than ever to make the *Griffon* project a success. He succeeded in recouping at least a portion of his credit and immediately ordered more provisions for his expedition.

Originally La Salle had planned to remain at Fort Frontenac to maintain close personal scrutiny over his business matters and to keep an eye upon those who would undermine his efforts, with Tonty in charge of the *Griffon* expedition. However, feeling the loyalty of his crewmembers suspect (except for Tonty's and Hennepin's), and with a strong desire to personally oversee the success of his enterprise, La Salle chose to accompany his men and lead the expedition in person. In early August, 1679, La Salle finally returned. Accompanying him, as a further spite against the Jesuits, were three friars from the Recollect order, one who would remain at Niagara, and the other two to engage in missionary work with the expedition along points west. With matters shored up in the east and his enemies and creditors behind him, La Salle was now prepared to sail west across the waters of the Great Lakes.

The men who had constructed the *Griffon* had not attempted to move the ship upstream in the Niagara River into Lake Erie, instead leaving her at anchor at the mouth of Cayuga Creek where she had been launched only a few miles above the roaring falls.

Tonty, suspecting that the men would encounter difficulties when they finally tried to move the *Griffon* out of the fast-moving river, took the ten-ton barque which had transported the advance party to Niagara the previous fall and sailed it along the coast of Lake Ontario to the site of the wrecked *Frontenac*. Anchoring into the shallow wreckage, Tonty attempted to salvage more of the equipment from the first shipwreck in the Great Lakes. While he leaned over the rail in an attempt to retrieve goods, the wind changed direction, his boat angled abruptly, and the anchor cable snapped. Tonty jumped at the oars lying in the hull, snapped them into the locks, and worked furiously for three hours to prevent this vessel from joining the wreck of the *Frontenac*. He had been able to salvage nothing, but an anchor, priceless here in this wilderness, had been lost.

On a day when the winds blew strong from one of the northerly directions, the crew hoisted the *Griffon's* sails, yet the ship could not cut through the river's strong current under sail alone. It ran the risk of being swept over Niagara Falls several miles downstream. The vessel could have been kedged, or winched, easily enough bit by bit out of the river except for one important fact -- Tonty was one anchor short to employ this method. Tow ropes were lashed to trees along the shoreline and men were set on shore to pull hard on those ropes, giving the sails vital assistance. With difficulty the men towed, and the *Griffon* inched forward. Hennepin wrote that "The Stream is so violent, that our Pilot himself despair'd of success. When it was done, we sung *Te Deum,* and discharg'd our Cannon and other Fire-Arms." By the end of a full day of hard labor, amidst the flash and roar of the cannon on her deck, the first ship to ply the upper Great Lakes finally escaped the grip of the Niagara River's current and sailed into the open waters of Lake Erie.

Now that the new vessel was ready for provisioning, La Salle sent Tonty and two men ahead in a canoe to see if they could learn something of the progress made by the 15 men La Salle had sent west to purchase furs the previous fall.

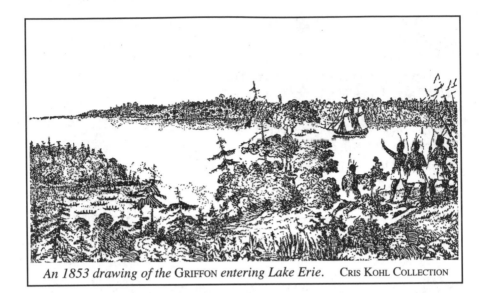

An 1853 drawing of the Griffon *entering Lake Erie.*   Cris Kohl Collection

Law-abiding, loyal to France, and faithful to God, La Salle perhaps had too much blind faith in human nature, politics and religion to have anticipated trouble when he turned the crowded *Griffon* into a veritable Noah's Ark of good and bad human types. On board congregated a total of 34 men: three Flemish friars frocked for religion in their gray robes with pointed hoods, sandals clinging to their thick-stockinged feet, crucifixes and rosaries swinging from their waistcords; a disgruntled, seemingly incompetent giant of a man who stood about seven feet tall, the perhaps Danish pilot who viewed freshwater sailing with disdain; a sincere and honorable Italian officer with a physical infirmity which did nothing to interfere with his natural leadership abilities; a Protestant Frenchman who was one of the great shipbuilders of his day; and an assortment of other professional and highly skilled French craftsmen, including carpenters and an iron worker, plus common laborers and sailors. It was a colorful cross-section of European society with a rainbow of human characteristics.

La Salle's enemies had tried to plant thoughts of failure in the minds of his crew in hopes of causing desertion: that the lakes were full of rocks and shallows certain to destroy their craft; that the Indians in the far west were hostile; that the men would never return; and myriad other tales (not without their elements of truth) to frighten them away and leave La Salle abandoned. So at the outset of the *Griffon's* voyage, sounding lines were kept busy to determine water depth. Fortunately, navigation proved easier than anticipated.

The crew encountered only one problem during the four days it took to cross the length of Lake Erie, and that occurred near the long, narrow point of land resembling the boney outstretched finger of a skeleton. La Salle described the incident off Long Point, known centuries later as the notorious ship's graveyard that it had become, in these words:

> *Night came on, and a thick fog concealed the shore, from which we supposed ourselves some ten leagues distant. I heard breakers about a league ahead of us. Everyone thought it was but the ordinary sound on the lakes when the wind changes, which is always heard from the side it comes from, and the pilot wished to crowd on sail to gain an anchorage before we stranded ahead; but as I knew that these two sand banks extended out very far, and as I was of the opinion we were near the one which was in fact just ahead of us, I ordered, notwithstanding everybody, that we change the course and bear east northeast, instead of as we were going, west northwest with a light wind from the southeast. We sailed two or three hours, sounding constantly, without finding bottom; and still we heard the same noise ahead of us. They all insisted that it was only the wind, and I, that it was the sand-bar which made a circle and surrounded us on the north side, from west to east. In fact, an hour later, we suddenly found only three fathoms. Everyone worked ship, I tacked and bore to the southwest, always sounding without finding a bottom. At length the fog lifted, my conviction proved true, and they all saw that they owed their escape from danger to me.*

La Salle's description (despite his unabashed Hennepin-like self-promotion) indicates that the *Griffon* had trapped herself between the mainland and the peninsula after sailing blindly into Long Point Bay. Fortunately, La Salle's keen observations saved the ship and crew.

Before reaching the western end of Lake Erie, the *Griffon* caught up with and collected Tonty and his two men, who had encountered very few Indians along the way and learned nothing of the advance party.

Upon reaching the wide mouth of what the French called "The Strait" -- the Detroit River -- on August 10th, the *Griffon* had to drop anchor against the strong current and wait for a suitable brisk wind to carry it upstream. On both sides of this river, the men observed open fields dappled with wild plum trees, groves of walnut, oak and chestnut trees, and lofty forests in the distance, teaming with game such as deer and flocks of turkeys. Hennepin noted that everything was "so well-dispos'd that one would think Nature alone could not have made without the Help of Art so charming a Prospect." Hennepin encouraged La Salle to establish a settlement on "this charming Streight [strait]" at some point in the future. But it would be another 22 years before a different explorer would do that: Cadillac would

After sailing up the Detroit River and across Lake St. Clair, the GRIFFON *proceeded through the marshy St. Clair Flats before the strong current at the river's mouth forced crewmembers once again to tow the ship upstream.*

ARTWORK BY GEORGE CUTHBERTSON, COURTESY OF THE CANADA STEAMSHIP LINES

name his settlement Detroit.

The *Griffon's* crewmembers were not the first Frenchmen to travel up the Detroit River. In 1670, nine years earlier, two Sulpician priests, traveling by canoe, made the first recorded passage of this waterway which Hennepin later found so delightful. What Francois Dollier de Casson and Abbé Brehant de Galinée found along the riverbank, however, appalled them: an enormous rock, fashioned in the likeness of a human figure and decorated with paint, which the Indians worshipped as some pagan god. The pious priests, filled with anger and hatred of this false god, attacked it with their axes and cast the broken pieces into the river. The *Griffon's* crew had no such experience, although in his revised 1697 recollections, Fr. Hennepin placed himself as one of the axe-wielding priests.

On August 12, 1679, the day which commemorates the feast of St. Clair, the *Griffon* left the river and sailed into the wide waters of a shallow, little lake which La Salle promptly named after that day's saint.

Across this small lake, the men noticed several fast-moving streams cutting through marshes. They had reached what we today call the St. Clair Flats, with its seven main channels distributing the waters of the river which flows powerfully out of Lake Huron about 30 miles upstream. The men patiently sounded each possible entranceway, intimidated by the many shallow, sandy reefs which would not provide water deep enough for the *Griffon* to proceed. Finally, one broad channel was sounded which gave a minimum depth reading of three fathoms (18 feet), more than enough clearance for the ship.

Approaching the river's north end, the crew of the *Griffon* was forced to drop anchor. The current of water trying to funnel itself out of Lake Huron with the force of a miniature Niagara Falls through that narrow bottleneck of a river's mouth delayed the ship for several days before a favorable wind from the south arose. La Salle quickly ordered the anchor raised, but still the ship could make no headway against the strong current. A previously proven method would have to be utilized here. A dozen men were sent ashore with ropes to haul the *Griffon*, itself under full sail to make whatever use it could of any assisting wind, and tow the ship along the river's edge where the current is at its weakest. After considerable hard work, they finally succeeded in dragging the *Griffon* out of the narrow channel mouth and into the wide-open expanse of vast blue water which is Lake Huron.

Pausing briefly at the foot of the lake, all gave thanks to the Almighty, sang the *Te Deum*, and set sail into the open waters. It was August 23, 1679.

Before long, La Salle's favorable winds died down, leaving the *Griffon* in disquieting doldrums just off the islands of Thunder Bay along the western shoreline of Lake Huron. It proved to be a two-day calm before a storm. When it struck, furious gales out of the west tossed the sturdy little ship for hours upon the suddenly unfriendly, churning waters. The uncontrollable vessel bobbed and dipped at the mercy of wind and waves.

So dire was the stormy situation that even La Salle thought all was lost, enticing his men to kneel on the deck and prepare for death. All except the pilot did so. Lucas the Dane instead spent his precious time cursing La Salle in his loudest voice for having brought him there to perish in a "nasty Lake, and lose the Glory he had acquir'd by his long and happy Navigations on the Ocean," according to Father Hennepin's journal. By now, La Salle suspected that Lucas was in the pay of his enemies, trying to sabotage his expedition.

Neither La Salle nor Lucas nor anyone else on board was destined to perish in that storm. When the winds finally subsided, the collective sighs of relief from the *Griffon's* intact crew were probably heard by the deer on shore. Prayers of thanks emanated from everyone on the ship "except the Godless pilot, who could never be persuaded to pray," according to Hennepin. Again, the crew sang the *Te Deum* in thanks for their salvation.

As the storm clouds slowly disappeared in the east after the lake waters grew quiet, La Salle and his men spied the wooded cliffs of Bois Blanc Island in the sunlight. With the ship nearing the Straits of Mackinac, the sound of one of the *Griffon's* cannons announcing their arrival caused a variety of residents to emerge from their dwellings: shouting Hurons spilled out of their bark houses, painted Ottawas raced out of their wigwams in the distance, curious black-robed Jesuit priests edged to the shoreline from the log chapel, while swarthy French traders, most with a shadowy past and no use for invaders, ambled slowly from their cabins to see the cause of this disturbance. That evening, August 27, 1679, La Salle's vessel dropped anchor behind the tranquil point of St. Ignace in the harbor of the Jesuit mission and trading post, established by Father Marquette in 1671, at Michilimackinac, "where there was a good bottom of potter's clay" in six fathoms of water (today's East Moran Bay). This settlement provided the last trace of civilization on the edge of the vast, unknown, western wilderness.

La Salle, knowing that he was envied or hated by virtually every inhabitant of St. Ignace, decided to enter the village in truly fearless, successful fashion. Donning his finest formal clothing, which included a scarlet cloak bordered with broad gold lace, a plumed hat and a scabbarded sword which glinted impressively in the sunlight, he strutted ashore with his usual imperial dignity from one of the many canoes manned by curious residents paddling around in awe at the novel ship. When most of his crew (some armed guards remained on board) also reached shore and the new arrivals were welcomed, they traversed the open expanse of land to the bark chapel, where mass was heard and thanks were again given for a safe passage. The *Te Deum* was also sung.

At the settlement of St. Ignace, La Salle found four of the 15 men who had been sent ahead eight months earlier with a large quantity of trading goods to be used for buying furs from the Indians in western Lake Michigan. These deserters had used a share of La Salle's goods for their own personal gain. Questioning revealed that another two deserters were up at Sault Sainte Marie, about 50 miles north, but no one knew the fate of the other nine men. La Salle had the first four deserters arrested before sending Tonty with six men to take the two at the Sault into custody.

With time passing all too quickly, and La Salle noticing the jealous eyes of some of the local inhabitants upon his ship, he determined to push on at once. He had also been warned that the winds in the beginning of the winter made navigation of the lake very dangerous. Despite Tonty with six men being on their mission to Sault Sainte Marie, the *Griffon* departed St. Ignace in early September and sailed easily through the Straits of Mackinac and across *Lac des Illinois* (named by the French after the Indian tribe at the southern end of the lake, also called *Lac St. Joseph* and *Lac Dauphin,* but today called Lake Michigan) for a distance of "about forty Leagues from Missilimackinac [Mackinac]" to the islands at the mouth of Green Bay, or *Baie des Puants* as the French called it. Here the ship dropped anchor and the expedition's luck took a long-awaited turn for the better.

An Indian chief with a few of his tribe members canoed to the *Griffon* when, upon learning that La Salle was a friend of Count Frontenac, with whom the chief had his own warm friendship, the most cordial welcome greeted the new arrivals. The chief also informed La Salle of a nearby encampment of French fur traders. La Salle had found the faithful remnants of the party he had sent ahead to procure furs and to wait for him.

And what a treasure in furs now awaited La Salle! The crew moved the *Griffon* to Detroit Harbor, an ideal, protected anchorage at the southeast side of Washington Island (although recent archaeological evidence suggests that the location may have been Rock Island), where the earlier fur traders had taken up residence while waiting for their leader. La Salle inhaled the fresh air of relief and independence while his men loaded the several thousand pounds of furs valued at 12,000 French *livres* into the *Griffon's* hold. The expedition leader's financial troubles could now be put behind him. La Salle's creditors would no longer pound upon his door with the persistence of an unpaid madam. They would all receive their money with interest, and La Salle would become a free man again, wriggled loose by this fortunate windfall from under the crushing thumbs of his enemies back in Montréal and Québec.

During this financial highlight, La Salle's obsessive ambition and thirst for discovery blinded him to the reality of his situation. His original plan had been to put Tonty in charge of that branch of the expedition which would head down the lake, cross the watershed, and begin building the second ship for eventual use on the Mississippi River, while La Salle and a crew would return on board the fur-laden *Griffon* to Niagara. However, La

La Salle's men loaded the Griffon *with furs.*   MICHIGAN HISTORICAL COLLECTION

Salle had sent Tonty north to capture deserters, and the expedition leader had run out of trustworthy lieutenants. All of La Salle's means for silencing his creditors and his critics lay in the holds beneath the barque's decking, but, put in a position where he had to make a quick decision, La Salle's vast dream overcame his ability to recognize his immediate priorities, and the course of his empire-building began to spin out of control.

La Salle's new plan was for the *Griffon* to return to Niagara with a skeleton crew led by Lucas -- the suspicious pagan pilot who had already cost La Salle one ship -- while La Salle with most of his men would travel in four canoes south along the lakeshore to the foot of these waters until they reached the land of the Illinois tribe, from whom they could learn the location of the watershed portage which would place them in the Mississippi River basin waterways. The *Griffon* would unload her precious cargo at Niagara, where the furs would be hauled overland to Lake Ontario, reloaded onto smaller ships, and transported to Fort Frontenac. As fast as possible, the *Griffon* would be reloaded with the equipment required to build another ship quite similar in proposed size and design to the *Griffon*, but the construction would take place on the far side of the watershed after this equipment had been hauled over the portage from Lake Michigan. How much easier it would have been if they could have carried the *Griffon* over that portage! On board the new ship yet to be constructed, La Salle would sail down the mighty Mississippi River, and perhaps ultimately find some way to reach China!

On September 18, 1679, a fully loaded *Griffon*, sitting deeper in the water than ever before, fired a parting shot from one of her cannons as she started in a northeasterly direction for Niagara. On board were Lucas the Dane and five other men (or four men and a boy, according to one report). Hennepin and the other priests had protested La Salle's unwise decision to let the godless pilot, Lucas, captain the *Griffon*, as he could easily turn out to be a thief. But La Salle knew that his choices were extremely limited. He felt that he himself had to keep moving forward, to proceed south to locate the watershed to the Mississippi River, and Tonty, the only other person whose capabilities and honesty La Salle trusted, was still indisposed on his mission to the Sault.

La Salle had ordered Lucas to stop at Michilimackinac-St. Ignace to unload the tools and ship's wares for which La Salle had no room in his canoes. The *Griffon*, moving as quickly as possible, would pick up these items upon its return trip from Niagara after having replaced its precious cargo of furs with more nautical hardware which La Salle needed to construct his Mississippi River ship. How the ship was going to get back up the St. Clair River and into Lake Huron with only six men on board was not recorded; perhaps a plan existed for more crew to be added at Niagara. The *Griffon* would meet La Salle and the rest of the expedition at the mouth of the Miami (today the St. Joseph) River at the extreme southern end of Lake Michigan. The overly ambitious La Salle hoped to squeeze in yet another load of furs which the *Griffon* would take back to Niagara before winter would set in and close any maritime activities on the lakes for a few months.

With the *Griffon's* full complement of sails filled with a west wind and growing smaller over the horizon of Lake Michigan, La Salle, with Hennepin and 14 others, embarked on a southern course in four heavily-laden canoes.

Hardly had the two expeditions begun their respective voyages when a severe storm suddenly swept the lake. La Salle's men experienced great difficulties in keeping the canoes together with their shouted directions while struggling to reach the shore, a feat they accomplished only after nightfall. For four miserable days, the violent storm refused to subside. Huddled under their overturned canoes in wet conditions, La Salle's cheerless encampment existed on Indian corn and pumpkins. During those many wretched days, La Salle thought only of the *Griffon* and her crew, out there somewhere in these conditions. His concerns were certainly real, as he himself had just recently experienced a much shorter storm of equal violence on Lake Huron. He knew what his crew faced. Forlorn and pathetic, he sagged down in the soggy discomfort of his makeshift shelter, hoping beyond hope that his men were safe and that his furs would reach Montréal.

His whole future and the fate of his Mississippi exploration rested upon the *Griffon* reaching Niagara safely. La Salle regretted that he could not be in two important places at once.

Historian Joan Forsberg at the Lake Michigan monument to La Salle near Algoma, Wisconsin. The 1930 marker reads: "Storm-driven and without food in October, 1679, Robert La Salle with fourteen men on a voyage to explore the interior of America, landed at this place. Expecting hostile Indians, he erected a barricade, but instead of war, they brought provisions and saved his life."

PHOTO BY CRIS KOHL

*　　　*　　　*

A man of such immense determination that it bordered on madness, La Salle continued on his course after the storm with his four canoes and weatherbeaten men. But summer was over, and the season of the witch was upon the Great Lakes. Storm after storm forced their retreat landward, and their progress southward was slow, particularly when they reached the steep, high bluffs which made landfalls extremely difficult. These delays also dug heavily into their food supplies to the point where the daily cuisine consisted of corn augmented with freshly picked hawthorn berries. A short distance further south, game suddenly became abundant, and the little canoe expedition finally reached the mouth of the St. Joseph River. Little did they know it then, but they had overshot a more direct route to their destination, namely the Chicago River, which provided access to the portage and to the interior of the continent.

On November 1, 1679, 43 days after leaving the island on the edge of Green Bay (historians hotly debate whether that island was really what we today call Washington Island, arguing that from the description of the anchorage, it could also have been Rock Island or Summer Island, and considerable archaeological evidence has been located on Rock Island to prove that the French encamped there for some time during the late 1600's), La Salle and his four-canoe expedition reached the mouth of the Miami (today the St. Joseph) River where a crude fort, named Fort Miami, had been constructed. To their dismay, neither Tonty nor the *Griffon* was to be found. The rendezvous was totally deserted. Finally, on November 20th, Tonty and his men arrived by canoe to a much relieved La Salle.

Tonty, however, had heard nothing about the fate of the *Griffon*.

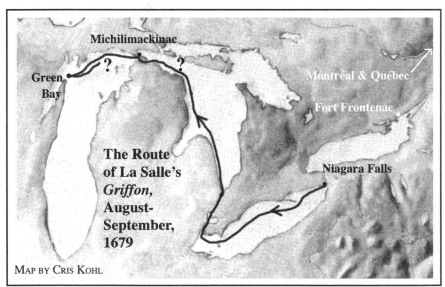

Michilimackinac

Green Bay

Montréal & Québec

Fort Frontenac

Niagara Falls

The Route of La Salle's *Griffon*, August-September, 1679

MAP BY CRIS KOHL

La Salle immediately sent two experienced *coureurs des bois* to return to Michilimackinac and make further inquiries about the *Griffon*. If they were to find the missing ship, her instructions were to sail to Fort Miami immediately, where any cargo the vessel was carrying would be unloaded and stored in the fort while the ship would be made secure and as safe as possible from the winter elements.

Meanwhile, with ice forming on the waterways, the stubbornly determined La Salle pressed on. He, Tonty, Hennepin and a party of men set out on December 3, 1679, up the St. Joseph River to the Kankakee portage, onwards to the Illinois River, hoping to reach the waters of the mighty Mississippi.

*   *   *

Volumes have been written about La Salle's incredible struggles and progress from this point, often reading like Homer's *Odyssey*, but as fascinating a story as it is, La Salle played no further role in the discovery or the development of the Great Lakes, so for our purpose, we must return to the tale of the ship named the *Griffon*.

In February, 1680, while wintering at Fort Crevecoeur on the Illinois River west of Lake Michigan and constructing the new ship for use on the Mississippi River, La Salle summoned Tonty, Hennepin and seven other men to his quarters. He appeared irritated and despondent as he expressed his concerns over the missing *Griffon*. From Washington Island, he had sent the ship on its return journey laden with valuable furs, but also with ship's hardware, such as rigging and cables without which the half-completed vessel which they had begun to build at Fort Crevecoeur could not be finished. These precious components were irreplacable, and La Salle cursed himself for having left them below deck on the *Griffon*. He decided that his concern for the *Griffon* was so overpowering that he and five men would proceed on foot through snow-covered forests and across frozen rivers to determine what had happened to the *Griffon*. Tonty would remain in charge at Fort Crevecoeur. If the overdue vessel was not at Fort Miami, they would keep going until, sooner or later, La Salle would find out what happened to his ship. He was prepared, if need be, to walk all the way back to Fort Frontenac at the extreme eastern end of the Great Lakes.

La Salle pretty much had to do just that. Between March 1 and May 6, 1680, he and his small expedition trekked and canoed across the wilderness back to Fort Frontenac. Reaching Fort Miami on March 24th, La Salle found only the two men whom he had sent the previous fall north to Michilimackinac to seek word of the *Griffon*. They had completely

37

circumnavigated Lake Michigan, darting into every river mouth, peeking into every natural harbor. They had questioned every Indian they encountered along the way.

Nothing was learned.

Bitter, La Salle almost resigned himself to the fact that the *Griffon* was lost. In early April, 1680, when the overland party reached the Detroit River, the ever hopeful La Salle directed two of his men to build a canoe and head north to Michilimackinac while checking every nautical nook and cranny along the way where a vessel might be lodged, and asking everywhere along the way and at their destination for any word on the *Griffon*.

Nothing was discovered.

In the summer of 1680, a huge wave of fierce Iroquois flooded west, attacked the Illinois Indians in a massive and bloody land takeover, and burned Fort Crevecoeur (although at least one historian has suggested that the retreating French explorers purposely set torches to their fortification just prior to their retreat). Tonty and a few men had been scouting the Starved Rock area as a possible sanctuary, and the men left behind at the fort deserted just before the Iroquois arrived. A few words had been hastily scrawled onto a plank of the unfinished ship on the stocks: "Nous sommes tous sauvages" ("We are all savages") followed by "a 15, 1680" (the date: "a" for aout -- August -- 15, 1680). Interpreted possibly as a philosophical statement about the meaning of life, this message predated Joseph Conrad's famous, symbolic line, "The horror. The horror." from his novella, *Heart of Darkness,* by more than two centuries. Perhaps the obsession on the part of the Europeans to control this wilderness, and the struggle by the natives to maintain a degree of independence and power had a strange and horrifying effect upon both groups. But the meaning behind the inscription was simpler than that. The loyal Frenchmen who had not deserted left this message to show that they had joined the Illinois in their retreat from the Iroquois on that date.

This native warfare did not signal the epitaph for La Salle's Mississippi expedition. The indomitable explorer returned to Fort Crevecoeur in autumn, 1680, with another expedition in search of Tonty and the men he had left behind. La Salle found unspeakable horrors graphically depicting the merciless Iroquois' invasion: the grounds of Illinois Indians' villages blackened by fire; cornfields burned to the roots; grimacing human skulls perched upon the charred poles of log houses; wolves retreating into the brush dragging remnants of human bodies; buzzards swooping up from a huge mound of rotting corpses; partially eaten bodies of Indian women still hanging from stakes where they had succumbed to unspeakable tortures; and small corpses of children with eyes gouged out and vital organs violently removed.

La Salle, desperate to discover the fate of his dear friend Tonty and the other men, quickly scoured each head and skull; any remaining tattered hair was clearly Indian. La Salle and his worried men located several remnants of French cloth and a debris field of utensils, but no other traces of their lost comrades. Before setting fire to it, the Iroquois had scavenged the new ship under construction on the stocks, removing all of the precious iron nails and bolts (one historian believes that the French themselves were able to remove most of the precious metal from the incompleted ship before their retreat).

At least half of the Illinois nation of Indians had been annihilated by the Iroquois, and La Salle shared their emotional anguish and pined for news about Tonty and the other faithful expedition members.

That winter, La Salle joyously received word from some friendly Indians that Tonty and his men were safe at Green Bay.

But he heard absolutely nothing about the _Griffon_.

Much later, in 1683, La Salle received a report from a teenage Indian, given to him as a slave, claiming that, three years earlier, he had seen a huge white man fitting the description of Lucas as prisoner of an Indian tribe west of the Mississippi. This man had reportedly been captured, along with four other whites, while they were making their way in heavily laden canoes towards the Sioux' lands. The other four had been tortured, killed and eaten by their captors, but the Goliath was kept alive as their prisoner.

La Salle was convinced that these men were his lost crewmembers, and that they had stolen his furs and other goods, somehow hidden or destroyed the _Griffon_, procured canoes with which to reach and join either the explorer du Lhut or a tribe of Indians not friendly to La Salle, but fell prisoner to yet another tribe while enroute. What ultimately became of the prisoners is not known. Indeed, this evidence is inconclusive, as verification was impossible.

*   *   *

Father Louis Hennepin, after numerous further adventures and misadventures, including being held captive by the Sioux Indians for several months and taken to Minnesota, was rescued and returned to France in 1681 where, two years later, he wrote the largely truthful _Description de la Louisiane (A Description of Louisiana)_, the first of two books about his adventures among the savage tribes in the New World. When Hennepin sought to add to his glory and honors in 1697, he did what many writers have done -- he wrote another book about the same topic and gave it a new title: _Nouvelle Découverte d'un tres grand Pays situé dans_ *l'Amérique (A New Discovery of a Vast Country in America)*. Here Hennepin's memory and pen went astray. Both books recounted the tale of the *Griffon*, only in the later volume, Hennepin enlarged upon his adventures of 1678-1681, making himself appear as the hero in numerous tricky situations, at the same time appropriating information and material from other explorers. Ultimately discredited and disgraced, Fr. Louis Hennepin died in obscurity.

Hennepin, writing about the fate of the *Griffon* in his first book, concluded (original spelling retained) that

> *...there is no Doubt, but that she perished....The Barque having anchored in the north of Lake Dauphin [Lake Michigan], the Pilot against the Opinion of some Indians, who assured him that there was a great Storm in the middle of the Lake, resolved to continue his Voyage, without considering that the sheltered Position where he lay, prevented his knowing the Force of the Wind. He had scarcely sailed a quarter of a League from the Coast, when these Indians saw the Barque tossing in an extraordinary Manner, unable to resist the Tempest, so that in a short time they lost sight of her, and they believe that she was either driven on some Sandbank, or that she foundered.*

In his second book, Hennepin described the last episode of the *Griffon* this way:

> *They sailed the 18th of September with a Westerly wind and fir'd a Gun to take their leave....The Ship came to an Anchor to the North of the Lake of the Illinois, where she was seen by some Savages, who told us that they advised our Men to sail along the Coast, and not towards the middle of the Lake, because of the Sands that make the Navigation dangerous when there is any high Wind. Our Pilot, as I said before, was dissatisfy'd and would steer as he pleas'd, without hearkening to the Advice of the Savages, who, generally speaking, have more Sense than the Europeans think at first; but the Ship was hardly a League from the Coast when it was tossed up by a violent Storm in such a manner, that our Men were never heard of since; and it is suppos'd that the Ship struck upon a Sand and was there bury'd.*

La Salle's strongest workers and allies were visionaries like himself, possessing a sense of the future. That rascal Hennepin, in spite of spending a mere six years (1675-1681) of his life in the New World and despite his later proclivity for enlarging upon history, assessed the Great Lakes with a prophet's foresight. As a captive of the Sioux in 1680, having experienced only scattered fur trading posts and warring Indian tribes in this part of the world, he wrote

> *It were easy to build on the sides of these small great Lakes, an Infinite number of considerable Towns which might have Communications with one another by Navigation for Five Hundred Leagues together, and by an inconceivable Commerce which would establish itself among them.*

Two centuries would pass before Hennepin's forecast of "considerable Towns" and "an inconceivable Commerce" for the Great Lakes came true.

The one-handed explorer, Henri de Tonty, continued to live and work in the Mississippi region. In 1699, 20 years after the *Griffon* disappeared, a missionary traveling under Tonty's escort stated that "He is beloved by all the *voyageurs*...It is with deep regret that we parted from him;...he is the man who best knows the country;...he is loved and feared everywhere...." History tells that in the year 1702, Tonty joined D'Iberville in Lower Louisiana, and was sent by that officer to secure the Chickasaw tribe in the French interest. Tonty died in a French colony in Louisiana, probably from yellow fever, in 1704. He was 54 years old.

La Salle's exploits took him down the Mississippi River, but his hopes for sailing a large ship on that river never materialized. He did claim for France the enormous tract of land which he named Louisiana (at that time exceeding by far the geographic limits of today's state of Louisiana) and he attempted to colonize the Louisiana-Texas area of the Gulf of Mexico. But his problems never ceased to cause him great grief, whether they related to his finances back in New France, to his inability to locate the mouth of the Mississippi River from a Gulf of Mexico approach, to his confrontation with the Spanish empire using his army of 200 Frenchmen and 15,000 Indians (a move which prompted his detractors to question his sanity) or to disgruntled expedition members who worried about their back pay or where La Salle was leading them.

Unfortunately, this intense and controversial man was ambushed and tragically murdered with a single gunshot to his temple by three mutinous members of his expedition somewhere in the swampy wilds of Texas near the banks of the Trinity River not too far west of the mouth of the Mississippi. The assassins stripped the body of its clothing and threw the human remains into the underbrush for the wild animals to devour. The traitors then seized La Salle's possessions, including his famous scarlet cloak with the gold trim which he had so proudly worn upon the *Griffon's* arrival at Michilimackinac eight years earlier. Like La Salle, the cape had survived every one of his shipwrecks, but it finally succumbed to a mutinous crew.

Thus ended a frenzied pursuit of fame. The date of La Salle's death was March 19, 1687; the great explorer had been in his 43rd year of life.

How often throughout history do we have a case where a truly great man, such as La Salle, was brought down in the prime of his existence by some lowlife who was not fit even to carry his boots.

When Tonty learned about La Salle's death, he wept openly and sobbed, "One of the greatest men of the age is dead." So genuine was his friendship with La Salle that he might just as well have spoken Shakespeare's immortal words written in a story about the death of a true friend: "And flights of angels sing thee to thy rest."

La Salle's life was brief but fiery. Hollywood could not have written a better script.

*   *   *

La Salle, the remarkable explorer, tried to revolutionize the fur trade by the use of European-style sailing ships on the Great Lakes and the Mississippi, and he established an empire for France in the West. But his vision was too vast for achievement with the resources available to him under the conditions in which he labored.

With so much lost when his ship, the *Griffon*, disappeared somewhere in the Great Lakes, and with the continued, and even increased, pressure and malice of Montréal merchants maintaining financial strain upon him, it is to La Salle's credit that he was able to move on and still attain so many of his ambitious aspirations.

La Salle had his weaknesses -- claims of unsociability, impulsiveness, autocratic leadership, and particularly his inability to place the proper people in positions of responsibility or to see that unpaid help would mutiny -- but his name lives on in history due to his honesty, his ambition and his physical determination. His successes aroused the antagonism of those who remain in obscurity, e.g. the men who maliciously competed with him in Montréal have been completely forgotten by history.

La Salle's efforts were not in vain. His explorations of the western Great Lakes and the Mississippi basin from Illinois to Louisiana formed the basis of France's claims to the western lands of North America, a vast area which France later sold to the fledgling country called the United States in 1803 in a transaction of great significance called the Louisiana Purchase.

Without La Salle's work, these lands may very well have become entrenched by British or Spanish domination in the late 1600's, and this could

La Salle left a significant legacy in the Great Lakes -- not to mention the lakes' first two shipwrecks! PUBLIC ARCHIVES OF CANADA

have blocked the expansion of the United States to the regions west of the Mississippi River, in spite of the much later doctrine of "Manifest Destiny." At the very least, without La Salle's accomplishments, the expansion of the United States across the continent would have been made more difficult, taken more time and probably cost more human lives. It is entirely plausible that the United States may very well be a geographically smaller country today had it not been for La Salle.

Likewise, the *Griffon*, La Salle's ship which helped shape history, is also far from forgotten. It is simply waiting to be found.

*　　　*　　　*

The fate of the *Griffon* has not been conclusively determined in the more than 325 years since the ship "went missing" with all hands. Five scenarios are most commonly presented as the most viable solutions to the greatest riddle of the freshwater seas:

1. The *Griffon* foundered with all hands in a storm in northern Lake Michigan not far off the shore where the ship was last reported seen by Indians. One theory holds that the summer heat had opened her seams easily to the storm's pounding waves because the vessel was built of green wood.
2. The *Griffon* became unmanageable in strong winds, stranded and broke up on some shore, pounded to many pieces with no survivors, or the survivors were taken prisoner by Indians and disappeared from the historical record.
3. The *Griffon* was burned and the entire crew slain and scalped by the Ottawas or some other Indian tribe which resented French, or at least La Salle's, intrusion into their region. It has been

suggested that the Indians concocted the tale of a storm causing the *Griffon's* demise to camouflage their own responsibility.

4. The *Griffon* was scuttled by the suspicious pilot, Lucas, after he and the crew sold the furs and took the money for themselves.

5. The *Griffon* was seized and stolen by unscrupulous fur traders, enemies of La Salle, possibly saboteurs hired by the Jesuits, who killed the crew, scuttled the ship and sold the furs.

The last three are usually discounted among historians who claim that there would have been talk and there would have been evidence had the case been one of these. Both French fur traders and Indians were viewed as braggarts unable to keep secrets, so if they had had anything to do with the loss of the *Griffon*, word would eventually have leaked out. Indians destroying the ship would have salvaged her precious ironwork, and their possession of such materials would have drawn attention to them. The sale of stolen furs, especially in the quantity stowed aboard the *Griffon*, disposed of in as sparsely populated a land as the Great Lakes region was at that time, would have produced demanding inquiries into their source.

That leaves the strong possibility that the first ship on the upper Great Lakes was destroyed by forces of nature, leaving no survivors, at least none who lived long enough to inform the outside world of the fate of the *Griffon*.

In the spring after the *Griffon* disappeared, La Salle received word from some natives of the discovery of flotsam washed up on the eastern side of Mackinac Island, the side facing Lake Huron. A hatch cover, a cabin door, two pairs of torn and tar-splattered linen breeches, a few bits of ship cordage and several bundles of rotted beaver pelts had to have come, by process of elimination, from the *Griffon*, as she was the only ship sailing on the upper Great Lakes, and hence the only candidate for loss.

Over time, several reports reached La Salle offering clues or hints as to what might have happened to the *Griffon* and her crew. These include the report about the ship having been destroyed by a sudden storm, "tossed on a Sand and there buried" close to shore in northern Lake Michigan, the report of the *Griffon* being helplessly driven "out" through the Straits of Mackinac towards the Huron islands by the force of a strong west wind, the report of items washed ashore on Mackinac Island's Lake Huron side, and the tale of the large, white prisoner, possibly the *Griffon's* pilot, Lucas, captured by Indians and paraded as a prisoner. But reports are not always true or accurate.

"I know the thing that kind of sours me after all these years is how many reports there are that turn out to be way off," commented writer and long-time shipwreck hunter Clive Cussler to me in April, 2004, when we, for the second time in as many years, discussed the possible fate and whereabouts of the *Griffon*. His long quest for the Confederate submarine, the *Hunley*, waylaid and delayed by faith in faulty reports from alleged eyewitnesses, became for him "a classic example" of why one should reserve judgment about statements in reports. Despite this, he succeeded in locating the *Hunley*.

"The *Griffon* is out there," he concluded, "but it would be a tough one to find."

*   *   *

O ver the past 200 years or so, virtually any time someone located an unknown wooden shipwreck, people wrote letters to the local newspaper stating emphatically that the vessel had to be the remains of the *Griffon*. Often these letters reflected wrong ideas about La Salle and the *Griffon* which had seemingly become ingrained in the minds of the general public. I came across one such letter in the mid-1980's when I was researching my 1987 book, *Shipwreck Tales: The St. Clair River (to 1900)*.

A hardhat diver, searching for a body at the bottom of the St. Clair River early in 1904, "had an adventure and found a treasure that would make 'Jules Verne' green with envy," according to a newspaper article. This diver (referred to as "Diver Reed," so it was probably Jim or Tom Reid of the famous Reid wrecking family from Sarnia, Ontario) told of having found a wooden shipwreck "with the hatches all securely fastened down. He also found a wagon load of brick and the skeleton of a team of horses, which had drowned while crossing the ice two years earlier." The wreck, a schooner, "was without masts," (which could have broken off during the sinking or from the current), and the diver planned to return to the site to uncover the hatches "to find out what cargo the boat carried." This diver made no mention of finding the missing body which he had gone down there to locate in the first place.

On March 17, 1904, not long after the diver story was published, this enthusiastic but disturbingly inaccurate letter appeared in the *Sarnia Daily Observer*, proving that people had the *Griffon*, and many incorrect details about that ship, on their minds:

> *Mr. Editor,---I noticed in your issue of the 4th that a diver, in exploring the bottom of the St. Clair, had come across the hull of a schooner with the masts gone and the hatches battened down, near Courtwright [Ontario]. As the oldest inhabitant, and that must reach back about 70 years, cannot remember any vessel going down in that neighbourhood, it is just possible that the schooner may have foundered in Lake Huron and in the course*

of many years, may have oozed down that far by the current. And as there was no local paper then published in this part of the province, the catastrophe could occur without people along the river knowing anything of it. I have not heard of any theory put forth. But what if this vessel should prove the hull of the old "Griffin" [sic] of La Salle, the French explorer? This is merely a thought; yet not a chimerical surmise. The "Griffin" was built at the mouth of the Cayuga river, above the Falls, and as soon as she was launched and ready to start on her first, last, and only voyage, through Lake Erie, entering the St. Clair river on the 12th August, 1679,.... La Salle, putting her in charge of his chief officer, continued his journey west by land, till he reached the Mississippi. In the meantime, the "Griffin" began her return journey, but the rich furs never saw Paris, for the unfortunate "Griffin" was never heard of afterward.

The considerations, in favour of her being intact somewhere, are as follows: The "Griffin" was built in a locality abounding in wood, where the workmen had the pick of the very best timber. The planks would be made by whip saws, and every article entering the construction hand made and subjected to close inspection and by practical, experienced ship builders, under the immediate inspection of La Salle, so that nothing of inferior nature or workmanship would be allowed in the building of the "Griffin." Nor was she got up for the waters of Lake Erie or our inland rivers, but with the capacity of navigating any sea or ocean La Salle might meet between Lake Erie and the Indies. Although only 12 tons burden, she was a stout craft, built of the best material by skilled workmen, and as it is only 225 years since she left the stocks, there exists no good reason why the hull of "Griffin" should not be sound yet. When her valuable cargo was stowed away in her hold, the hatches would most likely be securely battened down. I hope a further exploration of that sunken vessel at Courtright will be made.

The writer's use of the word "chimerical" hints at an education, but this contrasts with the unlikely description of a shipwreck that "foundered in Lake Huron and... may have oozed down that far [into the St. Clair River] by the current," suggesting little knowledge of how water currents work.

If nothing more, this letter may very well be representative of what the Great Lakes public generally knew about the history of the *Griffon* two hundred or so years after that ship's mysterious disappearance.

*   *   *

Dead men tell no tales, and if any of the *Griffon's* crew survived the ship's demise, whether that end came from natural foundering or stranding in churning seas, intended burning at the hands of crew or Indians, or resolved abandonment in some secluded backwater, then live men told no tales either. With all witnesses killed or otherwise silenced, the fate of the barque *Griffon* has remained a Great Lakes puzzle for centuries.

Numerous locations have at one time or another claimed to be the site of the lost *Griffon*. Chronologically, they include:

1 & 2. The inaugural *Griffon* site claims, made in about 1805 and in 1848 at Hamburg, New York, along the Lake Erie shore.

3. The Fitzwilliam Island discovery, north of Tobermory, Ontario, in 1860.

4. In the 1870's, the shipwreck in the harbor of St. James on Beaver Island.

5. The alleged *Griffon* anchor, found in Green Bay in 1887.

6 & 7. Two claims made in the "Straits of Detroit."

8. An unidentified shipwreck at Fisherman Shoal near Summer Island to the northeast of Green Bay in Lake Michigan.

9. The shipwreck buried in Mud Lake, connected by Tawas Bay with Saginaw Bay, uncovered in 1897.

10. The shipwreck found near the mouth of the Saugeen River at Southampton, Ontario, on Lake Huron in 1897.

11. The old shipwreck on the rocky shoreline and several skeletons in a nearby cave, western end of Manitoulin Island, Ontario, at the Mississagi Straits, claimed publicly to be the *Griffon* in 1927.

12. An old shipwreck off Birch Island near Hessel, Michigan, in the Cheneaux Islands, publicized in 1933.

13. Orrie Vail's shipwreck (the Griffon Cove Wreck) site at Russel Island near Tobermory, Ontario, with nearby skeletons, publicized in 1955.

14. The North Channel wreck near Thessalon, Ontario, made public in 1969.

15. A portion of an unidentified shipwreck sticking out of the bottom of northern Green Bay, claimed in the summer of 2004.

Each of these sites will be examined in more detail.

*   *   *

A letter from James W, Peters of East Evans, Erie County, and D. Eddy of Hamburg, New York, to the editor of the *Commercial Advertiser* of Buffalo, New York, published on January 26, 1848, appears to be the first *Griffon* shipwreck claim. This letter recounted an earlier discovery, made some time between 1805 and 1808 in the Lake Erie sand at Hamburg, New York, of a large quantity of iron rods weighing about 700 or 800 pounds. A tree about 12 inches in diameter had grown over these rods, indicating that they had been there for quite some time.

At that same site, embedded in sand but uncovered by a storm in January, 1848, were found "...a beautiful anchor and two small cannon, one above the other with French lettering...." These cannon "were defaced with age and rust, filled with sand, the horns or trunions knocked off, and an inscription in French on one of the guns." Peters, in his letter to the newspaper, claimed that these relics were from La Salle's *Griffon*.

These two eastern Lake Erie sites, one "above" the other, were identified in 1881 by Great Lakes historian Captain J. C. Van Cleve to be from the wreck site of a small British man-of-war which had stranded and wrecked there in the late 1760's. After 1763 and the end of the Seven Years' War, in which the victorious British took over New France from the defeated French, British military vessels on the Great Lakes often carried and used the spoils of war -- and this included any confiscated French cannons.

*   *   *

In 1860, two commercial fishermen named Alexander Munroe and George MacAuley from Southampton, Canada West (the province of Ontario was called Canada West prior to Canadian Confederation in 1867) claimed to have located the wreck of the *Griffon* near the southern tip of Fitzwilliam Island off the southeastern end of Manitoulin Island north of Tobermory in Georgian Bay. In clear water close to shore, the men found wooden shipwreck remains while they were setting their nets. They claimed to have recovered from those shallow, broken timbers an old brass cannon weighing about 200 pounds with French markings on it, and a pair of old muskets. On their return journey, however, their sailing craft capsized near Chantry Island close to Southampton, with the cannon and one of the two muskets sinking to the lake bottom.

The men survived, only to learn later that they had found the wreck of the 60-ton schooner, *Alice Hackett,* which had been accidentally stranded and wrecked by a drunken military crew at that spot along Fitzwilliam Island on November 8, 1828. The *Hackett* had been transferring a garrison of soldiers and their belongings from Drummond Island to Penetanguishene.

Again, the presence of a French cannon on board a post-1763 British ship on the inland seas was considered normal. It is not known what became of the remaining musket which the two fishermen had recovered.

* * *

Beaver Island, by far the largest of a chain of islands in northern Lake Michigan, would have been one of the first islands encountered had the *Griffon* sailed in a straight line between northern Green Bay and Michilimackinac. At the northern end of Beaver Island is the protected harbor named St. James. An old shipwreck in this harbor was, at one time, claimed to be the remains of the *Griffon*. Captain Dominick Gallagher, keeper of the Beaver Head Lighthouse, has been quoted as saying, "In 1875, it [the wreck] was partly above water. It was not a schooner, but a caravel style of ship of shallow draught with a high stern like the old saltwater ships, with no centerboard. As a boy, I swam and dived around the hull; it was so different to the ordinary sailing vessels, that I became convinced it was the long-lost *Griffon*."

Experts analyzing the probable track of the *Griffon* have stated that Lucas, the pilot, was most apt to head the ship back to Michilimackinac hugging the northern shoreline of Lake Michigan rather than casting fate to the wind and sailing straight out into the unbroken horizon where there were known trouble spots of islands and reefs. This does not totally eliminate these northern lake islands, but the wreckage in St. James harbor described by the keeper was, in all likelihood, a newer vintage barge of unusual design, or even the ship which belonged to Beaver Island's Mormon "King" Strang in the mid-1800's.

* * *

During the summer of 1887, an ancient anchor made of wood was grappled out of the depths of Green Bay "in a petrified condition." It looked so old and unusual that sailors immediately jumped to the conclusion that it must have come from the *Griffon*, which one newspaper at that time stated was "lost in that locality upward of 200 years ago."

This conversation piece of an anchor, placed on exhibit in the Transportation Building at the 1893 Columbian Exposition in Chicago, had, by that time, been evaluated as "not uncommon on trading vessels on the upper Great Lakes in 1792," fully a century after the *Griffon's* time.

Described as "a curious contrivance," the anchor "is about five feet across from tip to tip of the flukes and about four feet high. It is regarded as

EARLY ANCHOR OF THE LAKES

CRIS KOHL COLLECTION

a picturesque relic of early navigation. Three of the legs are a part of the stump which forms the head. The fourth leg, in front, is movable and is secured by an iron bar....This was moved outward in order to fill the basket with stones and then pushed back into place and nailed in again."

In all likelihood, the *Griffon* never actually sailed into the waters of Green Bay, remaining for its brief time in this area at anchor just off the Lake Michigan side of one of the islands (probably Washington Island or Rock Island) at the bay's wide mouth.

The nineteenth-century American historian, Francis Parkman, described how four of La Salle's men, "well stimulated with brandy," struggled to carry the heavy anchor up the Niagara escarpment to the site where the *Griffon* was being built. The anchor found in 1887, besides dating from the late 1700's, appears to have been of much lighter construction.

*   *   *

Maritime historian C. H. J. Snider made reference to two *Griffon* claims having been made in "the Straits of Detroit," but so little was reported about these that the only possible conclusion is that they turned out to be shipwrecks of newer vintage. It is unlikely that the *Griffon* made it as far as the Detroit River on her tragic return voyage, and any shipwrecks found in any other "Straits of Detroit" (and there were mentions made by early French explorers of other locations in the Great Lakes to which they gave that common name) have proven to be mistaken.

*   *   *

If one pictures the scenario of the *Griffon* having been seized and burned by Indians shortly after departing Washington or Rock Island, then that tragic event likely took place off Summer Island along the northeast side of Green Bay, for that isle was well-known as an old home of the Ottawas, who were wary and skeptical of La Salle's presence and angered by his ship.

One unidentified shipwreck at Fisherman Shoal just east of Summer Island was reported as a possible contender for being the long-lost *Griffon*, but an investigation concluded that this claim was based upon a desire for publicity and turned out to be a 19th-century wreck of a burned steamer.

*　　*　　*

Mud Lake, today called Lake Solitude, lies just inland from Tawas Bay, east of East Tawas, Michigan, on Lake Huron. This was the site, in 1897, of the discovery of shipwreck remains which yielded wooden spars, metal pieces reflecting ancient workmanship and massive chains of an unusual design.

By itself, this would make a weak claim for a _Griffon_ candidate, but in 1899, excavation of the site reportedly revealed skeletons, one with a sword rammed between its bones. The sword's hilt was decorated with French _fleur-de-lis_ and a French inscription with the date "1570" in it.

The man who found and excavated this shipwreck was T.E. Johnson, Superintendent of Education in Lansing, Michigan, and his report to _Michigan History Magazine_ argued strongly that this was La Salle's _Griffon_ and the skeletons were those of Lucas and the other five sailors who had all died either from an attack upon their ship or from quarreling among themselves.

This shipwreck, along with the artifacts and human remains, has since disappeared.

*　　*　　*

During the digging of a well along the shore of the Saugeen River at Southampton, Ontario, in 1897, the Rowan family, reaching a depth of ten feet, hit what appeared to be the bow of an old sailing vessel.

More excavation resulted in the finding of a dinner bell about five inches tall, displaying a _fleur-de-lis_ (the flower displayed on the French flag) and seemingly of French manufacture. Reportedly the ship's prow displayed the carving of an animal which, if viewed from a certain angle with quite an open mind, resembled a griffin. This claim, while containing some elements of truth, appears to be mostly imagination. One source of information states that these finds were simply the buried remains of a crib or bridge abutment, along with some peripheral debris.

*　　*　　*

Canada's Manitoulin Island in northern Lake Huron has a strong claim to solving the _Griffon_ mystery. In late October, 1927, Mr. Harold G. Tucker, a lawyer from Owen Sound, Ontario, arranged

51

for a small party of journalists to join him at the site of a shorebound shipwreck about one and a half miles north of the Mississagi (also spelled Missisagi and Missassage over the years) Straits Lighthouse at the extreme western end of thinly-populated Manitoulin Island, the largest freshwater island in the world. Tucker was convinced that this wreckage was the remains of La Salle's *Griffon*.

Tucker and other people had known about this shipwreck for years. The lighthouse at Mississagi Straits was built in 1877, and the first lighthouse keeper, Albert Cullis, who worked there until 1899, was aware that this shipwreck had lain north of his light for a long time already.

Others knew about the shipwreck, too. In the early 1800's, Indians reportedly took white explorers to see what they and their forefathers called the "White Man's Ship." A general name like this would seem likeliest to have been applied at a time when there was little or no competition from other ships for such a title. From the remains of this wreck, the Indians had recovered hand-forged spikes and handmade bolts, lead which had been used as caulking, and old tools which they showed to the white men. Some time after the lighthouse was constructed in 1877, Indians and white fishermen set fire to the shorebound wreck to obtain more of the lead caulking, which they melted down, remolded and used as lead for bullets or weights on their fishing nets. Reportedly some timbers were hauled away for use as firewood.

By 1927, barrister Tucker, who had been visiting that far end of Manitoulin Island for years, believed this shipwreck was the *Griffon*. The non-nautical newspapermen in his 1927 beach outing, staring at a pile of boards which to them did not much resemble a ship, were not as assured.

However, an interesting side story adds much to the tale of this shipwreck.

In the late 1890's, aging lighthouse keeper Albert Cullis, with assistance from two young helpers named William Grant and John Holdsworth, both of whom lived nearby, built and sold small sailboats in his spare time to augment his paltry income.

One day, Cullis scoured the nearby forest along the shoreline for a tree which would make a suitable small boat mast. He ventured towards a small canyon just to the south of "the old wreck" and immediately viewed a number of straight white spruce trees, any one of which would serve his purpose. As he entered the canyon, a rabbit jumped out ahead of him and scurried into a hole formed by the upturned roots of a large, toppled tree. Hoping that this hole was shallow and exitless so he could catch the rabbit and feast on a stew dinner that evening, Cullis went in pursuit. As he peered into the hole, he saw no rabbit, but something else caught his eye. A long watch chain lay draped over one of the tree roots. Digging it out, Cullis reached a tarnished silver watchcase, between three and four inches in diameter, which had held a type of "turnip watch" with the works rusted away, attached to the chain. More digging revealed three coins or tokens made of copper or brass, two of them triangular in shape, the other square, each about one-and-a-quarter inches in diameter with a round center which was slightly raised, all bearing dates from the 1600's.

The excited Cullis, aware of the close proximity of "the old wreck," connected these discoveries to whatever crew had been on that vessel. Looking further around, he noticed the mouth of a small cave formed by the lean of a long, straight slab of limestone. Peering inside this cave, Cullis saw three human skeletons lying neatly in a row, as if they had retreated into this shelter but perished from the cold or starvation.

Lighthouse keeper Albert Cullis found artifacts.
COURTESY OF THE MISSISSAGI LIGHTHOUSE MUSEUM AND PARK

Cullis quickly ran back to the lighthouse, his quest for a sailboat mast completely forgotten, and he summoned his two young helpers. William Grant (who became the Mississagi Lighthouse keeper in 1915 and remained in that position until his retirement in 1940) and John Holdsworth, both feeling the tingles, joined Cullis in returning by boat to the site of his discoveries.

The trio of men found more coins or tokens, several shipbuilders' tools and two mysterious, round brass items. These latter were later identified by an elderly British sea captain who visited the lighthouse as small cannon rams from which the wooden handles were missing through intent or corrosion. An examination of the three skeletons showed one to be of extraordinarily gigantic size; Grant, himself over six feet tall, could place the jaw bone of the large skull completely around the outside of his own face.

Although the men thought there could easily be a connection between the items they had found around the cave and "the old wreck," they did not know the story of La Salle's *Griffon*, nor did they know about the immense size of Lucas the Pilot. They took the skulls and some of the larger bones, as well as all of the relics, back to the lighthouse with them.

Not long afterwards, news of these finds reached the nearby town of Gore Bay, also on Manitoulin Island. Before long, a group of historians, including Gore Bay's F.W. Major and Dr. Frederick J. Conboy of Toronto, visited the site by boat. These men, familiar with the story of La Salle, the *Griffon* and her last crew, scoured the area near "the old wreck" in quest of more clues. About a mile up the shoreline heading north, and a bit inland, a second small cave was located. This contained another three skeletons. Now the total was six, the exact number of the *Griffon's* final crew. Another report divides the number of skeletons into four from the first cave and two from the latter, but the total remains six, with both reports placing the largest skeleton in the initial cave. Despite many more searches, no more caves containing skeletal remains were located.

However, archaeological techniques were not known or applied, and considering their genuine interest in history, the group was surprisingly sloppy. Four of the skulls and some of the large bones were placed in a macabre setup along the lighthouse dock, and ended up kicked into the water and lost, reportedly either when some of the boys whooped it up during a celebration one night, or when Cullis suddenly turned superstitious at the onset of a storm. Another of the skulls was kept by Dr. Conboy, and the largest of the skulls, which could have been that of Lucas the Dane, allegedly ended up somewhere in the National Museum in Toronto.

Lighthouse keeper Cullis had kept the old coins and tokens, but he retired and moved to Bruce Mines, Ontario, near the Canadian Soo (Sault Ste. Marie). These items disappeared after his death, although another report states that he had given these items to someone in the Soo. John Holdsworth kept the large watch, which was definitely dateable to the time of La Salle, and it went with him when he moved first to Michipicoten Harbour on the northeast shore of Lake Superior, and later to the Canadian Soo. It, too, has disappeared. Of the

What remained of the Mississagi Straits wreck in 1927 measured 30 feet long and 15 feet wide, with the original full beam estimated to have been 20 feet, about the size of the Griffon's width.

COURTESY OF THE MISSISSAGI LIGHTHOUSE MUSEUM AND PARK

brass cannon rams, one was cut into wedges to repair the lighthouse's oil tank, while the other went missing. The old tools and remaining bones became souvenirs for tourists to carry away with them from the lighthouse.

Another lighthouse helper named Jack Allen reportedly found many brass buttons in the gravel of the cave where the first skeletons had been located. A coffee can which was about two-thirds full of these buttons sat on the shelf of the old foghorn shed at the Mississagi Straits Lighthouse when the shed burned down. The buttons were all destroyed by the flames.

Virtually all of the evidence which might have decidedly help identify this shipwreck as that of the *Griffon* was thoughtlessly scattered or destroyed. The waves and the wind and the ice of hundreds of seasons in the Great Lakes had already taken their toll. Then axes and saws and fire and removal, all directed by humans, not Nature, further degraded the shipwreck remains.

A group believing the Mississagi wreck to be the *Griffon* worked hard to prove it. Roy F. Fleming of Ottawa, Ontario, under the auspices of the Department of Public Works, removed a screw bolt and nut about 30 inches in length, one which was used to join the keel, ribs and keelson, and submitted it to the National Academy of Arts and Trades in Paris, France, for examination. Their analysis found that "the bolt was manufactured by a process used in France previous to the 18th century and bears all essential characteristics of that process." This was strong evidence that the bolt was part of the *Griffon's* ironwork which had been manufactured in France from so-called "Swedish iron" and conveyed to Niagara at great financial expense.

The lead caulking is a strong argument in favor of this being the *Griffon* wreck site, as this author knows of no other Great Lakes vessel which utilized

"The old wreck" at the western end of Manitoulin Island north of the Mississagi Straits Lighthouse, as it appeared in 1934.
COURTESY OF THE MISSISSAGI LIGHTHOUSE MUSEUM AND PARK

this old European (originally Scandinavian) shipbuilding method. Numerous authorities -- the Smithsonian Institute and the Marine Department of Canada among them -- have not found any record of lead caulking ever being used in North American ship construction.

Analysis of the wooden frames has also indicated that their source trees could have been mature and from the Niagara area (which produced a noticeably different type of white oak than that found in the northern Great Lakes regions) at the time the *Griffon* was built.

Two cannon balls, one weighing three pounds and the other just under five, were found on Manitoulin Island near the Mississagi wreck site.

Commander Eugene F. McDonald of Chicago chatted with his 16-year-old nephew from Buffalo, Gene Kinney, an experienced hardhat diver, while Gene's sister, Mary bid him farewell at the outset of McDonald's 1937 Griffon *expedition to Manitoulin Island's Mississagi Straits.* CRIS KOHL COLLECTION

Commander Eugene F. McDonald of Chicago spent several years in the late 1930's attempting to solve this Mississagi Straits shipwreck puzzle. He took his yacht, the *Mizpah*, a luxury vessel about three times the length of the ship he hoped to identify and loaded with salvage equipment, to the shoreline wreckage on Manitoulin Island to try to locate and raise that portion of the hull and/or the anchor which had been snagging fishermen's nets in the deep water just off shore. But this water depth drops almost immediately to 180 feet and slopes deeper from there. Even the hardhat diving equipment McDonald had on board was inadequate for that depth.

The records of McDonald's August, 1937, expedition and examination (made along with Dr. George R. Fox, President of the Michigan Archaeological Society) indicated that the white oak timbers were hand-hewn, the vessel was flat-bottomed, of sturdy and heavy construction (built by shipbuilders trained to engineer vessels for ocean use), with ribs being spaced less than one foot apart, appearing to be of the Dutch and Flemish galliot type, with a beam not exceeding 20 feet and a length of about 60 feet. It was McDonald's theory that the *Griffon* struck the nearby Magnetic Reefs and broke in two, with both parts being blown over to Manitoulin Island.

If he were to find the *Griffon*, McDonald had already told the press that efforts would be made to reconstruct the old ship so that she could sail along the Chicago waterfront during the city's jubilee Carnival of the Lakes.

McDonald claimed to have found a small section of the Mississagi wreck in the waters off shore, but he

Hulk Is Studied Anew for Clew to LaSalle Ship

CHICAGO, Aug. 9—Eugene F. McDonald, Chicago manufacturer and yachtsman who set out to prove, if he can, that the hulk of an old vessel in Mississauga Strait, off the western end of Manitoulin Island, is that of the lost ship Le Griffon, radioed Mon-

Eugene F. McDonald of Chicago often made headlines during his 1930's Griffon expeditions. CRIS KOHL COLLECTION

failed to locate the reputed anchor or a cannon which would have simplified identification. His expeditions stopped with the onset of World War II.

The shipwreck remains, those which sat on the rocky shoreline and had not been torn apart or burned by the locals, disappeared in 1942, washed away by a violent storm. Some of the timbers which had been removed earlier and stored are today shared by three museums on Manitoulin Island.

In 1947, an elderly resident of Manitoulin Island told the recent tale of two men on a visiting boat who had lost their anchor "right opposite the lighthouse." In their attempts to snag that anchor, they had instead brought to the surface a brass cannon. While clumsily trying to land this heavy, slippery catch, the men watched the cannon suddenly drop back into the depths. Another report states that commercial fishermen have snagged their nets on obstructions "lying in the passage above the light" at a depth of 180 feet, one of which is a portion of a shipwreck (which could be the remainder of the *Griffon*), while the other is supposedly a large anchor, too heavy for the fishermen to raise in their nets from that depth. These tales could be true, or they could just be a couple of the spurious stories to surface in recent times. The claim that swords were found in or near the cave with the skeletons is pure imagination. Another claim that a hardhat diver died while searching in the Mississagi Straits for any remains of the *Griffon* or its cannon or anchor is unsubstantiated.

The Gore Bay Museum has some of the lead caulking, as well as excellent information about the various expeditions from the 1900's, including scuba searches made between 1954 and 1962 which scoured the

Mississagi wreck timbers and lead caulking, possibly from the Griffon, *at the Gore Bay Museum on Manitoulin Island.*

PHOTO BY CRIS KOHL

area, above and below the water, for clues to that shipwreck's identity.

Scuba (or s.c.u.b.a. -- for self-contained underwater breathing apparatus), was developed in 1943 in France by Jacques Cousteau and his team, but it was not until World War II ended in 1945 that scuba diving started to slowly catch on among water lovers in Europe and North America.

The first documented group of scuba divers to show up where the Mississagi wreck once lay arrived in 1954 when two members of the Underwater Club in Toronto made only one dive and recorded notes on conditions such as bottom topography and water current. If they located anything pertaining to the shipwreck, it was not noted.

In 1958, four scuba divers from Detroit and Grosse Pointe, Michigan, with the goal of locating shipwreck material near the Mississagi wreck site, discovered nearly 200 square hand-threaded nuts, washers, spikes, iron bars and lead caulking, all of which they donated to the Gore Bay Museum.

Norman McCready, an Indianapolis insurance executive who had served as a Navy commander during World War II, and his team of divers spent time at the Mississagi wreck site on board his white, 35-foot boat, *Penmanta,* equipped with electronic underwater detection devices, during two summers. In 1960, McCready brought up shipwreck railing, planking and ribbing from a depth of over 200 feet in the Mississagi Straits, and in 1961, his divers recovered a ship's bell broken in two from the same area. But conclusive evidence that these items came from the *Griffon* remained elusive.

Another group of scuba divers, from the Central YMCA Skin Divers Club of Cleveland, Ohio, in 1962 loaded up two station wagons with gear, including a trailer with a 16-foot aluminum boat, a portable generator, a trailer-mounted air compressor, marker buoys and underwater photography equipment, and headed to the rocky shoreline where the shipwreck remains had rested prior to 1942. They located and recovered numerous bolts, handmade spikes, nuts, washers, pins and other examples of early ironwork, plus, from a depth of 75 feet, a 32-foot-long wooden beam which had several small ribs attached to it. All of the artifacts were donated to museums on Manitoulin Island. These divers had their experiences publicized in an article in the world's pre-eminent scuba magazine at that time, *Skin Diver Magazine*, a California publication, in the December, 1962 issue. Coincidentally, that same issue carried an article called "Our Vanishing Wrecks," about the need to conserve our submerged cultural resources ("We have the most to lose when our wrecks disappear....our underwater regions will soon be stripped of their wealth of shipwrecks...") written by future *Skin Diver Magazine* Editor-in-Chief Paul Tzimoulis, a man clearly ahead of his time.

In July, 1968, four boats worked with two museums at the Mississagi wreck site. Expedition leader Gene Kinney, who, as a young man, had done

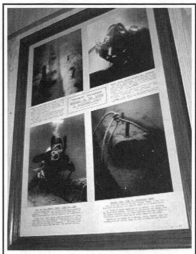

Part of the detailed 1962 Griffon *scuba search exhibit at the Gore Bay Museum.* PHOTO BY CRIS KOHL

the hardhat diving for his uncle, Eugene F. McDonald (by this time deceased) in the 1937 expedition, came up in his 58-foot yacht, the *VIV*. Joining him and the *VIV* were two other Illinois men and their vessels: famous shipwreck hunters John Steele of Waukegan in his boat, the *Lake Diver,* and Dick Race of Chicago in the *Neptune*. The *Neptune* came equipped with a sensitive magnetometer for detecting ferrous metal at considerable distances and depth, even picking up objects buried out of sight by mud, sand and boulders. The fourth vessel rounding out this exploration flotilla was the tug *Rocket,* under Skipper Jack Purvis of Sault Ste. Marie. The two organizations involved in this project were the Manitoulin Historical Marine Museum of Meldrum Bay and the Gore Bay Museum, both on Manitoulin Island.

Dick Race scanned near the "G" boulder (the Mississagi wreck's original location for years has had a large letter "G" painted by an unknown artist or artists on a large rock at the site, affectionately known by some as the "G" spot) in depths from 20 to 215 feet of water, picking up ten "hot spots" where the presence of ferrous metal was detected. The strongest signal came from the deepest "hit" in 215 feet of water, which no diver investigated.

With him on his tug, Jack Purvis had two divers, Dugal McQuarrie from Elliot Lake, Ontario, and Randy Stewart from Spragge, Ontario. The three of them spent considerable time experimenting with anchoring the vessel solidly and using the tug's propeller wash as a "sand sweeper" to blow away lake bottom debris from water less than 15 feet deep. The two divers also examined the shallow "hot spots" which had been detected, but with the limestone outcroppings giving way to a sand bottom at a depth of 15 to 20 feet and deeper, the men found no shipwreck evidence because it was buried.

Gene Kinney snorkeled in the shallows and did a scuba dive to a depth of 20 feet, but found nothing.

John Steele, on his first scuba dive at the site, explored at a depth of 120 to 140 feet for a length of 600 feet. Even though the water temperature at depth was 39 degrees (and 58 degrees on the surface), Steele stayed under for half an hour and later reported that the bottom was covered with "a layer of silt as deep as [his] arm up to the elbow." Nothing -- no beams or even rocks -- showed above the silt's surface. If there were any shipwreck objects at that depth, they were buried in deep silt. Another dive he made to 85 feet just south of the "G" boulder was to check out something he had detected on his boat's depth sounder. The object turned out to be a 20-foot-long log, sawn at both ends, about 30 inches in diameter. Steele also snorkeled in the shallows just off the "G" boulder, but without finding any piece of shipwreck material, and also, as was an accepted practice at the time, he dragged a grappling hook from his boat for several passes in front of the "G" boulder in hopes of snagging buried wooden planks with lead caulking or perhaps even the elusive anchor from the Mississagi wreck. But his hook caught nothing.

Dick Race did one dive to 110 feet around two marker buoys which had been dropped at magnetometer "hot spots," but he, too, could see no wreckage. He also explored one of the shallow spots, with no luck. Race left the project early because his father was ill, and the rest of the expedition, disappointed at having found nothing for the museums, disbanded.

In 1992, a team consisting mainly of members of the Canadian shipwreck conservation group, Save Ontario Shipwrecks, led by Ken McLeod of the Ottawa area and funded by a government grant, hired Great Lakes shipwreck hunter David Trotter of Canton, Michigan, to bring his boat and sidescan sonar to the Mississagi Straits. Although the search covered the full length of the passage and water as deep as 270 feet, newspaper accounts of the expedition mostly rehashed what was already known about the *Griffon* and the Mississagi wreck, plus technical information about the modern sidescan sonar equipment being used. One newspaper, attempting originality, stated that Ken McLeod's goal was "to methodically search the beach where the Mississagi wreck was found. That's never been done. It might provide clues to what that wreck really is." The media fizzled on reporting any outcome.

Today, the cave roof where the first set of skeletons and artifacts were found has sunk so much that the cave is no longer penetrable. It is situated 150 feet inland up the shoreline cliff and a bit south (towards the lighthouse) from the Mississagi wreck's original location, marked by the "G" boulder. Huge rocky slabs at the cave form an inverted "V" similar to a teepee shape. The cave is just east of a sandy bay where, in the 1920's, a commercial fisherman named Finnie James fouled the anchor of his fishing tug on some lead-caulked wreckage on the bottom.

Could the *Griffon* have made it into Lake Huron? No one saw the ship sail through the narrow Straits of Mackinac, despite the presence of two Indian villages, a Jesuit missionary and sundry French-Canadian fur traders populating both sides of that narrow passage. However, nearly 200 years later, no one witnessed the schooner, *Cornelia B. Windiate,* either, as that ship hastened through the Straits in late November, 1875, just before early ice closed that connecting waterway. Simply because no one saw or reported seeing the ship does not prove that she did not sail through the Straits.

One report from Michilimackinac in 1679 did reveal that several of the inhabitants had heard the sound of a cannon being fired during one night of stormy weather, perhaps as a desperate signal from an out-of-control *Griffon*, possibly sailing with a damaged or lost rudder, being pushed through the passage into Lake Huron by one of the strong westwind storms so prevalent during the autumn season on the Great Lakes. Lucas the Pilot had been given orders by La Salle to stop at Michilimackinac and leave the equipment and rigging for La Salle's planned Mississippi ship there before proceeding to Niagara with his vital cargo of furs. The *Griffon* never made that stop.

It has been conjectured that the *Griffon*, if forced through the Straits of Mackinac by strong westerly gales, could have stranded on the treacherous Magnetic Reefs (which would claim many a ship years beyond the *Griffon*) just south of Cockburn Island. There, the vessel could have broken in two, with both pieces and a clinging crew then being driven ashore six miles further east on Manitoulin Island at the Mississagi Straits.

At least one expedition from Michigan is being planned for the near future to take a remote-operated vehicle (ROV) to the Manitoulin Island side of the Mississagi Straits for a good look at what lies on that deep bottom. Perhaps that elusive definitive evidence will soon surface.

*   *   *

Another story relates how, in the summer of 1933, a northern Lake Huron Indian, the descendant of chiefs, revealed on his deathbed the secret location of the *Griffon* to a summer resident. The wreck lay in shallow water off Birch Island. That location had been regarded with a superstitious fear by the Indians and avoided as much as possible by them. According to legend, it had been a trader's ship which was lost with all hands, and reputedly carried a treasure of unspecified nature.

Birch Island, Michigan (not to be confused with Birch Island, Ontario, which also lies in northern Lake Huron, but off the northeast point of St. Joseph Island) is a small but long, narrow sliver of land about two miles south-southwest of the town of Hessel, Michigan, lying just west of the much larger Marquette Island. Located ten miles northeast of Mackinac Island, Birch Island makes complete sense if one considers a northeast wind creating a perfect drift line for the flotsam which was reportedly found on the east shore of Mackinac Island several months after the *Griffon* disappeared.

The Hessel wreckage was first located in 1925 by Capt. Louis Goudeau, an experienced Great Lakes shipmaster. However, he died before he could make a close examination. Cannon balls, allegedly of the size corresponding to the cannons on board the *Griffon*, and a gun carriage were also found near Birch Island, adding to the belief that this shipwreck had been armed.

The Les Cheneaux Chamber of Commerce and the Michigan State Park Commission excitedly envisioned a high-profile future for this wreck, including raising it, rebuilding it, and setting it up for public exhibit on shore. Times were tough in the mid 1930's, and anything to attract tourist dollars to this remote area was welcomed.

But serious examination of the wreck, reportedly completed in April, 1934, by Dr. Franklin Cook, a marine scientist from Evanston, Illinois, declared the vessel to be no older than from the year 1850.

RAISES HULL OF LA SALLE PACKET

Michigan Park Board Think It Has Found 'Griffon,' Long Lost Fur Ship.

If success attends the efforts of the Michigan State Park Commission to exhibit the recovered hull of La Salle's long-lost fur packet, Griffon, at Mackinac Island this summer, the thousands of tourists who visit this region will be afforded a striking

This article from the summer of 1934 incorrectly implied that the Birch Island shipwreck near Hessel, Michigan, had already been raised.

CRIS KOHL COLLECTION

A few stubborn *Griffon* believers tried to keep their case alive. Dr. B.L. Corbett of the Milwaukee Safety Commission presented a piece of wood from the Birch Island *Griffon* site to the Green Bay, Wisconsin, Kiwanis Club in June, 1934, and during that summer, stakes were driven around the wreck, with hundreds of tourists enjoying boat cruises to the alleged *Griffon*.

By summer's end, the enthusiasm was tapering off with the realization that this was not the shipwreck people had hoped it would be. They accepted the fact that it was not the *Griffon* and tried to let this claim die down as quietly and as inconspicuously as possible. A letter to the editor in one of the Detroit newspapers, innocently asking about the status of this *Griffon* claim, received a response that "plans for raising the hulk...were abandoned by Les Cheneaux Chamber of Commerce officials after it was found the cost would be too great...." It was, after all, in the midst of the Great Depression, and costly historic projects such as this were seen as frivolous at a time when many people were struggling to put food on the family table. *Griffon* supporters were appeased with the announcement that the Chamber of Commerce had been advised that it would be cheaper to raise the hulk during the winter, so they would wait. But a quiet, inactive winter passed.

By the time a veteran hardhat diver named John Beattie from nearby DeTour, Michigan, offered his services for free during the summer of 1935 in an attempt to learn more about the identity of this shipwreck, it was already clear that this was not the *Griffon*. This wreck, it had been learned, was, at 120 feet, about twice the length of the fabled ship, and it had a centerboard, a device not invented until many years after the *Griffon's* loss.

*   *   *

Dozens of books have been written about the explorer La Salle, but only two, both slim volumes, devoting their entire contents to the *Griffon,* have been published. The first one, simply named *The Griffon*, is a sliver of an artistic hardcover book consisting of 23 pages of text and a few drawings printed on thick vellum paper, issued without a dustjacket and published in Toronto. This small story was written in 1956 by one of Canada's pre-eminent maritime figures, C. H. J. Snider (1879-1971), who had previously written half a dozen larger books dealing with Canada's early maritime history. His weekly "Schooner Days" articles published in the *Toronto Evening Telegram* newspaper between 1931 and 1956 had a devoted following. One-fifth of his 148-page 1958 book, *Tarry Breeks & Velvet Garters,* is also about the *Griffon*. Although Snider had initially supported the Mississagi wreck on Manitoulin Island as being that of the *Griffon*, he clearly had some reservations (he found the over-heavy construction, the absence of tree-nails or "trunnels," and the presence of heavy ironwork for so small a vessel to be the roots of his doubt), and after he studied the Griffon Cove wreck near Tobermory, Ontario, in the 1950's, he quickly changed sides.

The second book, *The Fate of the Griffon*, by Toronto journalist Harrison John MacLean, appearing in 1974, contained 118 pages, also in hardcover binding but with a dustjacket, and published in Toronto and Chicago.

Both books argue in favor of Orrie Vail's Griffon Cove shipwreck's being the remains of the old *Griffon*. Like Snider, MacLean wrote for the *Toronto Telegram,* and in his book, he expressed, among other things, concerns about rival newspapers beating him to the "scoop." He dreamed of being the one to break the story of Orrie Vail's shipwreck discovery of the *Griffon* to the world, something which MacLean succeeded in doing on August 16, 1955.

Large headlines in Toronto newspapers reported that Orrie Vale, 62, a retired commercial fisherman and boatbuilder, had, as a child in 1900, discovered a 40-foot white oak keel, studded with hand-hammered spikes, in a cove on an island just north of the small town of Tobermory at the tip of the Bruce Peninsula. Only after retirement did he finally find the time to take a serious look at this shipwreck and reveal its presence to maritime experts, who agreed with him that it was, in all likelihood, the *Griffon*.

Tobermory's Vail family knew for three generations about the existence of this small shipwreck with the blackened hull lying in a secluded cove within a cove on the northeast side of Russel Island. But Orrie Vail's father and grandfather brought no public attention to the wreck. Orrie learned about these timbers when his father took him there to collect lumber which had fallen off the decks of passing cargo ships and drifted ashore. Even before the Vail family arrived, Indians knew about this wreck. Orrie, who spoke their language, heard the story, handed down through the generations, of how a crew of white men were killed and their boat was burned.

One theory holds that the *Griffon* could have been seized by pillaging Indians who then beached the craft and burned it. Another possible scenario is that Lucas the Pilot had persuaded the five members of his crew to join him in absconding with La Salle's furs. Presumably the men had used some of those furs to purchase canoes from local Indians before hiding the *Griffon* in a remote backwater and setting the ship on fire.

Journalist MacLean relied heavily upon the opinons of two men during the investigation of the Griffon Cove wreck: Rowley W. Murphy, a noted marine artist, and C.H.J. Snider. MacLean called the latter "the dean of Canada's nautical historians."

Analysis of the wood showed that the ship had been constructed of white oak. Nothing, however, was mentioned about the fact that most wooden ships built on the Great Lakes were constructed of white oak.

The Griffon Cove wreck showed signs of having had two mast steps; the *Griffon* carried two masts.

The minimum of iron usage in the Griffon Cove wreck, compared with iron's more lavish use in other wrecks such as the Mississagi wreck, corresponded logically with Hennepin's account of its scarcity.

Centerboards were developed in about 1800; appropriately, neither the Griffon Cove wreck nor the Mississagi Straits wreck had a centerboard.

The Griffon Cove wreck was secured by bolts which were tightened, not by nuts on threads, but by means of wedge-shaped pins pounded into slots in the ends of the bolts. For many experts, this cinched the age of the vessel as corresponding to that of the *Griffon*.

In the mid-20th century, experts held that screw threads on iron bolts (like those found on the Mississagi wreck on Manitoulin Island) had not yet been invented at the time of the *Griffon's* construction. Research in old European building tools and methods has since proved otherwise.

Many experts, however, did not agree with Vail. George Fox, a Michigan archaeologist-historian, sided strongly with the Manitoulin wreck. A French naval archaeologist, as well as Commander-of-Frigate Vichot, head of the French naval museum, turned down the Tobermory claim several times, concluding that "the Tobermory wreck does not appear to be of French construction....its technique corresponds to the 18th century or later."

There was talk of dredging the cove in hopes of finding a "smoking gun" clue: an anchor or a cannon. But funds for such a project were not found. Documentation was sent to the National Historic Sites and Monuments Board in Ottawa. Their response, a year later, was that the identity of the Griffon "has not been proved."

With no funding available to him to pursue his claims or to conserve the many shipwreck pieces which he had removed and placed in his locked shed for safekeeping, Orrie Vail guarded his treasures with a shotgun and, if anyone was interested, for fifty cents he would show them the remains of the *Griffon*.

Orrie Vail passed away at age 83 in May, 1976, and was buried at Dunk's Bay Cemetery outside Tobermory. Thirteen years later, the "Griffon Cove Wreck's" claim to fame still had its supporters. I received a letter, dated April 23, 1989, from a gentleman named Chy Langford of Arkona, Ontario. Obviously familiar with the work of Orrie Vail at Tobermory, Mr. Langford was upset over the lack of government support for Vail's *Griffon* wreck claims:

> *Dear Mr. Kohl,*
> *I realize you don't know me, but I hope you may be able to suggest how to go about getting some help or possibly suggesting what to do....*
> *As an experienced diver, you probably have made several dives at Tobermory. I guess the actual story starts a few years ago when I read a book called* Fate of the Griffon. *It was written by Harrison John McLean. He did quite a bit of research and talked to quite a few people, plus he actually met and became a very good friend to one Orrie Vail. Orrie Vail was the man who found the remains of an ancient sailing vessel, the first one to*

sail the Great Lakes. With John MacLean's help in researching, with the aid of C. H. J. Snider and Rowley Murphy who were experts in their fields, authenticated, along with signed documents, that the remains of the ship which Orrie Vail found and his father and grandfather and generations before Orrie had known about, were those of the Griffon.

This was all well and good, but now comes the problem. I have met and talked to Orrie Vail's daughter and have been told some unbelievable news. Orrie, along with the other men I have mentioned, have all passed away. A company, who by the way owns the car ferry which runs between Tobermory and Manitoulin Island, purchased the land the company uses for the ferry now from the Vail family. When the land was purchased, it was agreed between these people and the family that the old Vail home and the ship's remains would be put on display at the local museum. Now I learn that the Parks people who run the museums still have not done what they agreed to do. Apparently they don't believe these remains are really those of the Griffon. *The only men who could argue differently now have since passed away. This seems so wrong since this was not the original agreement. Orrie's daughter said she would hunt these important papers up so she could prove her point. Would it not be a better idea that these remains be preserved and displayed for everyone to see and appreciate a great piece of history?*

I realize that maybe there is nothing you can do, but even a suggestion to what we might try to do would certainly be encouraging. I know how dedicated you are to saving Ontario shipwrecks and to save the remains of this particular ship instead of it rotting away in some shed, where it now is stored, would be a great achievement. Thank you for taking the time to read this. It is greatly appreciated.

With best wishes,
Chy Langford

Mr. Langford had taken the time and effort to express his concern over the welfare of one aspect of our Great Lakes maritime history, and I appreciated his letter. However, I knew that several authorities did not believe that this particular shipwreck was the famous *Griffon*. But I was certainly in a position to publicize Mr. Langford's plea for assistance, since, in the late 1980's and early 1990's, I was the editor of a widely circulated bi-monthly newsletter which I had begun and named *Great Lakes In Depth*, produced for the Windsor (Ontario) chapter of Save Ontario Shipwrecks, a provincial maritime conservation group.

So I printed most of Mr. Langford's letter on the "Letters to the Editor" page of *Great Lakes In Depth*. I also used the old "Editor-gets-the-last-word" privilege to comment upon "the enormous costs of effectively preserving shipwreck timbers" likely being the cause for delaying their preservation.

Aware of the larger picture, I also wrote, "This disputable wreckage may or may not be from the *Griffon*, but the stories behind the search and the claims have themselves become part of Great Lakes history...." I ended with a suggestion that perhaps someone from the government could provide a more official response.

In no time at all, I had a response from the government, specifically from Mr. Peter Engelbert, a shipwreck expert who was employed at that time by the Ministry of Culture and Communications in the Province of Ontario. He generously sent me a note and a photocopy of a document called "The Griffon Cove Wreck: A Case Study in Archaeological Reconstruction of Timber Hull Remains," a Master's degree thesis by Paul F. Hundley published in 1984 by the Australian Institute for Maritime Archaeology, Fremantle, Western Australia. Mr. Engelbert's note read:

> Read this carefully, then let that hoary old tale of Orrie Vail's wreck being the Griffon *rest in peace. C. H. J. Snider and Rowley Murphy were knowledgeable men, but they did not have the benefit of a full underwater excavation, such as Paul Hundley did....*

In 1978, staff members of Fathom Five Provincial Park, the first underwater park or preserve in the Great Lakes -- established in 1972 due to the high concentration of shipwecks within five miles of Tobermory (and which, in 1987, became Fathom Five National Marine Park) -- excavated the Griffon Cove wreck site. Paul Hundley's detailed research and technical study on the Griffon Cove shipwreck indicated, among other things, that there had never been any decking on this vessel. His Master's degree thesis, after 60 pages outlining the details and his analysis, arrived at this conclusion:

> Evaluation of the hull remains, artefacts [sic] associated with the wreck, and contemporary historical records has led to the conclusion that the Griffon Cove wreck is not the *Griffon*. These remains are from a vessel, probably a local variation of a Mackinaw boat, approximately 45 ft. in length, used and abandoned in the mid-1800's.

Even though experts in the 1950's had studied and analyzed the wood and iron at this site, and Rowley Murphy had made a detailed and impressive drawing of the shipwreck with its missing hull lines extended, the Griffon

Cove wreck had been a large, open fishing boat, an undecked vessel. Except for its length and beam, it was not at all like the *Griffon*.

This turned out to be a good thing, for, had the Griffon Cove wreck really been the long lost *Griffon*, with the amount of site disturbance that had been carried on over so many years (similar to the Mississagi Straits wreck site), much of what we could have learned from it would have been destroyed.

The irony hit with tremendous impact. The only two books about the most famous missing shipwreck in the Great Lakes, written by recognized authorities Snider and MacLean, turned out to be about the wrong ship!

Hundley's conclusion about the Griffon Cove wreck opened the way for Mr. Engelbert's closing comments about the *Griffon* in his note to me: "Look on the bright side. She's still out there waiting to be found...by me!"

As editor, I placed all that information in the next issue of *Great Lakes In Depth*, again using my editorial prerogative to get in the last word: "We won't tell Peter that a large portion of the *Griffon* has been sitting in my shed for years!"

After the episode with the letters, one more incident occurred involving the Griffon Cove wreck. One day in late November, 1996, I was glancing through the pages of one of the the local newspapers for items of interest when a large classified advertisement for a historical estate auction in London, Ontario, jumped out at me. I read the list of offerings:

> ...antique dining table, War of 1812 British officer's sword, 1885 patchwork quilt, 1812 mortar and pestle, 1894 buffalo robes, old area and Canadiana books, 1903 birchbark canoe, rare Great Lakes marine lamp, Victorian clothing and footwear, "Penny-Farthing" bicycle, unique historical records and components of the 1679 "Griffin" [sic] which was the first sailing vessel on the Great Lakes,....

I read no further because I could not believe my eyes. I went over those words repeatedly. Items from the wreck of the *Griffon*? To be sold at public auction!? This sort of thing just did not happen in the Great Lakes, particularly in the province of Ontario.

On the scheduled evening of the auction, I drove eagerly to London, stood in line, received my bidding number (#304) and took my time browsing among the many curious people viewing these unique antiques. Of course, I spent most of the pre-auction time scrutinizing the "Griffin" shipwreck items. The fact was not hidden that these shipwreck parts came from Orrie Vail's Griffon Cove wreck near Tobermory.

Knowing that the Griffon Cove wreck was identified as a much newer vessel than the historic *Griffon*, I seethed inside at the thought that some unsuspecting buyer was going to end up with phony historical artifacts. Determined to speak my mind when the *Griffon* items came up for bids, I sat down biding my time as antique after antique sailed by at a variety of speeds and prices. In the "Auction Catalogue," with its detailed description of each of the hundreds of lots for sale that evening, complete with color photographs of many of the more unique ones, I jotted down most of the final bids.

Color photographs in an auction catalogue are a sure sign that these items are expected to fetch high prices, but I was amazed at some of the reasonable acquisitions being made: the War of 1812 British officer's sword sold for $55.00 and the pair of 1894 buffalo hide robes went for $100.00. I sat waiting, restless as the lots inched forward. I re-read the booklet's description of the so-called "Griffin" items:

> ONE OF THE MORE IMPORTANT CANADIAN HISTORICAL RECORDS EVER TO APPEAR IN THE FORM OF A COLLECTION PERTAINING TO "THE GRIFFIN" WHICH WAS THE FIRST SAILING VESSEL TO APPEAR ON THE GREAT LAKES HAVING BEEN CONSTRUCTED NEAR NIAGARA FALLS BY SIEUR DE LA SALLE IN 1679; SHE LOADED FURS AT GREEN BAY IN SEPTEMBER OF THAT YEAR AND CLEARED HARBOUR SEPTEMBER 8TH WITH A CREW OF SIX AND WAS NEVER SEEN AGAIN with the burned wreckage later discovered at Russel [sic] Island near Tobermory with one theory she was taken by Indians who killed the crew and burned the ship partially confirmed by the 1912 discovery of the bones of six white men nearby which correspond to the crew members -- the collection comprises a display frame of labelled artifacts from the Griffin's remains, diorama of the ship by the late Walter Stansell, two exhibit plaques with one retaining extensive research, framed reproduction of a newspaper display regarding the diorama, pamphlet history of the ship and two copies of [the softcover books] "The Tobermory Shipwrecks" detailing the Griffin on page nineteen -- both spellings of "Griffon" appear but in one description of the vessel it is recorded that a figure of the mythological beast the griffin was painted on the ship and it appears that the builder intended that to be the name of the unfortunate vessel.

I waited for the moment when an opening bid would be requested.

At long last, the mystery of the Grif-fon appears to be solved -- at a public auction!

Photo by Cris Kohl

But a controversial incident occurred about an hour before the "Griffin" items came up. Bids opened for a glazed antique display case of "selected North American Indian relics, including a rare 1876 Blackfoot peace pipe...." What the auction program failed to include in its information was that the exhibit case contained portions of an Indian skull.

Three First Nation members (the Canadian equivalent of "Native Americans") arose and calmly protested this offered item before bidding began. The delegation formally requested that they be allowed to return these human remains to their tribal members for proper disposition.

The embarrassed auctioneer, wide-eyed and momentarily stunned, could not speak. His flitting eyes scanned the room for the man in charge. The man in charge shook his head. The auctioneer proceeded hesitantly, the audience gradually regained interest and the auction picked up speed. The controversial articles did end up selling for $625.00, a high price that may not have been realized had it not been for the drama prior to the bidding. There was no violence that evening, but the incident did make the next day's newspapers.

I realized that my qualms about the auction of the "Griffin" artifacts coming up in a few minutes were indeed "small peanuts" compared to the immorality of selling human remains to members of the general public. Theirs being a far nobler concern, the First Nation emissaries had a greater right to speak up than I did. Feeling a tinge of shame about the Indian "artifacts" episode, I decided to remain silent about my *Griffon* knowledge. I would let it be a case of "let the buyer beware."

The "Griffin" lot sold for the astonishing price of $1,500.00.

To this day, I wonder if that buyer was ever made aware of Paul Hundley's thesis on the Griffon Cove wreck or if he ever cast doubtful eyes upon his costly purchase.

*　　　*　　　*

I n mid-October, 1969, another claim site received media coverage when Detroit metallurgist Richard Browne announced that he may have found the *Griffon* and that he had formed an underwater search company to work at the site in quest of positive identification.

His wreck location was given as 12 miles off Drummond Island in the North Channel opposite Thessalon, Ontario. This clearly placed the shipwreck in Canadian waters.

Browne and his partners intended to raise the wreck of the *Griffon* with their 41-foot cabin cruiser, which would have been quite an accomplishment worthy of the history books on its own accord. However, nothing more was heard of this project, so it was likely another case of mistaken identity.

*   *   *

S imple things which I have learned about oral history are that "old men forget" and that it is human nature to embellish a story to achieve the implied, the intended, or the requested result. Native Americans of the Ottawa tribe have long passed down orally the story that their ancestors destroyed the *Griffon* in Traverse Bay. But has that tale changed over time?

Commercial fishermen have long been the best source of information about what lies on the bottom of the Great Lakes, but unless they wrote down information at the time they experienced it, what they recall years later may be invalid or too vague to use. I will never forget the sincerity of one retired commercial fisherman at Britt, Ontario, on the eastern shore of Georgian Bay, who in 1994 pinpointed the "exact location" of one shipwreck for me -- using a screwdriver aimed at the blue part of an Ontario roadmap! The slotted end of his screwdriver must have covered several square miles on his map, but the elderly gentleman was convinced that I could now easily locate that shipwreck based upon the information he had just given me.

Scuba divers who explore shipwrecks, like sailors of old, have a reputation for spinning many a tall tale about the history of a ship, the details of a ship's loss, and, in particular, their personal on-and-under water yarns about searching for, finding and exploring sunken ships. I have savored the stories of these sons of Neptune (archaeologists call them other kinds of sons) while camping at Tobermory, Ontario in the 1970's, bent a few elbows with them in pubs along the St. Clair River in the 1980's, and joined well-known wreck hunters on their boats for hours of electronic sidescanning for shipwrecks in the 1990's. The main thing which they have in common is their ability to shorten the hours with the flow of their effervescent anecdotes. One just has to learn which of their words require a few grains of salt.

THE GRIFFIN.
First sailing vessel on the lakes, 1679.

This drawing and caption, part of an 1898 newspaper article, helped promulgate the incorrect notion that the Griffon *was the first ship on the Great Lakes.*   CRIS KOHL COLLECTION

The ship named the *Griffon* and its legend have been known throughout the Great Lakes for centuries, among sailors and shore-huggers alike, with the latter succumbing to hyperbole as often as the former. Journalists who had never set foot upon the deck of a ship have written about the *Griffon*, free-riding on the ship's tale of mayhem and mystery while adding their own dramatic embellishments without even knowing how a ship moves. With their assistance, the *Griffon*, the Great Lakes' second shipwreck, somewhere in the course of history, graduated to first place in the public's mind, and even drifted into the myth of having been the first sailing ship on the inland seas, instead of really the fifth.

*   *   *

E arly summer of 2004 found the Great Lakes abuzz with the prospect of another *Griffon* claim. A man named Steve Libert from Virginia reportedly filed a lawsuit in federal court in Grand Rapids, Michigan, seeking to be named the custodian of a shipwreck he claimed to have found in State of Michigan waters and, in the long run, to be declared the exclusive owner of that shipwreck.

He did not divulge the name of the shipwreck, instead maintaining an air of both authority as well as mystery with the comment, "If I said what it was, everyone would jump out of the woodwork...find the ship and tear it apart." His company, Great Lakes Exploration Group, based in Ohio, did reveal in filed court documents that "the vessel was owned by a foreign research expedition operating with the authority of...a foreign sovereign until it became wrecked, lost and abandoned."

State of Michigan archaeologist/historian Dr. John Halsey speculated that "You don't have to have a doctorate degree to know how many vessels were under a foreign sovereign on the Great Lakes," an indication that the identity of this shipwreck is that of the *Griffon*, which would indeed be a significant archaeological find. I had pointed out several years ago in my book, *The Great Lakes Diving Guide,* that the *Griffon* is "fabled," "elusive," "the dream of marine archaeologists" and the "holy grail of freshwater shipwrecks."

Dr. Halsey was unable to discern any identification from his viewing of a "grainy" underwater videotape of the site, and suggested that a state archaeologist scuba dive to the site and examine the remains. At press time, agreement between the Great Lakes Exploration Group and an archaeologist on a mutually acceptable time to inspect the site has not been made.

The judge in Grand Rapids rejected Great Lakes Exploration's request, stating that the company failed to give any identifying information, other than its disclosure of the latitude and longitude coordinates to a large area.

Mr. Libert, an experienced scuba diver who had removed a small piece of the shipwreck in an effort to determine its age, reportedly claimed that it had taken him 30 years to locate this site. He was certainly no stranger to salvage claims of shipwrecks in Green Bay, having spent years unsuccessfully trying to obtain salvage rights to the wreck of the schooner _Captain Lawrence,_ supposedly the ship which sank immediately after it had found the legendary but spurious "Poverty Island Treasure" in the 1930's.

Later in July, another newspaper reported that Mr. Libert was "suing a shipwreck in federal court as a means to take ownership." The shipwreck's location was given as being "about 3.5 miles west of Poverty and Summer Island," which would place it at or near Poverty Island Shoal in Green Bay. This shoal rises from a regular bay depth in that area of about 80 feet to only 13 feet. To this day, there is no buoy or beacon warning navigators about this potential hazard.

The _Griffon_ headed northeast or north-northeast towards the Straits of Mackinac after departing Washington Island or Rock Island, at the same time that La Salle and his men canoed south towards the Door County peninsula. Both parties were out of sight of each other when a sudden storm of long duration interfered with their respective progress. Although contemporary reports suggest otherwise, no one can say for certain that the _Griffon_ did not change course and end up wrecked inside Green Bay instead of in the waters of Lake Michigan or Lake Huron.

Dr. John Halsey pointed out that, even if the wreck is the _Griffon_, anyone filing a legal claim to own or salvage it might have a more difficult time gaining control than expected. If federal and state laws protecting shipwrecks are not enough, the _Griffon_ would also fall under the jurisdiction of new international legislation.

On February 5, 2004, the U.S. Department of State published Public Notice 4614 in the Federal Register. This document sets forth the policies of the USA, France, Spain, Germany, Japan, the Russian Federation and the United Kingdom concerning each country's sunken warships, military aircraft and other sunken government property. Many such shipwrecks lie within the waters of the United States: German U-boats off the East Coast, Japanese submarines off Hawaii, Spanish treasure ships in Florida waters (with decision reserved regarding the rights of the natives of Central and South America from whom that treasure originally was allegedly stolen by the Spanish), and French vessels, notably the wreck of another of La Salle's later ships, the *La Belle*,wrecked off the coast of Texas in 1686 and which was discovered by archaeologists in 1995.

U.S. Department of State Public Notice 4614 provides this information regarding the Government of France's policies:

> In accordance with the 1982 United Nations Convention on the Law of the Sea (among others art. 32 & 236) and Customary Law, every State craft (e.g. warship, naval auxiliary and other vessel, aircraft or spacecraft owned or operated by a State) enjoys sovereign immunities, regardless of its location and the period elapsed since it was reduced to wreckage (general principle of non limitation of rights of States).
>
> The primacy of the title of ownership is intangible and inalienable: no intrusive action may be taken regarding a French sunken State craft, without the express consent of the French Republic, unless it has been captured by another State prior to sinking.
>
> But this primacy does not forbid the State to freely renounce, whenever it wants to and in a formal way, to use some of its right on the wreck (except its ownership).
>
> These principles have been applied in the Agreement between the Government of the USA and the Government of the French Republic regarding the wreck of "La Belle", signed at Washington, DC, March 31st, 2003, and the Agreement between the Government of the USA and the Government of the French Republic concerning the wreck of the CSS Alabama [a Confederate States of America warship wrecked in French waters during the Civil War], signed in Paris, October 4th, 1989. Source: Communication from the French Foreign Ministry, November 28, 2003.

Loopholes can be sought in any document. With the wording of this one, a salvager could conceivably argue that La Salle's *Griffon* was not a vessel "owned or operated by a State," although that argument would likely fail because La Salle required the permission of the King of France to proceed with his plans for western expansion. One could also argue that Indians destroyed the *Griffon*, hence the ship was "captured by another State prior to sinking." Proof that natives captured the *Griffon* would have to be provided by the claimant, who, if he succeeded in that overwhelming task, would then have to argue successfully that a group of Indians constituted a "State." This could become a long, costly and ultimately losing proposition.

The U.S. government and the discoverers of La Salle's _La Belle_ shipwreck in Texas worked cooperatively with the French government under details clearly spelled out in two documents: "Agreement between the Government of the United States of America and the Government of the French Republic Regarding the Wreck of _La Belle_" and "Administrative Arrangement Between the Texas Historical Commission and the Musée National de la Marine Concerning the Wreck of _La Belle_."

The first document, comprised of five Articles, makes it clear that "The French Republic has not abandoned or transferred title of the wreck of _La Belle_ and continues to retain title to the wreck of _La Belle_" but also that "The French Republic does not desire the return of the wreck of _La Belle_ to its territory." The French government also gave custody of the wreck of _La Belle_ to the Texas Historical Commission for a period of 99 years, with automatic renewal unless the Parties agree otherwise. Respectful treatment and burial of human remains found on _La Belle_ were also spelled out.

In the second document consisting of ten detailed Articles, the Musée National de la Marine in France and the Texas Historical Commission agreed upon the curation (including the security, storage, preservation and conservation), research, documentation, publication, and exhibition of the wreck of _La Belle_. Interestingly, the document also pointed out that in July, 1997, France formally asserted ownership of the wreck of _La Belle_ and provided evidence thereof, and that the United States and the State of Texas acknowledged France's title to that shipwreck.

New ground rules have been established, and are steadily being established regarding submerged cultural resources. If the _Griffon_ is ever located, the _La Belle_ will act as a precedent to help determine responsible control over the historic remains of La Salle's second shipwreck.

The world of conservation and protection has come a long way since the days when a shipwreck was burned for its lead caulking, or when a commercial fisherman removed pieces randomly from their original location for storage in his shed.

*   *   *

T oday, with thousand-foot freighters being most representative of the massive shipping on the Great Lakes, it appears dramatically ironic that researchers are devoting so much respect, concern, time and energy to one of the tiniest commercial ships ever to ply these inland seas.

The dwarf, however, is a historic giant. James Oliver Curwood wrote, in _The Great Lakes and the Vessels That Plough Them_ (1909), that "By all but a few the _Griffin_ [sic] is forgotten, or has never been known. Yet by the millions who live along the Great Lakes she should be held in much the same reverence as are the caravels of Columbus by the whole nation."

The day will come when someone will indisputably locate the remains of the _Griffon_. It will take strong proof: a brass (or they could have been made of bronze) cannon or an identifiable iron arquebus, or one of the carved griffins, from either the bow or the transom -- and in the cold, fresh waters of the Great Lakes, these wooden griffins could very well be identifiable, especially if they have lain under sand or mud for centuries.

When the _Griffon_ is definitely found, Great Lakes maritime history will receive a loud and unmistakable shot in the arm. Books about the _Griffon_ will fly, first off printing presses and then off bookstore shelves, because the saga will have been completed. The public's insatiable appetite for the details behind solved mysteries will generate a great many meals, big and small, with generous leftovers.

We must also brace ourselves for the expected consequences. Truth stretchers will stretch, detractors will detract, claim jumpers will jump; many will seek a piece of the action or a bit part in the drama. Websites about the _Griffon_ will spring up overnight, containing -- along with the accurate and responsible material -- every bit of trash, hearsay, nonsense and ghost story ever printed, spoken and imagined about La Salle and this ship. Instant _Griffon_ "experts" will flock to the media offering exclusive interviews, while a handful of scuba divers will proclaim that they've been diving on the _Griffon_ site for years.

However, the immense, intense, exciting world of Great Lakes maritime history will become much richer (intellectually and historically speaking), and the person who solved the Great Lakes' greatest mystery, if everything is handled properly and responsibly and the godsend does not turn into a millstone, will sing the _Te Deum_ for all the right reasons.

RETURN FROM THE DEAD: TWO RAISED SHIPWRECKS

W hen I give presentations about the excellently preserved ship-wrecks in the Great Lakes, I am often asked, "If those shipwrecks are so fantastic, why don't they raise one of them so everybody can see it?"

Someone did -- twice.

*   *   *

I n the summer of 1969, a shipwreck was raised from deep water in Green Bay by a well-meaning bartender and scuba diver named Frank Hoffman.

Two years earlier, in November, 1967, a costly trawling net had snagged onto something, and Hoffman, an avid shipwreck diver who had arrangements with commercial fishermen, donned scuba gear and freed the net. He also examined this obstruction -- an upright, intact shipwreck in 110 feet of water!

By late 1968, in the days when shipwreck artifact removal was not yet illegal and divers delighted in randomly bringing up pieces of history as "tokens of accomplishment," items were recovered and exhibited at Green Bay's Neville Museum -- among them a swallow-tailed captain's coat with a rolled collar, hobnailed shoes, three anchors, deadeyes, pulley blocks, mast hoops, belaying pins, an iron skillet, a silver plate, a captain's desk, a soup kettle, keys, crockery, an 1849 pepperbox pistol, a double-barreled percussion shotgun, a powder flask, a dinner bell, clay smoking pipes, compasses, binoculars, and a bottle of beer. It was an amazing trove. The

The merchant vessel documentation division of the U.S. Coast Guard issued number 3985 to the Alvin Clark -- the lowest set of numbers not yet assigned to a vessel. The assignment of vessel registration numbers began not long after the Clark sank in 1864.

PHOTOS BY AND COURTESY OF DR. RICHARD BOYD

only thing left down there still to bring up was the mystery ship itself.

On July 29, 1969, the shipwreck was raised. It took months of planning and hard work, both above and below water, by Hoffman, his partner, Jim Derusha, President of Marinette Marine, and their team of dedicated divers. First the masts were carefully removed onto a barge. Then a lift cable system placed with great difficulty by divers under the hull allowed the ship to be winched up. Hoffman and Derusha supervised. The mystery wreck, slung between two barges with its bowsprit breaking the surface, was proudly towed into Menominee harbor to the cheers of a thousand people lining the shore.

Clean-up of the mystery vessel went quickly, directed by Frank Hoffman. The masts were put back in place, and new rigging with an old look completed the ambitious picture of this museum ship. Bishop Salatka blessed the vessel, which now floated on its own hull, and large crowds loved seeing the oldest wooden cargo ship in the U.S.A.

The two-masted schooner, Alvin Clark (105'8" x 25'4" x 9'4").

ART BY AND COURTESY OF JAMES A. ANDREWS

Definite identification of the mystery wreck soon followed. Research and evidence, e.g. several coins, the newest one dated 1863, leaned towards the ship being the *Alvin Clark*.

The raised Alvin Clark *suffered dramatically when it came to tax and insurance evaluations. The appraisal firm hired by the city of Menominee in 1984 reported that although the ship had "significant historical value," the actual market value was "zero."*
PHOTOS BY AND COURTESY OF DR. RICHARD BOYD

During the Civil War, on June 29, 1864, the 218-ton schooner named the *Alvin Clark* sank in a storm northwest of Chambers Island in Wisconsin's Green Bay with the loss of three of the five lives on board. Among the lost were Capt. Dubbin and mate John Dunn, both of Racine, Wisconsin. The ship, built in 1846 at Truago (later Trenton), Michigan, a town near Detroit, rested undisturbed for 103 years until Frank Hoffman first saw it.

When the clean-up team located personal artifacts with the words "Mich. Cray, Toronto, C.W." on them, Hoffman knew they had raised the *Alvin Clark*. Michael Cray was one of the *Clark's* two survivors in 1864, and he was from Toronto in what was then "Canada West" (C.W.), today's Ontario. Cray's grandchildren in Benton Harbor, Michigan provided further identification.

Well into the twentieth century, the *Alvin Clark*, virtually forgotten for over a hundred years, instantly found itself elevated to the position of being the most photographed nineteenth century schooner in Great Lakes history.

Tourists paid to see the *Alvin Clark,* yet it failed to make money. It is well-known among pleasure craft owners that boat maintenance never ends, doubly so for a wooden boat. Add the words "very old" to the "wooden boat" picture, and you have a situation requiring full-time attention and unlimited funds. It had reportedly cost Hoffman $90,000 in 1969 to raise the ship, and maintenance now cost more than the *Clark's* income. During the fuel crisis of early 1974, Hoffman, worried that few tourists would drive to Menominee to see the ship, decided to take the ship to the tourists. In the summer of 1974, he would play the swashbuckler and sail the *Alvin Clark* to popular seaports on western Lake Michigan, culminating at Chicago.

79

Vintage schooner may be Muskegon bound

'History' ship is available — no takers

MARINETTE, WIS. (AP) — The Alvin Clark, a 105-foot wooden schooner built in 1846 and raised from the bottom of Lake Michigan in 1969.

If the deal is completed, plans call for moving the two-masted schooner to White Lake at Montague, Mich., a Muskegon area community in a region

which does not stop or even pass through Whitehall or Montague."
Use of the community's "beautiful

MENOMINEE (AP) — The titanic task of raising a 19th century freighter from the floor of Lake Michigan has

He said he has gotten inquiries from Sault Ste. Marie to Port Washington, Wis., but no satisfactory re-

In the 1970's and 1980's, Frank Hoffman tried hard to sell the schooner, Alvin Clark. *The ship's costly raising and ongoing maintenance had drained him financially. Various ports -- Sault Ste. Marie, Port Washington, Muskegon -- all considered, but ultimately rejected, owning the* Alvin Clark. CRIS KOHL COLLECTION

Frustrated owner burns 'Mystery Ship'

MENOMINEE, Mich. (AP) — An amateur scuba diver who salvaged a 19th Century schooner from the depths of

Clark ablaze Monday night, then wielding a rifle to ward off firefighters.
"I figured if it were gone I

gave the Alvin Clark a rating as the oldest , surviving documented merchant vessel of its kind. The Smithsonian

Hoffman said last year that he was "doing very badly" financially.
"We're not making any

offense."
Hoffman was arr Monday night after alle brandishing a rifle to

But his plans were torpedoed when insurance carriers refused to quote him a price because they could not set a value upon the old historic ship.

The *Alvin Clark* remained in Menominee but continued to sail rough seas. Hoffman wrote to the Smithsonian, to senators, to President Carter's wife, to many other potential sources. He could find no financial assistance to conserve this huge artifact. Several individuals, agencies and institutions told him to re-sink the ship, but he stubbornly refused.

Frank Hoffman's ship had come in, but his luck had run out, and the risen ship was slowly scuttling its salvor. Desperate to rid himself of the albatross slung around his neck, Hoffman, adrift in a sea of trouble and turning increasingly to demon rum, tried to burn down the uninsured vessel in June, 1985, but was stopped. He had originally asked $350,000 for the ship in 1978; in 1987, he sold it for $117,000. A bitter Hoffman retreated, retiring to a secluded mobile home in Florida, and he died not long afterwards.

Dry rot set in on the *Alvin Clark*, the museum closed, and the masts soon collapsed, damaging the deck. Finally, in May, 1994, the decayed and crumbled pieces were trucked to the local garbage dump. The ship would still be an impressive sight today -- had it been left on the bottom of Green Bay.

*   *   *

We could have learned from a previous mistake, had we only known about it. That story, less publicized than the one about the *Alvin Clark*, took place 70 years earlier, when a shipwreck was raised from the Thames River at Chatham, Ontario. The results of that experience should have sent warning flags fluttering in 1969 for the *Clark*.

The charred and battered timbers of an old ship whose skeleton-like frame was a reminder of difficult days during the War of 1812 was discovered in 1899 by two log salvagers, Capt. Tyler and his partner, Karney, probing the Thames River near Chatham. At that time, anything unusual about the Thames River was reported to Edwin Bassett Jones, the Superintendent of the Chatham Waterworks, because the river was the source of the city's water supply. In his memoirs, Jones recalled the story of this shipwreck:

> ...One day, two men dropped in to say they had been using pike poles to raise sunken logs and sell them, and had come across timbers so heavy they could not be budged.
>
> I went personally to investigate and after checking the location and other details, came to the conclusion that this was the wreck of one of the army supply boats on Proctor's retreat. On the second visit, I recovered some bottom boards that had been charred by fire, one of which had three large auger holes, showing that the vessel had been scuttled as well as burned.... As more was learned about the wreck,...the details...aroused considerable public curiosity and interest. Members of the Scientific and Literary Society and others, such as Captain J. S. Black of the Kent Militia, held meetings to discuss it. Greatly through the efforts of Captain Black and R.C. Burt, the Tecumseh Historical Society was formed with the idea of raising the hull and preserving it as a nucleus of a museum. From the Ministers of Militia of the Dominion [of Canada], and of the Province, they obtained permission to take charge of the hull along with considerable information not to be found except in Government archives. The wreck was not of a gunboat, as had been believed, but that of the two-masted schooner, *General Myers,* captured from the Americans and used as a supply boat by General Proctor from Fort Malden at Amherstburg. The two smaller schooners were the *Eliza* and the *Ellen*, owned by Richard Pattison of Amherstburg. These two, having shallower draft, had sailed further up the river.
>
> Sight-seers from far and near were carrying away souvenirs and even gathering [cannon] shells to be sold for scrap iron. With authority from the government, warnings against such acts were posted and a guard set at the wreck....
>
> Early in 1901, the hull was raised and placed on a crude timber raft and floated down the river to be placed on [sic] Tecumseh Park. Lying under water eighty-nine years, the solid oak ribs and planking were waterlogged and very heavy, and from the cargo of iron shells, the wood was black as ebony and took a fine polish.

One side of the hull had been sprung as if from an explosion within. The vessel had beautiful lines and had been built for speed as well as strength. Her keel and keelson were tremendous oak beams. Her ribs were so close-set they almost touched. Her stem had been shaped from the root of a noble black walnut tree. She had been built to ride with the winds and breast the waves for a century or more and, as an example of superb ship-builder's art and skill, was well worth preserving. We hoped to search for and raise what remained of the *Eliza* and the *Ellen* to form an historic flotilla housed, perhaps, in the old Barracks on the Park....

The raised shipwreck had been found in twelve feet of water in the Thames River, where it had long been kept naturally preserved. One account stated that "The tannic acid of [the shipwreck's] oak, mingling with the iron of the water of the Thames, turned to a sort of ink, and the wood of the boat is now like bog-oak, but tough as whalebone." The Tecumseh Historical Society's plans "to build a house over the boat and to preserve the wreck entire, with the cannon balls, shells, etc.," never materialized, perhaps because the shipwreck appeared to be so solid. The entire exhibit stayed outside in the open.

The number and names of the War of 1812 vessels which Proctor took with him up the Thames during his retreat have caused disagreement among historians for nearly 200 years. Cuthbertson (1931) states there were four ships named the *Colonel* [not *General*] *Myers*, *Eliza*, *Mary* and *Miamis*. Lauriston (1952) mentioned three being scuttled, but named only the *General Myers* and the *Ellen*. Pierre Berton, in his two-volume popular history of the War of 1812 (1980-81), wisely left all these ships unnamed, as Hamil had done earlier (1951). The testimony of Capt. Webb Crowther, 41st British Regiment, taken on January 12, 1815, only fifteen months after Proctor's retreat but considered at least slightly faulty, must also be viewed:

...I immediately went to the General [Proctor] who was at the head of the line, he informed me that he wished to stop the navigation of the river at Bowles's to prevent the Enemy's Gunboats from coming up, by laying the *Mary* and *Ellenor* in the best position, and scuttling them, and to destroy the naval ordnance stores. I proceeded to Bowles's and found that the Deputy Ass't Quarter Master General was destroying the stores that had been landed. I then went on board the two vessels, and with the assistance of the naval officers, we moored the vessels across the river. I took the entrenching tools and carpenter's tools and.... I commenced immediately destroying the naval and ordnance stores that were on board these two vessels, breaking them, and cutting them and throwing into the river such as would sink. I then gave directions to the master carpenter to scuttle the two vessels, which was done, and in their scuttling in the water set fire to the upper works....

This provides the origin of the name *Mary* for one of the wrecks, but the name *Ellenor* appears nowhere else. A formal request for compensation was made after the War of 1812 by Richard Pattison of Amherstburg for the loss of his vessel, *Ellen,* described by him as a 50-ton ship which had been on loan to the British since June, 1813. So the correct name is likely *Ellen,* not *Ellenor.*

Some background to these War of 1812 ships must be briefly told in order to comprehend the rest of this tale.

The War of 1812 was the second, and final, armed conflict between the United States of America and Great Britain, the latter allied with its North American colony, Canada. This war was launched only seventeen years after Jay's Treaty in 1795 formally ended the American Revolution's violent strife between the U.S. and Britain.

British General Isaac Brock surprisingly captured Detroit in August, 1812, without firing so much

The War of 1812 wreck, the General Myers, *was raised in 1901 from the Thames River near Chatham, Ontario.*
CRIS KOHL COLLECTION

The shipwreck contained a vast, impressive cargo of cannonballs, bayonets, knives, etc.
CRIS KOHL COLLECTION

The historic War of 1812 hull was placed in Chatham's Tecumseh Park for public perusal. PHOTOS ON THIS PAGE BY JOHN A. MCGREGOR. CRIS KOHL COLLECTION

as a single shot. The U.S. General William Hull surrendered his fort, along with his 2,500 troops, to Brock's 700 militia and 400 Indians. However, 14 months later, just after the defeat of Captain Barclay's British naval force on Lake Erie by Captain (later Commodore) Oliver Hazard Perry on September 10, 1813, the tables were turned. General Henry Proctor, who had held Detroit during those months, found himself abandoning the fort, dumping into the Detroit River any cannons and munitions which he could not take with him, and retreating with his 850 troops and 1,000 Indians (under their famous leader, Tecumseh) up the Thames River with more than 3,000 angry Americans, mostly backwoods fighters from Kentucky, led by a future president, General William Henry Harrison, hot on their heels.

With him, Proctor took a number of small, unnamed batteaux plus five larger boats: one two-masted schooner and four gunboats, probably named, respectively, the *General Myers, Ellen, Eliza, Mary* and *Miamis*.

The *General Myers* is believed to be the two-masted ship which the advancing U.S. troops found burning on October 4, 1813, in the Thames River about half a mile upstream from the Forks (where today's McGregor Creek flows into the Thames River, which is also the site of Tecumseh Park in Chatham). Harrison, in his report to military headquarters, wrote,

> ...At the first farm above the bridge, we found one of the enemy's vessels on fire, loaded with arms, ordnance and stores.... At Bowles' farm, four miles above the bridge, we halted for the night. We found two other vessels and a large distillery filled with ordnance and other valuable stores of the enemy mounting in flames....

The retreating Proctor destroyed his vessels and munitions so they would not fall into enemy hands. The two ships burning at Bowles' farm, at the end of the navigable part of the river, were probably the *Eliza* and the *Ellen*.

The next day, further upstream, Harrison and his troops captured Proctor's small batteaux loaded with provisions, and the remaining two gunboats, the *Mary* and the *Miamis*, along with eight cannons (including one or two from the Saratoga conflict of 1777), many cannonballs and other munitions. However, as these two larger ships and their armament, cannons included, were being returned to Detroit, they sank in soft-bottomed Lake St. Clair and were never recovered. Harrison knew where more cannons lay in the Thames River, and he likely retrieved those over the next year.

Tecumseh was killed, Proctor was courtmartialed, the War of 1812 ended in late 1814, and the three shipwrecks in the Thames River were forgotten. Canada and the United States went on to brag for many years about having the longest undefended border in the world, even though Canadian-American relations remained guarded.

Detroit's chief historian, Clarence Monroe Burton -- scholar, businessman, collector of source materials on Detroit and the Old Northwest -- read with great interest about the raising of the *General Myers* in 1901 at Chatham, which was only about 50 miles away, and the shipwreck's placement in a public park there. He also read, in the small print at the end of the article, that the other two War of 1812 shipwrecks lying in the Thames -- the *Ellen* and the *Eliza* -- had been located further upstream. Burton became determined that Detroit would have those remaining shipwrecks. They would be triumphant relics of Proctor's retreat in the War of 1812, perfect for public spectacle. Detroit would proudly exhibit Canada's shame.

Clarence Burton was slow to plan his attack and undertake action towards acquiring these shipwrecks, but once he started, he rolled with the blind zeal of a frenzied convert. In the summer of 1905, he reportedly headed an exploring party which quietly began operations from a boat that had steamed up the Thames River in Canada from Detroit. On board was a hardhat diver, and before long, Burton claimed that his expedition had located three sunken vessels in the waters above Chatham (he apparently was not aware that only two from the War of 1812 were left there).

A story was reported by numerous U.S. newspapers that when the *General Myers* and the other War of 1812 shipwrecks were first located, "a plan was originated to have them removed, brought to Detroit and presented to the city as memorials." The Canadians had never heard of this plan.

The flintlocks found in the hull of the *General Myers* had the words "New Haven, Conn." engraved upon them, proving that they had been removed from Detroit's munitions supply during the British occupation. This became an argument for the return of the shipwrecks to Detroit.

A Toledo newspaper article headline in September, 1905, declared "Two More British Battleships Found in Thames River Near Detroit," the implication being that these shipwrecks were found in the U.S.A. The caption beneath an accompanying old photo of the raised *General Myers* read, "Raising what is left of a British warship in Michigan," a decidedly incorrect location.

Finally, Burton proclaimed that his explorers possessed records which showed that chests of silver had been taken upon the boats!

Years later, in the early 1990's, Canadian commercial diver and shipwreck hunter Mike Fletcher faced a similar situation when California divers claimed to have discovered a "million dollar treasure ship" in Canadian waters of Lake Erie in 1991. It was the wreck of the historic but non-treasure-ship, *Atlantic*, which Fletcher could prove he had found a decade earlier. The salvagers used the "rich wreck" news to attract West

WAR TO THE KNIFE

C. M. Burton and Canadians Scrap Over Old Gunboats.

SUNK BY AMERICANS IN THAMES

Detroiter Wishes to Raise Hulks and Place Them on Belle Isle as Souvenirs—Dominion Patriotic Societies Are Stirred and Have Protested to Their Government.

"War to the knife" has been declared against president of the Michigan Historical and Pioneer society, Clarence M. Burton, by the patriotic citizens and societies of Canada an

Clarence M. Burton (1853-1932), referred to as "that indefatigable curio hunter" by one newspaper, ultimately bequeathed his vast collection of archival materials to the City of Detroit. He fought tooth and nail to acquire the War of 1812 shipwrecks from Canada's Thames River. CRIS KOHL COLLECTION

Coast investors to their company.

In 1905 and 1906, Clarence Burton tried very hard to erase the international boundary line between Detroit and those shipwrecks in Canada. One report stated that he "expected no serious difficulty as a result of interference by the Dominion [Canadian] government," and that he "declared the vessels were now private property" and that he "would be able to effect a bargain whereby he could take them over." He planned to raise the shipwrecks and place them in a specially constructed museum on Belle Isle [part of Detroit] in the Detroit River. Burton reportedly stated in late 1905:

> I am going to have them, if I have to go to war. I have interests at work to secure them and will succeed. If they belong to any government, they belong to the United States. I sent two men to the secretary of state at Ottawa and they were told that the Canadian government has no claim on the boats. So that settles it.
>
> It will cost $1,500 to raise the boats and put them on Belle Isle. I will pay the sum out of my pocket and present them to the city, if it will provide proper shelter for them....
>
> They don't belong to anybody now, but they will soon belong to me. Wait until spring. As soon as navigation opens, I shall proceed to raise them and the Canadian government won't interfere either. I took a diver up the river with me three months ago and we located the boats. I...think we shall find them in a good state of preservation.

Patriotic Canadians shouted, "You shan't have them!"

"Betcher I will," yelled back Clarence Burton.

Burton lost his war. It was finally contended, among other things, that to raise the shipwrecks would cause discord among friendly peoples. That exemplified the simple yet considerate state of international shipwreck diplomacy which existed between the United States and Canada a century

Recovered from the wreck of the General Myers *in 1901 were two tons of cannon balls of various sizes, quantities of grape and cannister shot, bayonets, flintlocks and military buttons. All that remain today are the few in the Chatham museum.* PHOTOS BY CRIS KOHL

ago. In today's more complicated world, we have the modern precedents of the famous U.S. War of 1812 military ships, the *Hamilton* and the *Scourge*, lying intact in deep (289 feet) Canadian Lake Ontario water. If Burton pressed his claims today, at least for the *General Myers,* he would likely win.

The New York *Tribune* reported in 1905 that: "...A feeling of resentment is growing among Canadians along the border, who say that the ships are not American property, and that to allow the relics to be preserved in Detroit would not only be a constant reminder of the defeat of their mother country, but would be an insult to all patriotic Canadians...." The *Tribune* was obviously unaware that the *General Myers* was already on public display in Canada!

Chatham, Ontario, displayed that shameful relic of a British retreat in its Tecumseh Park along the Thames waterfront. But no conservation technology was applied. Several years later, the decayed and crumbled fragments, those which remained after vandalism and tourist thefts had taken their toll upon the timbers, were hauled off to the local garbage dump.

STORY OF THE OLD GUNBOAT

Sketch of Historical Incidents Which Surround it in History.

Views of the Ancient Warrior.

The recent recovery from the bottom of the River Thames at a point near Chatham, of the British gunboat camped on Traxler's farm, four mile above Chatham, where at noon the kind-hearted housewives had been baking bread for their hungry, dis- since the day of Nelson. The lines of the boat are declared by experts to be beautiful. Her keel and keelson are tremendous sticks of oak; her ribs are set so close together

While historians in Detroit fought to acquire the War of 1812 shipwrecks in the Thames River in Canada, the one which was raised, the General Myers, *became a park attraction in Chatham. Before long, those parts of the ancient shipwreck which had not been stolen or vandalized while on public exhibit began to rot and crumble.*
CRIS KOHL COLLECTION

*   *   *

In an ironic twist in the mid-1950's, Canadian maritime historian, C.H.J. Snider, told this somber tale of the *General Myers'* fate to Tobermory's Orrie Vail, emphasizing the theft of shipwreck pieces by tourists. Snider did this as a warning of what might happen to the alleged wreck of the *Griffon* at nearby Griffon Cove, the existence and location of which Vail had announced to the world through the press. Vail speedily recovered most of the Griffon Cove wreck's pieces and locked them in his fishing shed for safekeeping. In so doing, however, he destroyed the archaeological integrity of the site.

Frank Hoffman also had difficulties with his wreck -- not because tourists might have pilfered pieces of the *Alvin Clark*, and not particularly because he had compromised the archaeological integrity of the site (the raising did allow us to learn maritime architectural design; it would have been impossible to complete an underwater survey of this silt-filled, embedded hull) -- but because time, that abstract concept which unfailingly conquers everything, defeated him and the *Clark*, just as it had crumbled the pieces which remained of the *General Myers* in that municipal park in Canada in the early 1900's.

THE DEAD SHERIFF'S SECRETS

T hin and unshaven, nearly dead from starvation and exposure, the stranger clutched a single oar and appeared frail as he attempted to stand up in his yawlboat as it struggled towards the village dock at Wiarton, Ontario, on a bitterly cold day in late November, 1867. The appearance of a lone mariner in an open boat coming off the treacherous waters of Georgian Bay was irregular, to say the least. A subsequent newspaper account revealed that the man arrived "in such an exhausted state that assistance was required to enable him to be removed from the boat to the tavern."

He said that his two crew members had been crushed to death below deck when the cargo of whiskey barrels they were trying to stabilize suddenly shifted forward as their small schooner struck the rocky shoal in harsh weather. He was barely able to free the yawlboat in time to save himself after waves had pulled the sinking ship back into deep water. He said that it had taken him eleven days to reach Wiarton and that he had only a small supply of biscuits and salt fish to nourish him during that time. He told them that his name was John Waddell, that he was once Sheriff of the Western District of Canada West, and that he was Captain of the lost schooner, *Explorer.*

What he did not tell them was perhaps far more important.

*   *   *

L ess than a year after he spent time in a hospital recuperating his "exhausted frame" after being the sole survivor from the *Explorer* shipwreck, Capt. John Waddell moved his family from Chatham,

Ontario, to the Lake Huron town of Goderich. The family made its new home at Ridgewood Park on the Maitland River's north bank overlooking both the picturesque river and the busy harbor. From there, between 1868 and 1870, Waddell reportedly made several trips of an undisclosed nature in a small sailboat to the Georgian Bay area.

Somehow, John Waddell was making money.

Chatham historian Victor Lauriston wrote about the public accomplishments of John Waddell, even delving into some personal aspects of the man, for example, making mention of his "bold and somewhat peculiar handwriting." Of the cyclical rises and falls in the prosperity of the former Sheriff of the Western District, historian Lauriston stated that John Waddell "was well away to the building of a new fortune when, in 1870, he was drowned when a pleasure craft upset near Goderich."

Captain John Waddell had been well known in the ports of Windsor, Sarnia, Port Huron, Goderich, Georgian Bay and, of course, Chatham, where he lived and from where he had been managing, as well as actually sailing, freight and passenger ships for over two decades.

Waddell, born in 1817 in England, moved with his parents and three siblings to Canada in 1832. His father, Capt. Walter Waddell of the Royal Dragoons, had been wounded at the Battle of Waterloo in 1815 and retired shortly thereafter. John engaged in business in Montréal before moving to the town of Chatham, in what was called Upper Canada, and later, Canada West, as a member of the Eberts Brothers firm.

The Eberts family began its Chatham dynasty when patriarch Joseph Eberts procured land on the north shore of the Thames River nearly opposite today's Tecumseh Park. He moved his family there from the Detroit-Sandwich (Windsor) area in 1818, not long after the end of the War of 1812. At the family homestead named "Orchard Place," Joseph and his wife Ann raised their three sons (William, Walter and Henry) and four daughters (Euphemia, Catherine, Nancy and Frances).

The Eberts brothers were known as energetic businessmen who also worked extensively as shipbuilders and navigators. Their list of nautical activities, with references to their ships, among them the *Hastings, Ploughboy, Brothers, Peerless, W.D. Eberts, Kent* and *Canadian*, alone would fill a volume.

In November, 1843, John Waddell married Nancy Almira Eberts, thus personalizing and cementing his business relationship with the well-known, enterprising family.

In November, 1848, Waddell formally left the Eberts Brothers merchandising firm (but informally continued to work for or with them) to take the prestigious position of Sheriff of the united counties of Essex,

Kent and Lambton, collectively known as the Western District of Canada West. However, this did not stop John Waddell from dabbling in business ventures. On the side, he worked at constructing and operating some of the finest ships in the area, such as the schooners *St. George* and *Belle of Chatham* and the steamer *George Moffatt*, and he owned lumber mills at Collins Inlet on the north end of Georgian Bay.

Things went well for John Waddell. In 1850, he built "the old stone house," an impressive structure with, according to Lauriston, "pretensions to architectural attractiveness," a domicile which still stands today on Chatham's Water Street overlooking the Thames River. Waddell claimed that the stones had traveled as ballast in his ships returning from Kingston, but a few people whispered that his house had really sprung up from materials which had disappeared from the large supply used in the construction of the new courthouse a block away.

1844.

CANADA WEST.

NEW AND DIRECT COMMUNICATION FROM
Buffalo to
Detroit, Goderich, & Chatham.

The British Steam Boat

KENT.

H. VAN ALLEN, MASTER.

WILL ply during the present season between Buffalo and Detroit, by way of the Canada shore. Leaves Buffalo every Monday evening, at 7 o'clock, and Detroit every Thursday evening, at 7 o'clock, touching at the following Ports, viz.:

Port Colborne, Port Dover, Port Ryerse, Port Rouen, Port Stanley. and Amherstburgh. On her arriving at Detroit, the Steam Boat Huron leaves immediately for Goderich, and Steam Boat Brothers for Chatham.

This route affords facilities to Emigrants and others, over any other, landing at Ports situated in and near all the Districts west of Niagara.

For further particulars apply to our Agents, viz :—H. S. Beecher & Co., Buffalo ; D. Bromley, 123 Broad street, New York ; H. Bromley & Co., 121 Pearl street, Albany ; T. Hardison, Port Colborne ; Henry Waters, Port Dover; Edward Ryerse, Port Ryerse ; John Kilmaster, Port Rouen ; G. R. Williams, Port Stanley ; Park & Co., Amherstburgh ; Watkins & Bissell, Detroit ; Eberts, Waddell & Co., Chatham.

June 7, 1844. 45 tf

Eberts, Waddell & Co., Chatham, Canada West, owned and operated many ships, including the steamer Kent.

CRIS KOHL COLLECTION

But Waddell's fortunes sank in 1857, the year of the great financial panic, augmented in his case by the wrecking of some of his ships. For five years, the Waddells lived quietly on Water Street, slowly using up the family funds and resources. When exciting tales of the British Columbia gold rush -- a gold rush was the nineteenth century's version of a major modern lottery, but with manual labor -- reached his ears in late 1861, John Waddell, bedazzled by dreams of quick wealth, a few months later impetuously moved his wife and their seven children via steamships and a railroad trek across Panama to the city of Victoria on Vancouver Island. However, Waddell found no gold, and Nancy missed Chatham. In 1865, they returned home.

In 1866, Waddell had a two-masted schooner named the *Explorer* (48′ x 16′ x 5′6″) built at Chatham. The Surveyor's Certificate of Admeasurement for Vessels states (handwritten parts are in italics):

This is to certify, that the Vessel called the *Explorer* of *Chatham*, Burthen *Thirty-two 66/130* Tons, whereof (blank) is at present

Master, is _British_ built, has _one_ Decks [sic] and _two_ Masts; that her length from the fore part of the main Stem to the after part of the Stern Post aloft is _forty-eight (48)_ feet (blank) inches, her breadth at the broadest part is _Sixteen_ feet, (blank) inches, her height between deck or decks, is _five_ feet, _six_ inches; that she is _Schooner_ rigged, with a _Standing_ Bowsprit, is _Square_ sterned, carved, built, has _no_ Head, and appears to be the same Vessel described in the (1) _Builders Certificate_ dated the _Thirtieth day of May 1866._

Given under my hand, at the Custom House, this _Thirtieth_ day of _May_ in the year _One thousand Eight Hundred and Sixty-six._

(signed) _John Duck, Customs Officer_

The new vessel was owned and captained by John Waddell, who took the _Explorer_ on cargo runs mainly from the Windsor and Chatham area up to northern Lake Huron. After the ship sank in late 1867, rumors questioning the published account of the loss of the _Explorer_ reportedly circulated, and these whisperings may have prompted Waddell to move his family to Goderich in 1868. He never returned to Chatham.

The Lake Huron fate which John Waddell had escaped when the _Explorer_ sank in 1867 caught up with him less than three years later. Accompanied by his teenage son, Waddell sailed in a light skiff from his residence in Goderich north towards the mouth of the Au Sable River. It has been suggested that Waddell was beginning another of his clandestine trips to Georgian Bay. Off Pine Point (today Point Clark), they were overtaken by a storm which capsized their skiff. The son clung to the boat and was rescued at about midnight, but the father had drifted away. His body washed ashore fifteen miles south of Goderich and the dead sheriff was buried in that town's Maitland Cemetery. In the Waddell family plot, the tombstone inscription describes him as "eldest son of Wm. and Isabella Waddell, Late Sheriff of The Western District of Upper Canada and Major Unattached of the Militia of Said Province Accidentally Drowned 20th July - 1870, Aged 53 Years" (see page 136).

*   *   *

In 1876, several years after Capt. John Waddell died, on a day when the lake was particularly calm and clear, a commercial fisherman near Tobermory spied the top of an upright mast rising from about 100 feet of water. He had accidentally located the old wreck of the _Explorer_.

Mariners, aware of the _Explorer's_ cargo, with their attention perking at

92

the mention of the whiskey barrels, attempted several times unsuccessfully to raise the shipwreck. In early June, 1881, the steamer, *Josephine Kidd,* of Goderich, with Capt. McDonald of Kincardine on board, grappled for the vessel and snagged it, but the cables broke once the wreck was lifted and turned around (the *Explorer* weighing more than expected). The crew departed, determined to return with more efficient salvage equipment.

The 48-foot-long, short-lived 1866 schooner, Explorer, *may never have been photographed, but this vessel, the 47-foot-long, twin-masted, single-decked* Lettie May, *built at Green Bay, Wisconsin, in 1874, closely resembled that vessel.* CRIS KOHL COLLECTION

The several salvage efforts had succeeded only in inflicting considerable damage to the wooden remains. Early in 1882, Mr. E.N. Lewis of Goderich purchased the wreck from the company which had held the insurance on her. Lewis secured the services of professional wreckers (salvagers) from the H.N. Jex company in Port Huron, who struggled for ten days to recover the wreck from 94 feet of water using the steamer *Victoria* and two hardhat divers. When the *Explorer* was raised, the concern was not about how much damage previous salvagers had done. Instead, a grim story emerged.

The cargo of "saw mill machinery and ardent spirits" was gone, entirely replaced by heavy stones. The two dead crewmembers were found locked below deck, and a dozen one-and-a-half-inch-diameter auger holes had been bored into the centerboard box near the keel. The speculation was that Capt. Waddell, with his crew, had removed and hidden the valuable cargo along the shore, then he got the crew drunk, locked them below deck, sank the ship and collected the insurance money.

Waddell's mysterious trips to Georgian Bay were explained as retrieval missions to recover portions of the covert cargo supposedly hidden in a cave on Cove Island's Northeast Point.

Several newspapers in the U.S. (at Port Huron, Detroit, Chicago, Sturgeon Bay, etc.) printed the sensational story, and for several weeks in the late summer of 1882, U.S. and Canadian papers waged war while

A CAPTAIN'S CRIME.

Discovery and Raising of the Schooner Explorer After Five Years' Mystery.

A Terrible Crime Brought to Light by the Successful Operations of the Wreckers.

The Vessel Sunk for the Insurance, and the Crew Foully Murdered.

The unknown sunken schooner which Captain Jex's wrecking expedition went to has been raised, and proves to be the schooner Explorer, which went down several years ago. With the recovery of the vessel the particulars of a great crime came out. It is not often that mysterious "disasters" can be so fully explained. Late in October, 1867, the Explorer was fitted out at Chatham, Ont., with a stock of goods to trade with the Indians around Georgian Bay

Dramatic headlines screamed the Explorer's *story. The story quickly spread around the Great Lakes, this article appearing in the Chicago Inter-Ocean. Note: "Five Years" should read "Fifteen Years."*

CRIS KOHL COLLECTION

respectively condemning and supporting the long-dead former sheriff.

It is cowardily easy to circulate malicious lies about the deceased, since they cannot defend themselves. However, John Waddell's acquaintances picked up the torch in his defense.

On July 28th, the Goderich *Star* claimed that the *Explorer's* $2000 cargo was insured for only $1500, while the new $5000 ship was insured for only $2500, so it made no financial sense for Waddell to sink them. Besides, he supposedly had never filed a claim for the insurance money on the cargo. The *Star* stated that they had seen no signs of auger holes when they inspected the raised ship. They argued that there were no skeletons found in the vessel, and that the cabin door had been pulled off by someone grappling for the wreck.

A reply to the Goderich article came from hardhat diver R.G. McCulloch, who sent this letter to the local paper:

To the Editor of the Port Huron *Daily Times*:

Dear Sir: -- I see by your valuable paper that the Goderich *Star* denies the fact that the schooner *Explorer* was scuttled and sunk, as published in the local papers. I was one of the divers that worked on the *Explorer* and gave the report to the press concerning the scuttling of that craft, and from personal knowledge know that the *Explorer* was scuttled.

If the editor of the *Star* will get the harbor master of Goderich, and go on board the *Explorer* and lift the "limber" boards, the harbor master (who thoroughly understands his business) will show the editor of that paper where he can find twelve one-inch-and-a-half auger holes, eight on the starboard side and four on the port side.

I will further state that the schooner was stripped of all her sails, rigging and booms, and the sheet blocks were cut with a cold chisel, and part of the links left on the traveller; and the lamp and compass were taken out of the binnacle box.

The schooner was weighed with (as near as I could judge without weighing) fifteen tons of stone, and thirteen lockers in the cabin were also filled with stone. There was one perfect body found on board with a shirt and a pair of pants on, and the bones

94

and putrid flesh of another were found on the deck, having evidently floated out by the surging of the water while we were working at the wreck. The hatches were spiked down, and the hatch bars on; and securely fastened. I also found seven of the plugs in the hold of the vessel that had been used to stop the holes until all was ready. The small door leading from the cabin to the hold of the vessel was also out. The cabin door had been locked and the key left in the lock, but the door was lying on deck, having been torn off with an anchor or grapnel. I have no hesitation in saying that the schooner was scuttled and then sunk.

Mr. Lewis, who claimed to own the schooner, asked me to say nothing about it in Goderich, as, he said, "The least told, the sooner mended." The schooner had been under water for several years, but the name was perfect on the quarter and on the stern, as follows: "Explorer, of Chatham." Who scuttled the schooner, I do not know, but the facts which I have stated can be proved by a dozen witnesses.

Hoping you will publish this, I remain yours truly...

R.G. McCulloch, Sub-Marine Diver.

Port Huron, August 3, 1882.

This was strong, virtually irrefutable evidence. A J.D. McDonald of Port Lambton, Ontario, sent his response to the Sarnia *Canadian Observer*, claiming that he had examined the *Explorer* in Chatham just a few days before the ship was launched in 1866, and that he "took notice of a certain number of plugs in the centre board box." He further stated that he asked about the holes at the time, wondering what they were put in for, but "the party of whom I made the inquiry could not inform me. But the holes were there...." He thought it totally acceptable that a new boat would have holes bored into it just before it was launched.

Another hardhat diver, Duff Fecteau of Detroit, who claimed to have "first found the *Explorer*" (possibly he was the first diver on the wreck) called at the Port Huron *Daily Times* office and stated that he "found the holes in the bottom of the schooner and plugged them up. In the cabin he found one tea-cup, one mustard spoon and two teaspoons, and several clay pipes," and that the vessel "presented a deserted appearance, everything that could be taken away having been removed." He was positive the *Explorer* was scuttled.

John Waddell himself returned from the grave to defend himself. A reporter from the *Detroit Free Press* interviewed Customs Officer Baby, of Windsor, Ontario, and obtained the following account of the loss of the *Explorer* from Capt. Waddell's own pen, written 15 years earlier. Mr. Baby had requested a note asking for the particulars of the disaster. Capt. Waddell's letter was dated January 26, 1868, at Chatham, Ontario:

You want a narrative of my voyage north on the last trip of the *Explorer,* and though I am almost tired of this subject, I will endeavor to give you an idea of what occurred....

...I fitted her out for a trading trip on the north shore and intended to locate William (my son) at Little Current all winter with a small stock of goods to see what he could do with them. Accordingly, we cleared from here and went down to Windsor to finish our load. This was on the 1st of November (which was getting rather late). Having completed our load there,.... I then engaged two good sailors [subsequently identified as William Starnes and the other only as Jack] to go with me, and on the morning of November 3 we got away from Windsor.... we made sail and ran out of the [St. Clair River] rapids on the morning of the 8th of November....

...It began to snow and the wind was very changeable, still blowing a violent gale and the lake one sheet of white foam. The land on shore speedily began to get white, which...confused me badly in calculating distance, point of land, etc....

...we found ourselves in shallow water with the sea breaking clear over us, and throwing the vessel down on her beam ends, which shifted a lot of barrels of whiskey in her hold and gave her a bad list to port.

...one of my hands proposed to go into the hold and try to stow the barrels which were shifted, but it was impossible to take the hatches off, and I directed them to take the ax and chop a passage through the cabin bulkhead, which they did, as the moveable part of the bulkhead was jammed tight with the cargo stowed against it.

After chopping the hole out one man went in with a lantern, and when he came out reported some whiskey barrels stove in and a considerable shift of cargo on the port side and he volunteered to take the other man and fix it as good as ever in fifteen or twenty minutes if the vessel could be kept steady. I had been steering from about 2 o'clock p.m., and I told them I would watch her sharp and give them notice of any danger. We then got the hand pikes aft and I kept one to sound on the deck with as a signal of danger, or if I wanted the men on deck.

The hands came out once after being in the hold about twenty minutes, lighted their pipes and went in again. A few minutes elapsed and one of them handed me some whiskey in a tin mug which he got out of the broken barrel. I cautioned them about drinking too much at this time. They then went to work again for over a quarter of an hour and I thought I was coming to shallow water again, so I knocked and both came up.

They were both pretty jolly with the grog they had drank, and after waiting about for some time the biggest of the two said that five minutes more would complete the job, and they would finish it. I tried to persuade them to stay up as we were drawing pretty well off Yeo Island into the Ship Channel, and would soon square away into Georgian Bay, but they went in again nevertheless.

After they had been about twenty minutes or more in the hold, a big sea breaking shore drew my attention, when it was pretty clear I was getting on some shallow place again. I immediately knocked on deck, but by this time a huge breaker was roaring along to windward, and I kept the vessel away before it to ease her. This wave lifted her stern clear up almost perpendicular and broke over both sides near the forerigging, jamming her nose under water. She struck with force enough to tear the masts out nearly, and her bow settled on the shore....

The next sea was a sea of foam and roared like Niagara Falls, and just before it struck I saw it was going to sweep her clean, so I jumped into the port main rigging, but it tore her cabin door off, threw the yawl on the top of the cabin, capsized the vessel clear over to starboard, the water poured into the cabin and filled the hold right off. All this happened in less than three minutes, and when she struck with her fore foot on the rocks the shock was so violent that I could feel the cargo slide forward in a solid body right into the bow of the vessel, and the men in the hold must have been jammed to pieces before she filled with water, and I hung on to the rigging, expecting that my time was up.

...after awhile I found she was in deep water, drifting along into Georgian Bay with a heavy current. Although half an hour or more elapsed when I began to think if I could save the boat till daylight I might get off to shore....

...I employed part of my time in catching the little scraps of biscuit which floated out of the cabin window. I now began to suffer from numbness in the joints and cold.

So having drifted away below Flower-pot and Ben's Plumb, and the wind being round to the northwest and blowing straight on the main shore, I got into the boat and left with my pail and one oar. I was about ten miles off shore then and it took about four hours to get there. The beach I picked out to land on was bad and the surf came very near capsizing the boat. However I got ashore and let the boat beach herself the best way she liked.

A good deal of snow on the ground and all my matches wet except a few in my vest watch pocket which were just damp enough not to go off. Picked out a snug place under a big cedar to make a fire and get some shelter and then started and raced up and down the beach for hours till I got pretty warm.

Four or five hours after being ashore I got a match to light and set my combustible afire, which was a great comfort, enabling me to dry my feet. Kept hunting wood and firing up all night.

For three days... I could not get away from this place, wind being northwest and a gale all the time. Nothing to eat but wet biscuit which had fallen out of the pail into the bottom of the boat and were full of sand, etc., and only about a pound of this altogether.

The third day after being ashore, I launched the yawl and with the wind southwest worked round the point into Wingfield Basin near Cabot's Head, where I found a poor old Indian all alone with a few salt fish only to live on..... I stayed here three days living on salt fish entirely, and then got a supply of fish and left with a south wind, intending to get to Owen Sound the best way I could.

After ten days of misery and suffering I reached Cospoz's [Colpoy] Bay, ill and exhausted as you may suppose. The idea was entertained that the vessel would float ashore somewhere, but I had two men and a Mackinaw boat out for three weeks and they report having seen nothing of her.

When the raised _Explorer_ first arrived at Goderich to great public and press fanfare in mid-July, 1882, the newspaper there wrote that "...notwithstanding her long immersion and rough usage, [the _Explorer_] is still in excellent condition, her hull being of good oak timber. Mr. Lewis intends fitting her up for service again, and will undoubtedly find her good for a long term yet." Lewis paid the $1000 salvage bill, and decided to use the _Explorer_ as a combination pleasure yacht and coastal trader.

*   *   *

In January, 1993, a collection of over 700 historic documents called the Eberts Papers, dating from 1818 to 1895, came my way on approval for purchase. Included were numerous business documents, nautical and otherwise, signed not only by the Eberts brothers, but also by Capt. John Waddell, in his "bold and somewhat peculiar handwriting."

Here were authentic documents from the 1840's and 1850's pertaining to Eberts brothers' ships: the _Hastings, Ploughboy, Brothers, Peerless, W.D. Eberts, Canadian,_ and others. My eyes opened really wide when the original "Surveyor's Certificate of Admeasurement for Vessels," dated May 30, 1866, for the schooner _Explorer,_ was among the many ships' documents.

Realizing that this one-of-a-kind collection of historic documents belonged in, and ideally owned by, the city of Chatham, I spearheaded a fundraising drive which, due to the generosity of several individuals and business-es, particularly one very charitable person who requested anonymity, soon acquired the several thousand dollars needed to secure the Eberts Papers. These documents now repose in the Chatham-Kent Historical Museum.

In late April, 1993, I received a letter from someone in the Toronto area:

> Dear Sir:
>
> Congratulations on your excellent book, *Dive Ontario!* I picked it up last week and read every page. I was however quite interested with the *Explorer* (pg. 167). I was shocked to see my ancestor's name as the infamous captain of this vessel.
>
> My family originally settled around the town of Sunderland near Lindsay, Ontario, when land in Canada was deeded to military personnel in lieu of a pension. Our family name is reasonably rare, and doubtless, this fellow was my great grandfather's brother or uncle....
>
> I would value any information you might have on either the man or more about the wreck. I would greatly appreciate you calling (collect) if you could point me to other information sources....
>
> Yours truly,

I looked at the signature and nearly dropped the letter in shock. There, in that "bold and somewhat peculiar handwriting" which had become so familiar to me, was written the name "John Waddell." I had heard about

The Eberts Papers in-cluded the Explorer's *original Surveyor's Certificate of Admea-surement.* CRIS KOHL COLLECTION

unusual circumstances where a person's handwriting could, for some inexplicable reason, be the same as, or very similar to, that of an ancestor. Nonetheless I fully expected to hear the theme music from "The Twilight Zone" as I gazed at that signature. After a while, I just shook my head, still in disbelief, and mailed John Waddell whatever information I had about John Waddell.

✝   ✝   ✝

But that's not the end of the story. Three further episodes bear mention. Firstly, the *Explorer,* raised in July, 1882, repaired, rerigged and returned to service, sank in eleven feet of water after striking a pier at Kincardine, Ontario, on June 19, 1883. Easily raised and again repaired, the bad luck ship was only two months away from her third and final strike.

Secondly, on September 4, 1883, a late summer gale drove the salt-laden schooner yacht onto Greenough Shoal off Stokes Bay, Ontario, on the Lake Huron side of the Bruce Peninsula. Coincidentally, the location was about eighteen miles south of Tobermory, where the *Explorer* had lain on the lake bottom for fifteen years. But in this final sinking, as spectators on shore watched helplessly, all four men on board perished after they had clung desperately for hours to the stranded vessel's rigging: Capt. Charles Woods (the 30-year-old bachelor son of London, Ontario Capt. Joseph Woods), John McDonald, a Mr. Heals and Walter Crane, son of Albert Crane of Chicago. The *Explorer* was still owned by Mr. E.N. Lewis of Goderich, who had arranged both of the ship's salvages during the previous year.

One newpaper account in September, 1883, concluded:

> Only a few weeks ago, she [the *Explorer*] was cruising around the coast of the [Bruce] Peninsula with a large party of ladies and gentlemen from Goderich on a pleasure trip. Her loss is now complete having been broken to pieces on the rocks. The bodies of the crew will probably be recovered on the shore this week. The history of the *Explorer* is a romantic one, and her final complete loss with her crew will doubtless have the effect of reviving many peculiar superstitions common among sailors.

Thirdly, nearly a century later, in 1975, the wreck of the *Explorer* was discovered by scuba diver Paul LaPointe. Paul, who operated a charter boat at Tobermory and ran a scuba dive shop (one of the first I ever entered) out of his garage, coincidentally lived just outside Chatham, Ontario, the old home of Capt. John Waddell.

Unfortunately, when Paul LaPointe died in February, 1995, the location of the lost schooner *Explorer* went with him.

"...UNLESS SOME DIVER
DISCOVERS HER"

T he scuba diver lifted the flexible corrugated rubber hose, pushed on
the end plunger and let the air out of his buoyancy compensator to
sink slowly below the surface of the cold lake. His partner remained
on board their small boat. The diver, excited and curious, followed their
vessel's anchor line towards the bottom, hitting a thermocline -- a sudden,
chilling drop in water temperature -- at a depth of 85 feet. From that point,
the water grew darker and he grew colder as he descended.

By the time he reached the lake bottom at 185 feet, the diver felt the
numbing pain of a "cold headache" caused by the 38-degree fahrenheit
water. "Just like what happens when you eat ice cream too fast on a hot
summer day," he thought. He knew this wouldn't go away until he returned
to the surface and warmed up. Despite his aching head, he proceeded.

At that deep depth -- and it was well past recommended sport diving
limits -- he maneuvered in total blackness, and only the thin beam from his
underwater light allowed him to see anything at all. What he saw initially
was disappointing -- only the sand, silt and small stones fading into blackness
away from that small anchor secured at the end of the long line which he
had just used for his descent. He did not see the large object which he knew
was down there somewhere near him in the total darkness, the thing which
had displayed all the characteristics of a shipwreck when the men picked it
up electronically on the old ELAC sidescan unit aboard their boat.

Scuba courses teach you never to dive alone. But this diver, just like
the man who remained on the boat, knew that when you are already breaking
the "scuba rules" by diving this deep, you might as well be diving alone. If

you run into a problem down there, you could rely only upon yourself.

He ventured a very short distance away from the security of his slim lifeline, memorizing the location of his slender trail back to the surface, but still he saw nothing. As he began a slow, 360-degree rotation, he unwittingly ascended from the lake bottom only a couple of feet, and his shoulder hit something. It caught him by surprise and temporarily restrained him. His drysuit had snagged onto some part of a shipwreck, and, in turning away from it, the zipper had opened merely a tad. But it was enough. The diver felt the instant chill of freezing lake water creeping insidiously into his protective suit, and he knew that he would be cutting this dive short.

But at least he had found it -- a shipwreck which, in all likelihood, no one had ever seen before. Visibility was low -- only a few feet -- but he followed what appeared to be a wooden railing. At this point, there was no way of telling if it was the port or starboard rail. Soon his narrow light beam circled an object above and slightly away from the railing -- a window with bars on it. The diver immediately thought that this looked like a prison ship! Simultaneously it dawned upon him that this window did not appear to be in the vessel's hull, but rather in a deck cabin. If that was the case, then this was a very unusual find, since the deck cabins of most ships which sink are blown off the hull, usually destroyed by the powerful air pressure seeking escape as the invading water quickly and mercilessly displaces the seeming emptiness inside the hull. This displaced air, not being able to escape from the sinking hull faster than the water entering it, almost always blows off any wooden deck cabins and hatch covers.

The diver did not venture away from the railing, but sank down slightly below its base. Suddenly his light caught a couple of letters carved into a wooden nameboard attached to the ship's hull. He began reading: *E...L...* He struggled to maintain the thin light beam's position as he swam steadily towards the right ...*I...A...B...W...I...N...* This was an awfully long and unusual name, the diver thought. At that depth, with his breathing compressed air, his mind was already playing tricks on him with the help of the narcosis-inducing pressure. He was having trouble remembering this odd arrangement of letters. The cold water and the pitch darkness did not make it any easier. But this feature -- a readable nameboard -- turned out to be another shipwreck rarity conveniently giving him the name of this find.

He gazed at the alphabet soup ensemble again, from beginning to end, just to make certain that the letters were still in the same order.

In his mind, he repeated the name over and over. This would not be one of the Great Lakes' many "mystery wrecks" with an untraceable history!

Just to be sure, he returned to the beginning of the carved letters a third time and memorized each one of them again.

He could not press his luck any further, alone in the cold darkness with a leaking drysuit. Cautiously and fortunately he found his way back to the anchor line which he had used to make his descent, the string of Theseus to help him find his way out of this black labyrinth in a controlled manner.

The diver headed up slowly and he impatiently waited out the long minutes of his mandatory decompression stop near the water's surface. He was bursting with excitement about this shipwreck discovery and his gloved hands clenched and unclenched with the itch of wanting to surface immediately and tell his companion on the boat about the wondrous things he had just seen on the lake bottom: seemingly an upright, intensely intact sailing ship.

Illinois diver Paul Ehorn had just become the first person to explore this virgin shipwreck. Back on the boat, he gave his colleague, well-known shipwreck hunter John Steele, who owned the boat and the sidescan unit, a detailed description of the shipwreck without any mention of the nameboard.

"So, what wreck do you think it could be," asked the seasoned shipwreck hunter after listening to Paul's enthusiastic description of it.

"It's the *Cornelia B. Windiate*."

John Steele's jaw dropped. He had once joked that Paul wasn't playing with a full deck on the surface, and he sure as heck wasn't going to get any cards down there at 185 feet. He figured Paul was still a bit dopey from nitrogen narcossis -- the so-called "rapture of the deep."

"How do you know it's the *Cornelia B. Windiate*?" he asked with raised eyebrows, a bit bemused.

"Heck," replied Paul off-handedly in his usual good-natured way. "The name is right on the side of the wreck!"

The two men were having an excellent day of wreck hunting. Luck came early -- at nine o'clock in the morning -- on Sunday, May 11, 1986, when they found the intact steamer, *Norman,* in 210 feet of water. John had been at the helm when the sonar picked it up and he was also the one to do a solo dive to check it out. After that deep dive, tired but happy to have located this shipwreck so fast, John took a nap while Paul took the helm. It was on Paul's watch that the sonar resounded with that day's second shipwreck discovery.

In his dive into the deep, Paul Ehorn had managed to find indisputable evidence that this shipwreck was indeed the schooner *Cornelia B. Windiate*, a vessel which John Steele knew had gone missing with her entire crew many years ago in Lake Michigan.

But there was just one problem. Paul was diving in Lake Huron.

*   *   *

103

The winter of 1875-1876 was severe. By November 24, 1875, fourteen inches of snow had fallen at Sault Ste. Marie, and the ice at nearby Mud Lake was two inches thick. At Mackinac, the temperature was 22 degrees Fahrenheit and there was "considerable floating ice in the Straits."

This early cold spell, instead of quickly dissipating, spent several days worsening. A dispatch from Sault Ste. Marie on November 30th reported "Snowing. Wind light, northeast. Mercury 17 below last night. Ice fast forming in the river. It is quite impossible for ships to force their way through the [Soo] canal now. The [steamers] *St. Paul, Missouri* and *Norman* are reported frozen into Mud Lake by a man arriving from there yesterday."

In the southern part of the Great Lakes, Cleveland reported that its "creeks, canals, slips, etc., were all frozen over with ice" and that the steamer, *Starucca,* arrived "covered with ice and had a pretty rough passage."

Thick, restrictive ice had formed over many Great Lakes waters by the first two days of December. Sailors, struggling to squeeze in one last profitable cargo run of the season, found themselves instead struggling for their lives.

On Lake Ontario, the large schooner, *James R. Bentley,* ran ashore on Simcoe Island near Kingston, her crew being saved with great difficulty by a local steamer. The sea pounded the *Bentley,* reportedly "washing her masts and rigging thirty or forty feet high, and under the action of the frost, giving them a thick coat of ice." The ship was later recovered.

The bark, *Parana,* suffered ice and storm damage, requiring that the ship be drydocked for repairs after it was towed into Chicago. Her crew suffered terribly from the cold during their frightful ordeal. One crewmember, Joseph Trombley from Saginaw, Michigan, lost a foot after doctors concluded that amputation would be necessary.

The largest Great Lakes schooner at that time, the 1,444-ton *George W. Adams*, only six months old, beat a hasty retreat while northbound on Lake Huron towards the Straits of Mackinac. The ship returned to Port Huron, where it was reported that it "will probably lay up in Sarnia Bay. It is hardly possible she will venture again with such unfavorable weather in prospect."

Steam-powered ships fared no better. The *Belle Cross,* with the barges she was towing up Lake Huron, had to return to Port Huron, being unable to reach Saginaw on account of the thick ice.

The small steamer, *Favorite,* with a cargo of hoops, froze solidly in Saginaw Bay several miles off shore. With only a three-day supply of food, the crew was in danger of starving to death. A tug hired to rescue them made no headway whatsoever as it attempted to break through the thick ice. One newspaper, aware of the sailors' very precarious and desperate situation, reported that "the only chance for the crew would seem to be that they can hold out until the ice has become sufficiently firm to enable them to walk ashore."

One of the most tragic tales to emerge from this icy storm involved the loss of an 18-year-old wooden barge on Lake Huron. The 371-ton *Waurecan,* stranded on Austin Reef in northern Saginaw Bay, held her frozen crew captive in the icy grip of early winter for an entire day before the steam barge, *Burlington,* could rescue them. Crewman George Courter had to have both feet amputated. Another sailor, from England, lost one foot. Crewman Anthony Wood froze both of his ears. The barge's master, Captain McKenzie, required the amputation of one foot. Unfortunately, he had brought his wife and their baby along on this dangerous trip; she was so badly frozen that both of her feet ultimately had to be removed, but the infant, placed under its mother on top of the deck load with a piece of canvas thrown over them, was saved from injuries. The seas washing over the mother and child had frozen the canvas so solidly around them that it had to be chopped loose by their rescuers.

Mother Nature displayed one of her worst temper tantrums on the Great Lakes that late autumn.

The nearly new, three-masted schooner, *Cornelia B. Windiate*, under Captain Mackey of Chicago, departed Milwaukee with a load of grain for Buffalo on Saturday, November 27, 1875, just before these horrid conditions developed. The weather, undistinguished when the captain and his Chicago crew left Milwaukee, turned into an icy maelstrom within hours.

The *Windiate* unfortunately had lost three precious days of time. Returning from Buffalo with 500 tons of hard coal in her holds, the *Windiate* broke her jibboom in a collision with the schooner *San Jacinto* on Lake Huron on November 20th, then damaged her headgear upon entering the Chicago River when the barge, *Sandusky,* ran into her on November 22nd. While other ships which reached Chicago by November 23rd unloaded their cargoes and stripped their canvas for winter layup, the *Windiate* was quickly being repaired so she could complete just one more trip of the season. One Chicago newspaper, on Thursday, November 25, 1875, stated that "Repairs to the *Windiate* (a new stem) will be completed today, when she will leave for below in tow of the propeller *Garden City*. The *Windiate* goes to Buffalo."

In the maritime lingo of the day, "for below" meant heading to a port somewhere "down," or downbound on the lakes, that is, following the general current towards the ocean. Buffalo, at the extreme eastern end of Lake Erie, certainly was "below" from Lake Michigan. The *Windiate's* delay for repairs meant that the crew would have to sail later into the dangerous season.

The *Windiate* was towed by the steamer, *Garden City*, through the Chicago River, already thronged along both sides with silent ships in winter lay-up, and out into Lake Michigan before heading up to Milwaukee, sailing light, that is, without any cargo. At Milwaukee, she quickly took on 21,000 bushels of wheat, and waited until the next day to depart. The *Windiate* could have left on Friday, November 26, 1875, but a longtime superstition among sailors has a Friday departure portending bad luck on the voyage. No one aboard the *Cornelia B. Windiate* wished to attract misfortune by sailing on a Friday.

On Saturday, the schooner, towed out into the chill waters of the open lake by the steamer, *Egyptian*, sailed for Buffalo on her final run.

On Sunday, less than one day after the *Windiate* left Milwaukee, a devastating storm raged across the entire Great Lakes system. The *Cornelia B. Windiate* disappeared without a trace. During this blizzard-like tempest, and afterwards, no sighting reports were ever filed anywhere about the *Windiate*. No wreckage or bodies were ever found floating or washed ashore, and the one-year-old schooner became one of the many ships on the Great Lakes which mysteriously and tragically "went missing with all hands."

The lost schooner, rated A2 and appraised at $18,000, was insured for

This lookalike to the schooner Cornelius B. Windiate *is the three-masted* Granger. *Note the location of the stern cabin, the davits and the yawlboat.* PHOTO COURTESY OF PATRICK LABADIE COLLECTION, THUNDER BAY SANCTUARY RESEARCH CENTER

106

$14,000 (no company in the 1870's insured a vessel for its full value). Her cargo had insurance coverage for more than a dollar a bushel among a variety of insurance companies: Amazon, $5,000; Inland Union, $5,000; Merchants' Mutual, $5,000; Orient, $4,000; Bangor, $2500; St. Paul Fire & Marine, $2500; and Northwestern National, $1200, for a total of $25,200 for 21,000 bushels of wheat.

Ironically, a brief heat wave hit the Great Lakes just before Christmas, 1875, prompting newspaper comments such as "Poor weather for skating" and "The prospect of a sleighride on Christmas day cannot be realized."

Just before Christmas, traditionally a happy time when families are together, the Chicago newspaper offices were inundated with requests for the names of the *Windiate's* eleven crew members, something which no one could provide beyond the identities of the captain, the first mate and the second mate. This situation prompted the influential Chicago *Inter-Ocean* to editorialize:

> ### ANOTHER LAKE HORROR.
>
> The Schooner Cornelius B. Windiate Founders on Lake Michigan.
>
> And Captain Mackey and His Entire Crew Find Graves Beneath the Angry Waters.
>
> Crew, Cargo, and Craft Are Sacrifices to the Canal Style of Construction and the Grasping of Owners for the Eternal Dollar.
>
> A Poetical Tribute to the Brave Men Lost with the Jenkins—Miscellaneous Marine News.
>
> LOSS OF THE WINDIATE.
> THE WORST FEARS CONFIRMED.
> A week ago the INTER-OCEAN alone of all the lake papers announced that the schooner Cornelius B. Windiate, grain loaded from Milwaukee and bound down, was overdue at Port Huron and Detroit—that is, that she had not passed those points—and that there were inquiries as to her whereabouts. Since then our marine reporter has asked every arriving captain

The Chicago Inter-Ocean *newspaper evoked the tragedy and implied greed behind the loss of the* Cornelius B. Windiate *[sic; the real name is* Cornelia B. Windiate*], while claiming the ship sank in Lake Michigan.* CRIS KOHL COLLECTION

"NAMES UNKNOWN"

THE INTER-OCEAN is written to frequently by the families and friends of sailors inquiring as to their whereabouts. At present we have letters from relatives of several men who are supposed to have been lost with the schooners *Minnie Williams* and *C.B. Windiate,* but as the names of the unfortunates are not known and cannot be learned, we are powerless to answer them.... The crew of the *Windiate* [shipped] from Chicago. The ships' books contain all the names, but the books went with the vessels to the bottom, and as no record is kept ashore the only resort is to visit the shipping offices. This has been done by the reporters in the case of the *Windiate,* but to no avail. The proprietors of one office knew they had got berths for two men on the ill-fated craft, but did not know their names, and thought it probable that the remainder of the crew had been picked up on the dock. Thus it is. A sailor ships on a vessel at his home port, and at the vessel's port of destination he is discharged and obtains a berth on another craft just leaving the harbor. There is no time to write to family or friends, and his whereabouts of course become unknown. The close of the season this year, as usual, finds hundreds of sailors missing. Many have doubtless deserted their families, but many others have found watery graves, and their parents, wives, children, or others interested have not even the melancholy satisfaction that certain information would afford....

All this might be different and without any extra expense, and with very little extra labor to the Custom House clerks. All the customs regulations now exact of vessel captains in this respect when clearing is the *number* of men on board. If there was a general order making the captains furnish the *names* of the sailors and the Custom House clerks put them in writing, to be preserved, we would always have a record that might be consulted at any time and there would not be the uncertainty that at present exists; and on the occasion of the loss of a vessel, with sacrifice of life, thousands of sailors' relatives and friends other than those of the victims would not be needlessly anxious. When a vessel goes down and the crew are referred to as "names unknown," it is easy enough to imagine the anxiety that is felt in the home of every sailor whose whereabouts are in doubt.

Will the department or Congress make the reform suggested?

Eventually these recommendations were followed, also using Canada's "Seamen's Agreement Act" which went into effect on January 1, 1876, as an example. This agreement made it mandatory for the captain of a ship to "enter into an agreement with each seaman employed in their crews," outlining such terms of employment as the particulars of the intended voyage, the seaman's job and the amount of his wages. This agreement had to be made and signed by both master and sailor in the presence of a "respectable" witness or the Chief Officer of Customs, and a copy of the agreement remained on shore. This must have sounded terribly bureaucratic to sailors of that era.

At the end of the year 1875, one Great Lakes newspaper listed a month-by-month " Death Roll" from the Lakes Marine for the year 1875. Regarding the *Windiate* under the month of November, it wrote: "Captain Mackey, First Mate Harvey, Second Mate Burch, and eight others, were lost from the schooner *Cornelius* [sic] *B. Windiate*, which, beyond a doubt, was [sic] foundered on the night of Nov. 28 [1875] on Lake Michigan near the Foxes."

The year's end "Incidents of the Season," published in late December, 1875, in the shipping news section of one of the Chicago papers, succinctly reported: "Nov. 28---Schooner *C. B. Windiate*, grain laden, lost on Lake Michigan with all hands." Another report stated, "It is known that she did not pass off this lake [Lake Michigan], as had she got through the straits and into Lake Huron, some one would have seen her."

We know now that these reports erred regarding both the date of the

THOMAS WINDIATE

Left: *Thomas Windiate of Manitowoc, first owner of the* Cornelia B. Windiate, *named the ship after his daughter.* PHOTO COURTESY OF MANITOWOC MARITIME MUSEUM. Right: *No photograph positively identified as being that of the* Cornelia B. Windiate *has been discovered yet, but this three-master, the* G. C. Trumpff, *constructed at Manitowoc in 1873 by those who built the* Windiate *a year later, was similar.* PHOTO COURTESY OF PATRICK LABADIE COLLECTION, THUNDER BAY SANCTUARY RESEARCH CENTER

Windiate's loss, which is understandable, and the lake in which the ship sank, which remains hard to believe. It came up as late as April 25, 1911, when Thomas Windiate, "the last surviving member of the Masonic lodge at Manitowoc," died in that city at the age of 84. His long obituary noted that he "constructed many prominent boats... [including] the *Cornelia B. Windiate*, one of the noted wrecks that went down on Lake Michigan with all on board and no trace of her was ever found."

*   *   *

Thomas Windiate, born in England on January 16, 1827, into an unusually large family of 20 children, arrived in America with his parents in 1836, settling in Pontiac, Michigan. In 1852, he married Canadian-born Cornelia Elizabeth Wallis in Pontiac, and they moved to Manitowoc, Wisconsin in 1855, where Thomas began a series of successful businesses. Before securing an extension of the railroad to Manitowoc, Thomas Windiate established a stagecoach line to Sheboygan, worked at farming, and built the original Manitowoc harbor piers for the government, as well as a high school in that city. He constructed the Windiate House hotel in 1869, described as "second to none in the Northwest" by the Manitowoc newspaper, and that establishment soon entertained many leading men of the country as guests. The Windiate family resided in the Windiate House, which quickly became Manitowoc's social center. A Grand

WINDIATE HOUSE,

THOMAS WINDIATE. Prop'r.

TOURISTS, TRAVELERS AND PLEASURE SEEK-
ERS will here find large, elegantly furnished rooms
in one of the healthiest localities in the State.

A "Tip Top" Livery

In connection with the House. 1T-19-tf

Thomas Windiate built the hotel named the Windiate House in Manitowoc, Wisconsin, in 1869; he and his family also resided there, hosting so many entertaining annual events that it quickly earned the reputation of being the social center of the entire region in the late 1800's. CRIS KOHL COLLECTION

——The Windiate House received a new boarder on Saturday in the shape of a very young lady. She was heartily welcomed by the happy landlord who vowed he would keep her free gratis in everything just as long as she wanted to stay.

Manitowoc's front page newspaper announcement of the birth of Cornelia B. Windiate in the one-month-old Windiate House hotel on Saturday, September 4, 1869, was coy. Thomas Windiate was so proud of his first child that he later named a ship after her when she was only four years old. CRIS KOHL COLLECTION

Ball was always held just before Christmas, where "a good time may be expected. Good music and supper will be provided." A report after one of these events stated that

> The Christmas Dance at Windiates' was a splendid affair, there were about thirty-five couples present, who enjoyed themselves hugely, and the supper was excellent as it always is when prepared by Mrs. Windiate. Tom surpassed himself in attention to the company and in the most refined urbanity towards the beautiful circle of blooming happy ladies.

A party at the Windiate House in February, 1874, was described as having

> ...passed off most pleasantly and to the entire satisfaction of all concerned. The dance was carried on especially lively until supper, which was served in excellent quality. Messrs. Severance & Williams' Band played in their usual superior style so that the dancing was continued until four o'clock Saturday morning. From Two Rivers the party was attended by beautifully dressed ladies and handsome young gentlemen. Sheboygan sent her late Mayor and his estimable lady. Milwaukee her brave captain Vance. Menasha her lively Mr. Dunbar, and Neshota the indefatigable Mr. Jones, thus furnishing the best possible representation of our neighboring localities. All expressed entire satisfaction with the whole entertainment of the evening and we learn that preparations are already in progress for another similar party immediately after the Lenten season.

Into this very sociable family arrived a daughter named Cornelia B. Windiate on September 4, 1869, the first child born in the new Windiate House.

During the 1870's, the ambitious Thomas Windiate also engaged in shipbuilding. In early 1872, he and a partner repaired the schooner, *Dan Tindall,* which had been wrecked at and recovered from the Straits of Mackinac and towed to Manitowoc. He partnered with well-known shipbuilder James Butler in their home port of Manitowoc, Wisconsin, for the construction of two new schooners to be used in the grain trade from Lake Michigan to eastern ports. The first one, the *G.C. Trumpff,* was launched on July 12, 1873; but Thomas Windiate had sold his share of the ship by then.

The second one was launched the following April.

The Chicago *Inter-Ocean* newspaper reported on April 11, 1874, that "The new canal schooner being built by Messrs. Windiate & Butler, at Manitowoc, is, we understand, to be named the *Cornelia B. Windiate,* after a daughter of the senior partner of the firm." This created some confusion because Thomas Windiate's wife was named Cornelia E. Windiate.

Ice still blocked the Great Lakes in late April, 1874 (the mid-1870's were notoriously cold years for the inland seas, with late springs and early winters predominating.) Proud of his new 332-ton schooner of respectable dimensions (138'6" x 26'2" x 11'6") and anxious to get her underway, Thomas Windiate sent the new ship out into ice-flecked Lake Michigan. A problem arose and the *Cornelia B. Windiate* had to return to Manitowoc because of a leak. Embarrassed repairs were quickly made, and the ship sailed for Milwaukee on the first leg of her maiden voyage. There, the press described the new schooner as "a good model [which] from her draught promises

> **Arrival of the Windiate.**
> The new schooner Cornelia B. Windiate is in port on her first trip, bringing a light cargo of hay, etc., from Manitowoc, where she was built. She is full canal size, and withal a well-constructed vessel. She is the property of Windiate & Butler, of Manitowoc, who are also the builders. She took her departure from Manitowoc on Saturday last, but was found to be leaking when some distance up the lake, and put back. This fact accounts for her non-appearance here several days ago.

On her maiden voyage in May, 1874, the Cornelia B. Windiate *began to leak enroute to Chicago.* CRIS KOHL COLLECTION

to be an excellent carrier." The *Windiate* had a freezing birth and a frigid christening, with the Milwaukee paper of April 29th reporting that "the vessels which arrived here had their decks covered with ice."

Thomas Windiate felt the financial pinch of low grain prices in 1874 and 1875. One mid-season report stated that "Vessel-owners generally, along the entire chain of lakes, feel greatly discouraged.... Their crafts have as yet not earned a penny, and they fail to discover a ray of hope for anything better in the future.... The lakes are largely overstocked with tonnage...." Thomas Windiate luckily found a buyer for the *Windiate* in November, 1875. Just before the ship disappeared with all hands, banker C.C. Barnes, whose State Bank of Manitowoc failed years later, became the proud, new owner of another bad investment, the *Cornelia B. Windiate.*

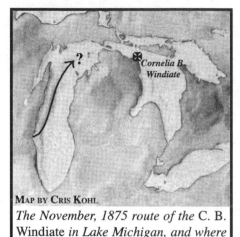

MAP BY CRIS KOHL

The November, 1875 route of the C. B. Windiate *in Lake Michigan, and where the shipwreck was eventually found.*

What six-year-old Cornelia thought about her father selling the ship which had been named after her, or, even more significant, how she was affected by the complete disappearance of the *Cornelia B. Windiate* and the crew, was never reported, if indeed it was ever observed.

Cornelia B. Windiate grew up in Manitowoc with the nickname "Cornie," and a few of her social activities went reported. When she was nearly 13 years old, "Cornie Windiate and Addie Hill supplied the gentlemen with button-hole bouquets" at Manitowoc's Young Ladies of St. James' Parish Festival in 1882. In the summer of 1898, "Tom Windiate [her brother] and Miss Cornie Windiate of Kansas City, Mo., [were] visiting their parents Mr. and Mrs. Tom Windiate of this city [Manitowoc]."

On Saturday, October 2, 1901, Cornelia B. Windiate married Henry A. Paine, a prominent businessman of Oil City, Pennsylvania, the ceremony taking place at Windiate House where Cornelia had been born 32 years earlier. The couple honeymooned at the Pan-American Exposition before taking up residence in Oil City.

Cornelia B. Windiate moved away from Manitowoc in 1901, her father, Thomas Windiate, died in 1911, and the historic Windiate House at York and Sixth Streets was sold in 1947 by Rev. Thomas Windiate, son of the original owner, for $15,000. In the 1950's and 1960's, a printing company occupied the first floor, with apartments on the two upper floors. The building was razed in late 1974, and today, a medical clinic building occupies the site.

*   *   *

The schooner *Cornelia B. Windiate's* forward mast, rising to a depth of about 93 feet, still sports a yardarm held precariously to the mast by a comparatively thin pin. Following this mast to the deck places the diver at a depth of 165 feet. The wisdom of attaching the mooring line for visiting boats to the top of this massive mast has been questioned; if that mast ever breaks or topples, any recreational boat tied to it will be carried down to create yet another shipwreck!

The forward mast of the Cornelia B. Windiate, *complete with rigging and yard-arm, rises from deck level at 165 feet to within 98 feet of the surface, providing a visual reference for divers, in this case, technical diver Jim Stayer, to drop straight down to the visually magnificent bow.*   PHOTOS BY CRIS KOHL

The bow displays both wooden stock anchors, catheads, a large windlass with an impressive amount of chain, bitts and part of the bowsprit. All hatch covers remain in place and the stern retains a magnificently intact deck cabin (indicating that the ship sank slowly) with unbroken windows behind protective bars and a "spiral staircase" (actually steps which make a 90-degree turn over five levels) leading below deck. The name of the ship appears carved into a wooden trimboard on the starboard side, and the stern is graced with several decorative iron stars attached to the

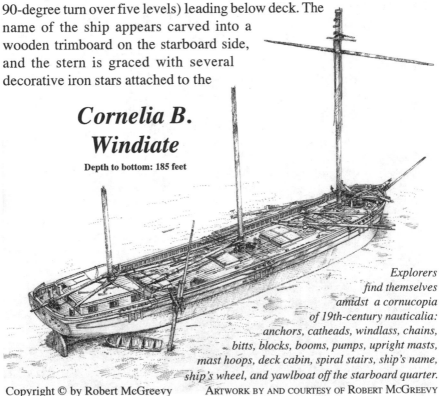

Cornelia B. Windiate

Depth to bottom: 185 feet

Explorers find themselves amidst a cornucopia of 19th-century nauticalia: anchors, catheads, windlass, chains, bitts, blocks, booms, pumps, upright masts, mast hoops, deck cabin, spiral stairs, ship's name, ship's wheel, and yawlboat off the starboard quarter.

Copyright © by Robert McGreevy   ARTWORK BY AND COURTESY OF ROBERT MCGREEVY hull. The lifeboat lies along the starboard quarter. No damage to the hull can be seen anywhere, not even along the lake bottom. As no human remains have been located on the ship, and as the lifeboat was not launched, the implication is that the ship became trapped in the ice, slowly sinking, and that the desperate crew attempted to walk the several miles to shore, but did not make it. Their bones probably lie on the lake bottom somewhere between the shipwreck and the shoreline.

*   *   *

S pring arrived late again in 1876, half a year after the *Cornelia B. Windiate* disappeared with all hands. The severe winter, which had roared in early like an angry lion, was determined to go out in similar

A broken bowsprit, boom and mast among deck and bow fittings and equipment still in place add to the unequalled sense of history, drama and tragedy one feels when exploring the incredibly intact and preserved Cornelia B. Windiate. PHOTOS BY CRIS KOHL

 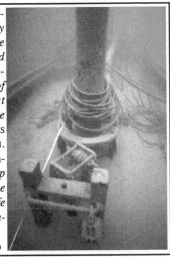

Left: *The* Windiate's *deck closely resembled the one on this unidentified Great Lakes schooner. Note the use of the wooden mast hoops to hold the sail to the mast.* CRIS KOHL COLLECTION. Right: *On the* Windiate's *midship mast, the hoops have dropped to the fife rail next to a centerboard winch.* CRIS KOHL PHOTO

fashion, and to take its time doing so. The St. Marys River was still frozen shut on May 9th, and Marquette, Michigan, reported that "there is no water in sight here outside the breakwater, but the ice is softening up." One huge steamer, the new *Commodore*, struggling to reach Cleveland from Milwaukee, found herself stuck in ice temporarily twice during that passage, aware that only her displacement of 2,082 gross tons plus her immensely heavy cargo had enhanced the ship's ability to cut through that ice and complete the trip. The shipping season suffered a very late start 1876.

Nearly half a year had passed since the *Cornelia B. Windiate* had sailed out of sight and into history. No trace of ship or crew had been found. The Chicago *Inter-Ocean* retrospectively and prophetically summarized the matter just prior to the commencement of the 1876 navigation season:

> It was the sad duty of THE INTER-OCEAN last fall to announce the loss of the schooner *Windiate* with all hands. The vessel left Milwaukee with grain for below, and was never afterward heard from. It was so late in the season when she set sail that there were comparatively few craft remaining in commission, and it could not be learned that the masters of any other vessels had even seen her after she was a day out of Milwaukee. None of the bodies of her unfortunate crew have [sic] been found, and while it is generally conceded that she foundered at the foot of this lake, it is not certainly known that she did not get through the straits, and meet her terrible fate in Lake Huron. A relative of one of the victims of the disaster writes THE INTER-OCEAN requesting that the masters of the first down and up fleets be asked to keep a lookout for the wreck, "as there is a bare possibility that some portion of it is above the surface at some

point." This request, we are sure, the masters will comply with, and promptly report if the whereabouts of the *Windiate* are discovered. But it is very probable that she went down in deep water, and it is not likely that she will ever be seen again unless some diver accidentally discovers her....

It was 110 years, almost to the day, before "some diver," namely two shipwreck hunters chasing history, located the *Cornelia B. Windiate*, solving a longstanding mystery. Paul Ehorn and John Steele spent time in June, 1986 filming the shipwreck with housed 16-millimeter movie cameras and lights.

"If you dive with a crowbar, you dive alone, but if you dive with a camera, you can take a thousand people with you," John Steele has often said.

The film was edited that fall, and both men went on the shipwreck show circuit in 1987 with well-received presentations on the wrecks of the *Norman* and the *Cornelia B. Windiate*. They had removed nothing from either shipwreck, but a diver who had followed them out to the *Windiate* in June, 1986 to steal its location went back in July, tied a line to the ship's wheel, attached the other end to his boat, and tried to yank up the choice artifact, succeeding only in wedging it firmly into the shipwreck on an unnatural angle.

"The *Cornelia B. Windiate* is an example of one shipwreck which the archaeologists should be working to protect and to survey instead of those lumber piles of broken up wreckage in 15 feet of water that they're spending so much time and money to examine and safeguard," claims Paul Ehorn.

Ohio's Joyce Hayward, a member of the Women Divers Hall of Fame, in August, 2003, organized a large group of divers, historians, photographers and boat captains, with the blessing of NOAA, the Thunder Bay National Marine Sanctuary and Underwater Preserve at Alpena, and the State of Michigan, in a survey project of this special shipwreck, mapping and cataloging the entire vessel and its artifacts to avoid any plundering. This group appreciated John Steele and Paul Ehorn's responsible stewardship of this distinctive shipwreck discovery.

The *Cornelia B. Windiate,* that exceptional example of maritime material history, is probably the best preserved of all the shipwrecks located so far in the Great Lakes -- and we respectfully remember this sad tale of the ship whose short history was spent mostly in ice.

THE SHIPWRECK
WHICH HELPED BUILD CHICAGO

One winter night a few years ago, several members of the Underwater Archaeological Society of Chicago shared camaraderie and a post-meeting meal at Ricobene's Restaurant, a historic landmark which preserves its original 1946 atmosphere on the south side of Chicago.

As usual, the topics of discussion revolved around Great Lakes ships, shipwrecks and the people who were involved with them.

"A lot of sailors have lived, worked, staggered and bragged along the Chicago waterfront, but nobody was as colorful as Cap Streeter," Keith Pearson, a man known for his strong views, suddenly blurted out.

A mischievous twinkle of recognition appeared in Pete Chval's eyes. Jim Jarecki, too, perked up at the sound of Streeter's name. Birds of a feather recognize one another, even when separated by a hundred years. These three -- Pearson, Chval and Jarecki -- introduced me and a few others sitting around the tables that evening to some of the tall tales about Chicago's adventurous, eccentric mariner of the late 1800's.

It is all too easy to get caught up in stories about the indomitable Cap Streeter. He was an out-of-control adventurer not afraid to stand up to lakefront millionaires and Chicago bureaucracy. He was the pioneer emperor of what he called "The Deestrict of Lake Michigan." He was a pirate born a hundred years too late. The more I heard my colleagues' anecdotes, the more I wanted to find out about Cap Streeter's legendary, comic-opera escapades, especially the unusual tale of how his shipwreck literally helped build Chicago.

*　　　*　　　*

117

Captain George Wellington Streeter guided his noisy, shuddering, steamer through moderate Lake Michigan waves northward from Chicago on a test run to Milwaukee. He had proudly painted the letters "Reutan" along the sides of the ship's bow, certain that he was going to take this vessel down to Central America, there to partake of the lucrative business of gun-smuggling. So certain was he of reaching his destination, an island called Roatan, that he had named his ship after it -- or as near to the spelling of it as he could muster. "Cap" admitted that book learning was not among his strengths.

While the *Reutan* strained under the pressures of Lake Michigan's wind, waves and rain, the five paying passengers also strained -- over the leeward railing -- from the roughest ride to Milwaukee they had ever experienced. Streeter, ever watchful for opportunities, had ensured that his test run would not cost him anything by taking along customers. Later, safe at their destination, the green-faced wayfarers informed Streeter in no uncertain terms that they would be taking the train instead of the *Reutan* back to Chicago.

So Cap, his wife Maria and their engineer faced the returning winds and waves on their own. The weather had worsened, and the engineer, his constitution weakened, retreated into one of the berths, leaving the ship's operation to the Streeters. Maria kept the engine's fires stoked while Cap, who had wisely lashed a sturdy line between himself and the rail, held the helm. Every time the waves washed his light frame overboard, the muscular Maria hauled him back in, hand over hand. She did this a total of seven times before the storm, although abating, slid the *Reutan* solidly onto a shallow sandbar about 450 feet off Chicago's shoreline just north of the river. It was three o'clock in the morning, and the Streeters turned in for a bumpy night's sleep.

A few months earlier, Cap and Maria had encountered a soldier of fortune named Captain Bowen who was generously buying rounds for an attentive but well-lubricated audience in a Chicago bar. He convinced the tipsy Streeters -- and many others in the wide-eyed throng aflame with booze-fueled dreams -- that gun-smuggling mercenaries in Honduras were paid in advance and would later be awarded generous land grants and lumber contracts when an appreciative new revolutionary government was in power. That, he was convinced, was a quicker way to riches than a gold mine.

Cap Streeter, the would-be smuggler-tycoon, immediately sold his share in the Apollo Theater and bought an old boat, a "handyman's special," which he spent the winter of 1885-86 repairing and equipping with a secondhand boiler. Cap and Maria hoped to take their 30-foot-long vessel down the Mississippi River and headquarter themselves at New Orleans while they ran remunerative runs to Roatan. But first, the *Reutan* had to prove her seaworthiness in Great Lakes waters, and if she passed, Streeter felt confident that the ship could handle the Gulf of Mexico. Their round-trip to Milwaukee on July 10, 1886, was fated to sail them into Great Lakes legend and lore.

Come daylight -- it was Sunday morning, July 11, 1886 -- the wind had died, the waters were becalmed, the sky was blue and the sun was shining. The three souls on board the *Reutan* faced a perfect summer day. However, the hull had opened in several places and appeared to be solidly embedded in the soft sand, which the storm had further shored up against the ship. Sadly the vessel which was to run guns in Central America had failed her foul weather test on Lake Michigan.

But the undaunted Cap Streeter had another idea.

Why not stay right where they were? The ship's deck hovered a foot above the water, and the cabin remained solid and dry. It was so shallow that the Streeters could easily wade those few hundred feet ashore to Chicago, but the shrewd, old devil already had visions of filling in a strip to construct a convenient causeway to the mainland.

At that time, Chicago's brisk and steady construction spree kept a vast army of workers busy, and Streeter quickly offered them, for a nominal fee, a place to dump their waste materials which was much closer than the costlier official dumping ground at the north end of the city. The general area several miles out in Lake Michigan had also been used steadily as a natural garbage dump site since the Great Fire of 1871, but Streeter offered construction companies an inexpen-

The steamer, Reutan, *stranded off Chicago in a storm on July 11, 1886, with dramatic results.* CRIS KOHL COLLECTION

sive water location right off the heart of the city. Over the next few years, the Streeters sifted through the rubble before hauling it out in their skiff from shore and strategically distributing it near the *Reutan,* picking out discarded iron, copper, lead and zinc and living comfortably from the sale of these scrap metals and from their dumping fees. Cap Streeter built a solid bulwark of thick, wooden beams around the *Reutan,* and Lake Michigan's ceaseless waves continued to do their work depositing sand around this new barrier. Before long, Streeter was able to position jackscrews under his boat, raise it completely above the water level so he could shovel fill to form a foundation, and repair the damage to the ship from the stranding while making his abode weatherproof. Cap and Maria spent cozy days and nights, and even snug winters, in their new home while the size of their surrounding property grew larger by the week.

Surprisingly, it took several years before the millionaires who owned the shoreline properties near the *Reutan* reacted to the outrageous Cap Streeter.

*   *   *

The illustrious George Wellington Streeter came from impressive all-American stock. His great-grandfather and grandfather had earned notable reputations fighting in the War of Independence and the War of 1812 respectively, and his mother was directly descended from Francis Marion, the Revolutionary War's legendary "Swamp Fox."

Born in 1837 into a large family on a wilderness farm outside Flint, Michigan, George W. Streeter ventured successfully into the lumbering business in 1855 at age 18. With some money put aside, he married local girl Minnie Waters while they were still teenagers, and they relocated to the Mississippi River where Streeter worked as a steamboat pilot. In the spring of 1860, the Streeters and two others took a wagon train out west simply to see what it was like. The Civil War broke out and Streeter, serving in the Fifteenth Michigan Volunteers and partaking of considerable action in a dozen battles, mostly in Tennessee, emerged with the rank of captain (so his title of Captain, or "Cap," had been legitimately earned, although not in a maritime sense.)

When the Civil War ended, the restless and unpredictable Streeter started a popular traveling circus with a menagerie of native animals -- bears, wolves, moose, elk, lynx, raccoons, eagles and an enormous white Normandy hog which weighed over 1,500 pounds and which Streeter passed off to the paying public as a "white elephant."

The circus success which gave the Streeters financial security in 1866 failed them the next year, and they went bankrupt.

*George Wellington Streeter
in his younger days.*
CRIS KOHL COLLECTION

Cap again changed directions. In the winter of 1867-68, he built a small steamboat named the *Wolverine* which he operated in the Great Lakes lumber trade. By late 1868, he sold the boat and the Streeters moved to St. Louis, where, the following spring, Cap invested in a riverboat which he named after his wife -- *Minnie E. Streeter* -- at the same time that she confiscated the couple's $700 nest egg and ran off to join a vaudeville touring group.

Between 1869 and 1872, Streeter hauled freight between the river cities of New Orleans, Cincinnati and Nashville. He moved to South Chicago in 1873 and built the *Catharine* -- named after his mother -- but within two years, the compulsive Streeter moved to Bedford, Iowa, investing in a livery stable, stagecoach line and hotel, all of which occupied his time for the next several years.

In the early 1880's, Streeter encountered an old acquaintance from the days when he was still married to Minnie. Maria Mulholland, a former school teacher in Ireland who shared Streeter's strong inclination and constitution for whiskey, had been living with her uncle, Detroit shipbuilder John Ward. George and Maria were soon married and living in Chicago, eventually listening to barroom tales about the fortunes to be made in gunrunning.

By 1889, three years after the Streeter's ship first stranded off Chicago, water no longer surrounded the *Reutan*. Instead, Cap and Maria resided on 186 acres of newly-created land. Drygoods millionaire N. Kellogg Fairbank, who owned the mansion and the shoreline nearest to the *Reutan* and who finally reacted to the distasteful view of Streeter's shanty ship, angrily reproached Streeter for having taken advantage of his tolerance. Fairbank, originally given the impression that the stranded vessel would remain in place only until it could be repaired, seethed as he stepped down from his fine carriage, flailing his arms and ordering Streeter off this vast expanse of near-barren land.

Cap Streeter eyed him quietly through squinting eyes, shifted his chewing tobacco, and then spoke.

"You're wrong, mister," Cap said as he pointed towards shore. "Your property goes up to there, where the beach used to be."

The red-faced Fairbank exploded with his claim to riparian rights (allowing a landowner with waterfront property to do whatever he likes with this footage, including alterations along the shoreline or in the water).

Streeter yelled back, "I've got squatter's rights, sovereign rights and the right of eminent domain. And I've got this." He pulled out his Civil War musket and ended the conversation with four words:

"Now git, damn yuh."

Some time later, when many wealthy landowners banded against him,

Streeter brought up that topic of riparian rights to a reporter:

"Do you know what them fellers claims? Lemme tell yuh what they claims. They claims ripairin' rights, that's what they claims. What is ripairin' rights? Lemme tell yuh what they is. Ripairin' rights is the rights to ri-pair yer shore where it's wore off by the water. Don't gi'en yuh no more right to fill in the lake an' own the fillin' 'an it does me to dig a hole in yer front yard an' own th' hole."

But to Streeter's simple way of thinking, the new land he had created belonged to him.

Fairbank made the mistake of not taking his grievance against Streeter to court. Instead, he ordered the police to oust the squatter, thus beginning many years of unsuccessful attempts to remove Streeter from the new land. Initially, five constables arrived at the *Reutan* to evict Cap, but once again he drove them away at the point of his Civil War musket, that legendary buckshot-spewing shotgun which, in later years, sported a mounted bayonet, more for psychological intimidation than for actual usage.

What the millionaire landowners kept hushed up was the fact that their mansions also stood on land made by filling in Lake Michigan. Chicago real estate and hotel tycoon Potter Palmer had begun the trendy influx to that area when he dumped vast amounts of dirt in the mosquito-infested swamp just north of the Chicago River, and, in 1884-1885, built his pretentious mansion styled after a castle on the Rhine River. However, unlike

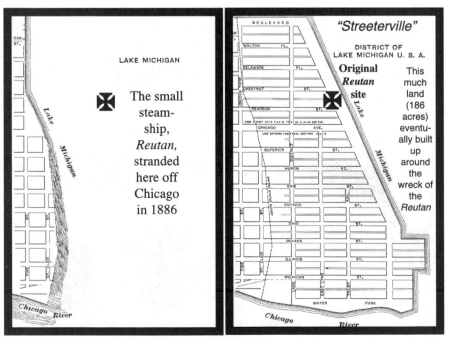

Streeter's situation, Palmer had first purchased the swamp land which he filled in.

Bureaucratic obstruction of Streeter's endeavors began in earnest in 1892, when he decided to repair the *Reutan* and use the ship again on Lake Michigan. A two-story scow became the new Streeter residence. When his work on the *Reutan* was finished, Streeter invited everyone in Chicago to view the launching, set for June 4, 1892. However, he was denied a launching permit, instead being told that the *Reutan* was a houseboat, and as such required a housemoving permit. But the street department refused to issue Streeter the needed permit. The press and most of the city's inhabitants sided with Cap.

Streeter eventually succeeded in returning the *Reutan* to service as an excursion vessel for the Columbia World Exposition in Chicago in 1893. He had changed the ship's name, some say to "Maria" (after his wife), while others say to "Squatter" (after himself), but Cap showed a preference for combining the two, not to mention his weakness in spelling, when he painted "Mariah the Squater" on the ship's bow.

Initially, of course, this new real estate resembled barren farm fields, but the opportunistic Streeter sold many of the lots to his friends. These new landowners formed a makeshift army to protect their property, particularly from those who owned what was formerly "lakefront"

Cap Streeter (right) *repairing the steamer,* Reutan, *for use at the 1893 Columbia World Exposition.*

CRIS KOHL COLLECTION

LAKE MARINE NEWS.

Police Still Keep Streeter's Steamer on Land.

PEOPLE INSPECT THE VESSEL

She Is by No Means a House, but a Handsome Craft.

Captain Shaack Is Roundly Censured—Shipping Master Biemel Acquitted.

The case of Captain Streeter, who was refused the privilege of launching his new steamer from the foot of Superior street, is attracting general

The Chicago Inter-Ocean *of June 11, 1892, reported Cap Streeter's problems with getting the* Reutan *re-launched.*

CRIS KOHL COLLECTION

Often, with the police in plain sight waiting for them to leave their residence, the Streeters avoided eviction simply by stubbornly staying put. CRIS KOHL COLLECTION

footage.

Streeter's legal arguments for his ownership of the new land involved an 1821 survey which clearly defined the Lake Michigan shoreline, and other documents outlining where residents' property lines ended.

Streeter and his "Army of the District of Lake Michigan" caused problems for the city, particularly once they formally claimed independence from Chicago and the state of Illinois in May, 1894.

"This here ain't part of Chicago or the State of Illinois. It's the Deestrict of Lake Michigan, subject to nobody but the President of the United States. Now git t'hell outta my Deestrict afore I plug yuh," was Streeter's informal proclamation.

The new "deestrict" operated under its own set of liquor laws, or rather, lack thereof. Streeter explained, "This is a frontier town, and it's got to go through its red-blooded youth. A church and WCTU [Women's Christian Temperance Union] branch never growed a town big yet. Yuh got to start with entertainment."

In 1899, with the expanding force of more wealthy notables such as

The Streeters made themselves comfortably at home on their newly-created land in various dwellings over the years -- from tents to two-story scows (above).
CRIS KOHL COLLECTION

124

Potter Palmer behind them, the police again tried to remove Streeter, only to retreat in yelping dismay after the scrappy Maria dumped a kettleful of boiling water upon them from the second floor.

To his opponents, Streeter was illiterate, hard-drinking and profane. Potter Palmer considered him "a rude, blasphemous, drunken thief." Streeter's invariable uniform, comprised of a silk stovepipe tophat and a dark frock coat at least a couple of sizes too big for him, did nothing to endear him to the wealthy.

The most famous Streeter controntation occurred in May, 1900 between 600 police officers and Streeter's ragtag army of squatters. Streeter or one of his men supposedly fired two bullets into the horsedrawn carriage of a police captain, who then decided that enough was enough. He ordered the army of Chicago constables to capture Streeter. An informant told Cap about the prospective attack, and Streeter was able to assemble a small brigade of tramps, hoboes and squatters armed with rocks, clubs, pitchforks, axes and guns. They quickly dug shallow entrenchments in the low-lying fields, threw together driftwood barricades and braced themselves for the police attack. When it came, the charging constables met with such an impressive barrage of gunfire from the ragtag army that they hastily retreated. Concerned about a more massive attack which they would not be able to repel, many of Streeter's cronies deserted. Cap and his few faithful followers waited for sunrise.

People reading their morning newspapers in the Windy City chuckled. Cap Streeter was at it again. Hundreds took up ringside positions at the lake.

But a maverick policeman walked into Streeter's camp, talked with Streeter, and the makeshift militia surrendered. Subsequent charges against them were soon dropped.

Despite its humorous edge, the warfare was real -- opposing sides had

An army of 600 Chicago policemen faced Streeter's squatter army, entrenched in makeshift forts, in May, 1900, along Lake Michigan's shore. Cris Kohl Collection

Cap Streeter often landed in jail, but just as often was released. CRIS KOHL COLLECTION

formed, entrenchments were dug, forts were constructed, guns took aim, blood was shed, people were hospitalized. The City of Chicago even built a navy of armed steam tugs, mounted with small cannon and Gatling guns, sent out to conquer a vast, treeless field of vagabonds armed with rocks, clubs and pitchforks. It was a bit of Wild West mayhem, a touch of the Gangs of New York, a dollop of Ma and Pa Kettle, all sprinkled liberally with grains of the Marx Brothers.

The preposterous, yet amusing, spectacle of a squatter defying an entire city -- the largest and most powerful city on the Great Lakes, no less -- captured the attention, and often the hearts and support of the public. In those days before radio, television and the internet, newspapers were experiencing their golden age with powerfully loyal readerships in the years between 1870 to 1920, and they reported every chortle, tittle and sigh from Streeter regarding each victory and defeat in this conflict between the common man David and the bureacratic Goliath.

Streeter often spent time in jail, but always had a lawyer secure his release. The battles, legal and physical, went on for years. In spite of Streeter's lack of good grammar and clear enunciation, he pleaded in court with logic and sincerity, almost always with success.

One occasion came close to ending Streeter's freedom. Found guilty of murder in 1904 when a man was actually killed during a skirmish, Cap was sentenced to life in prison. Brokenhearted at the prospect of never being with her husband again, Maria died within weeks of Streeter's incarceration. Eight months later, Illinois Governor Altgeld, reviewing the case and agreeing that Streeter's buckshot-loaded shotgun could not have been the weapon used in the crime, pardoned him. In deep mourning and extremely lonesome, Streeter watched time pass slowly for two years until he met and married Elma Rockwood, a woman about half his age, but with mettle and temperament equal to his. He called her "Ma" Streeter.

The legal battles continued. Just before Christmas, 1918, Streeter, 81 years old and going blind, was finally evicted from his makeshift residence. A combination of the Chicago Title and Trust Company wanting him removed, and Streeter's refusal to stop selling alcohol in his "deestrict" on Sundays, ultimately became his downfall. Forced off the property where he had lived for 32 years, Streeter, with "Ma" and their small dog, moved into a houseboat named the *Vamoose* docked in East Chicago.

By the time Cap Streeter died of pneumonia at the age of 84 on January 24, 1921, aboard his houseboat, the world had changed far too much since the *Reutan* had first stranded off Chicago in 1886. Steel ships 600 feet in length had replaced the 120- to 200-foot schooners and wooden steamers which had crowded Chicago's harbor by the hundreds. Automobiles and airplanes had been invented and

Ma and Cap Streeter.
CRIS KOHL COLLECTION

seemed to be everywhere. Motion pictures were well on their way to replacing vaudeville. Radio had just begun to broadcast to the masses, and Prohibition was in effect across the country (a societal condition which by itself would have been enough to kill Streeter). It was a strange, fast world which the slow-moving Civil War veteran no longer recognized and in which he no longer felt comfortable.

Upon Streeter's death, a huge, silent sigh of relief escaped from Chicago's establishment. The war was finally over. The enemy had been vanquished, not at the hands of those who opposed him and not put in his place by the courts of the land, but by the natural fate which awaits everyone. Cap Streeter, however, had been a worthy opponent; he had neither fallen into disgrace nor slid into dishonor in more than three decades of fighting for the land, which he honestly believed belonged to him, and for the unlikely

Cap and Ma Streeter continued their legal battles for land from the water; they lived cheaply on board a houseboat named the Vamoose. *Cap's death was no mystery, as one Chicago newspaper headlined.* CRIS KOHL COLLECTION

geographical and political entity which he had established and commanded.

The war actually still flashed, slow to die out, with Ma Streeter continuing the court fights. However, in 1925, her claims were dismissed because she was ruled as not having been legally married to Streeter, since neither he nor first wife Minnie bothered to obtain a divorce. Ma died penniless in the Cook County Hospital on October 19, 1936. The last suits by alleged heirs and ragtag landowners were dismissed in 1940.

Despite the large volume of newspaper ink which related Streeter stories to an amused and fascinated public, most people today are unaware of who he was and what he did. The amazing controversy of Cap Streeter made better newspaper copy than history text, and he has been either shrugged off as an eccentric bit player on a larger stage, or ignored altogether.

Today, the land created by his shipwreck is the site of impressive and valuable buildings such as the Drake Hotel and the Chicago campus of Northwestern University, while the illustrious rascal, Captain George Wellington Streeter -- pioneer, privateer, buccaneer, musketeer -- leaves a largely overlooked legacy in Chicago's history.

CAPT. GEORGE
WELLINGTON
STREETER.

CRIS KOHL COLLECTION

Cap Streeter's 40-car funeral, attended by many dignitaries (including Chicago's Mayor Thompson and the President of the Chicago Title and Trust Company), ended in Graceland Cemetery, home to the mortal remains of Chicago millionaires, many of whom fought Streeter during their lifetimes. Cap is buried among them, but a safe distance away in a noisy corner near the elevated train -- conditions he would appreciate.

PHOTO BY CRIS KOHL

PHOTO GALLERY 1

Above: Many members of the *Griffon's* crew had to get out and tow their ship through the fast-moving waters at the head of the St. Clair River so the vessel could enter Lake Huron in 1679. The *Griffon* holds the distinction of being the first ship on the upper Great Lakes. Unfortunately, it also became the first shipwreck there. What happened to this vessel on its maiden voyage and where it sank remain the greatest mysteries on the inland seas to this day. ART BY AND COURTESY OF STAN NORRIS, SARNIA, ONTARIO. *Below left:* The Province of Ontario set up this historic marker near the point where the crew towed the *Griffon* upstream. *Below right:* These artifacts, left behind by some of the earliest fur traders on Lake Michigan in the 1670 to 1720 period, were found on Rock Island where Green Bay begins. They could easily have belonged to La Salle's men. PHOTOS BY CRIS KOHL

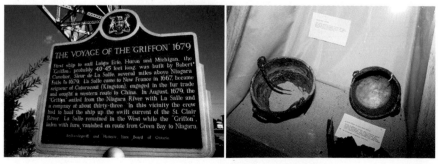

Left: The rugged shoreline of Lake Huron's Manitoulin Island, famous as the world's largest freshwater island, may very well have been the place where the *Griffon* wrecked. *Inset:* Three museums on Manitoulin Island, in this case the Net Shed Museum at Meldrum Bay, display timbers taken from "the old wreck" which had lain on the western shoreline for many generations already by the time the first settlers arrived on the island in the 1860's. *Below:* Sean Moore gazes at the runny, white letter "G" painted onto a rock marking the site where the remnants of "the old wreck" reposed before a 1942 storm washed them away.   Photos by Cris Kohl

Above: The Mississagi Straits lighthouse at Manitoulin Island's western end is a museum today, with extensive newspaper accounts and pieces of "the old wreck" purported to have been that of the *Griffon. Below:* The historic museum at Gore Bay offers the largest "old wreck" collection, including a chunk of the lead caulking. *Below left:* The author explored "Griffon Cove" on Russel Island near Tobermory by inflatable boats.   PHOTOS BY CRIS KOHL

Above: The *Alvin Clark*, built at Detroit in 1846, sank with the loss of three lives in an 1864 storm on Green Bay. ART BY JAMES ANDREWS, COMMISSIONED BY JOYCE HAYWARD, COURTESY OF BOTH. *Below*: The masts were removed first, then the hull was raised and towed to port. Frank Hoffman appears in the bottom photos.

PHOTOS BY AND COURTESY OF DR. RICHARD BOYD

Above: The *Alvin Clark,* once the masts had been restepped and rerigged, looked capable of sailing again on the waters of the Great Lakes with great ease. *Below*: Windlass, capstans and winches, all restored to their original working condition, awed the many visitors who initially flocked to visit the "Mystery Ship."

PHOTOS BY AND COURTESY OF DR. RICHARD BOYD

Below: Many of the *Clark's* tools were housed and exhibited in a building next to the ship. PHOTO BY CRIS KOHL

Above: Funding for the costly conservation of this large ship proved elusive for the man who had raised the *Alvin Clark*. Hoffman's vessel had become an increasingly heavy albatross around his neck. Frustrated by the mounting expenses of maintaining this museum, Hoffman tried to destroy the ship, but was stopped by authorities. By the late 1980's, 20 years after being raised from the icewater depths of Green Bay, the *Alvin Clark* was warping, sagging and rotting. Photos by Cris Kohl. *Below*: By 1994, all that remained of this once-magnificent Great Lakes sailing ship had crumbled. The pieces were trucked off to the local dump. Lesson learned. End of story.   Photo by and courtesy of Dr. Richard Boyd

Above: A War of 1812 ship was raised from the Thames River just upstream from Tecumseh Park in 1901, about the time this colorized postcard was published. CRIS KOHL COLLECTION *Left and below:* This Tecumseh Park cannon came from the Crimean War; today, no trace is exhibited of the War of 1812 "old soldier shipwreck." PHOTOS BY CRIS KOHL

135

Top: The Eberts family papers included documents pertaining to John Waddell and the schooner *Explorer. Middle:* Several Waddell family members repose in Maitland Cemetery at Goderich, Ontario, including John Waddell, "...accidentally drowned 20th July, 1870, aged 53 years." *Bottom left:* Local historians have told the tale which hints that Sheriff John Waddell "borrowed" generously from the supplies of stone used in the construction of the Chatham courthouse to build this nearby house, his private residence on Water Street. Ironically, today the house remains stable, while the courthouse needs replacing. *Bottom right:* Charter boat captain and wreck hunter Paul LaPointe, who resided just outside Chatham, John Waddell's place of residence during his mid-1800's tenure as Sheriff, located the wreck of the *Explorer,* originally owned by Waddell, in 1975. PHOTOS BY CRIS KOHL

Top, left: Paul Ehorn, tending lines on his own boat in this photo, was manning the helm of John Steele's vessel when the sidescan unit detected the wreck of the *Cornelia B. Windiate* on May 11, 1986. *Above:* John Steele at his usual shipwreck locating position.

PHOTOS BY CRIS KOHL

Above, left and right: One mast of the *Windiate* towers to within 93 feet of the surface, guiding Jim Stayer to the deck another 75 feet below. PHOTOS BY CRIS KOHL

1870's jug on deck

Ship's wheel on its strange angle (see story for details)

Port hawse pipe and chain

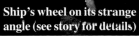

Technical diver Jim Stayer explores and videotapes the bow area of a true gem of the Great Lakes: the schooner *Cornelia B. Windiate* in 185

Above left: Joyce Hayward, shipwreck survey organizer, with historian Patrick Labadie and technical diver Darryl Ertel. *Above right, l. to r.:* Divers Cris Kohl, Joan Forsberg, Dave Mekker, Durrell Martin, Alan & Martha Jensen, Darryl Ertel and Pat Stayer. *Right:* The upright, intact *Cornelia B. Windiate* offers a wealth of archaeological information about an 1874 schooner. Bow items include the windlass, anchors, chains, a bowsprit portion, and copper capped bitts. Tangled rigging lies on the deck. Deadeyes line the port rail. *Below:* Darryl Ertel and Pat Stayer prepare to dive. PHOTOS BY CRIS KOHL

Above left: Captain George Wellington Streeter guards "his" new land. CRIS KOHL COLLECTION. *Above right:* A birdseye view of modern Chicago skyscrapers constructed on lakeside land created by Cap Streeter's 1886 shipwreck. PHOTO BY CRIS KOHL. *Below:* This 1920's postcard shows the rise (literally) of "Streeterville." CRIS KOHL COLLECTION

7:—The Drake, Chicago's Wonderful New Hotel.

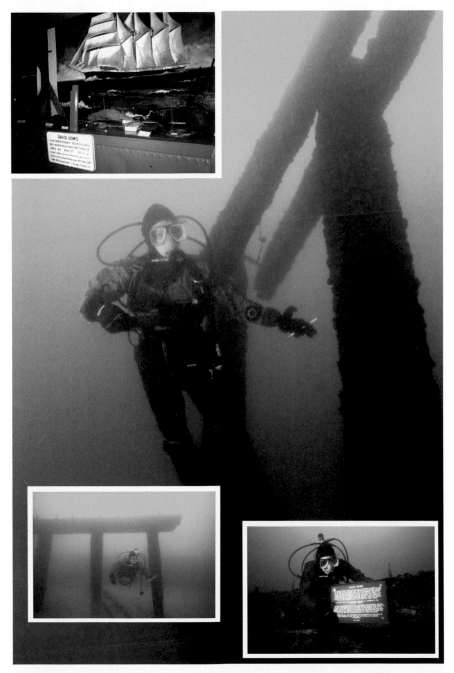

Above, left: Sault Ste. Marie, Michigan's Valley Camp Museum exhibits material from and about the *David Dows*, the largest sailing ship on the Great Lakes. PHOTO BY CRIS KOHL. *Others*: Diver Valerie Olson Van Heest explores the *Dows'* remains. A historic marker was placed on the wreck.   PHOTOS BY AND COURTESY OF JOE OLIVER

Above and below: The *Minnedosa,* the largest sailing ship ever built on the Canadian side of the Great Lakes, retains her deck cabin and tonnage numbers in deep water. PHOTOS BY AND COURTESY OF DAVE TROTTER/ UNDERSEA RESEARCH ASSOCIATES. *Left:* Great Lakes shipwreck hunter Dave Trotter spanned 16 years researching and searching for the *Minnedosa* before locating the elusive wreck. PHOTO BY CRIS KOHL.

Above: Very few wooden shipwrecks in the Great Lakes have been located with their superstructure cabin housings intact, for air trapped below deck seeking fast expulsion during the sinking normally causes the weak points in the deck, such as hatch covers and housings, to blow off. *Below*: Old-fashioned jugs and a knotmeter, a mechanical device for measuring ship speed, were found and placed on the wreck's deck by the first divers to explore the *Minnedosa*.

PHOTOS BY AND COURTESY OF DAVE TROTTER/UNDERSEA RESEARCH ASSOCIATES.

Left: The Mackinac Bridge as mariner's landmark. *Right and above:* Tom Farnquist on board the Great Lakes Shipwreck Museum's vessel, *David Boyd,* accidentally found the *William Young* while side-scanning for a body.

PHOTOS BY CRIS KOHL

The wreck of the schooner-barge *William Young* lies in 118 feet of busy water one mile east of the Mackinac Bridge. Highlights of this shipwreck site include anchors and the ship's wheel.

PHOTOS BY CRIS KOHL

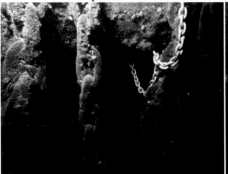

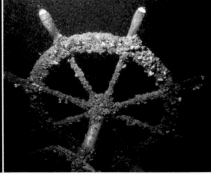

LEVIATHANS OF THE LAKES

B igger did not always mean better on the Great Lakes. Within a decade of each other in the late 1800's, both the United States and Canada built the largest sailing ships the freshwater seas ever produced. Unique in that one was a five-masted ship while the other sported four masts, these leviathans, it was hoped, would revive the use of sailing ships over steamships for commercial purposes on the inland seas.

Reportedly the Great Lakes system (both the United States and Canada) in 1882 consisted of 2,498 sail vessels, 1,398 steam vessels, 630 canal boats and 192 barges in operation, totalling an impressive 4,718 craft. However, a major change was underway, and the handwriting was on the wall. A visit to the vast majority of shipyards on the inland seas showed that steamer construction far outnumbered that of sailing craft. More and more, commercial schooners already in service were being demoted to barges, with their masts whittled down so only a couple of stumps remained for absolute emergency sail use, and these partially dissected ships, laden with heavy cargoes, were towed, often in a string of several vessels, behind a powerful steamship.

In a desperate effort to counteract this trend, Great Lakes shipbuilders constructed two of the largest bulk-carrying schooners the world had ever seen. Massive and magnificent, they turned heads in many harbors.

Their career records, however, ultimately proved disappointing.

*   *   *

T he largest sailing vessel ever built on the Great Lakes was the five-masted, 1,347-net-ton schooner, *David Dows* (265′4″ x 37′6″ x 18′), launched after successive misfortunes and amidst enormous fanfare

145

at Toledo on April 21, 1881. Built at the Bailey Brothers' shipyard for Toledo's M.D. Carrington for $90,000, named after one of Chicago's leading merchants and given official number 157029, she was designed to convey 140,000 bushels of grain or 3,000 tons of hard coal, a decidedly advantageous carrying capacity compared with other ships. The *David Dows* was the largest schooner in the world, a notable claim to fame for a vessel from the inland seas.

An idea of the *Dows'* size can be gleaned by the height of the ship's five masts: respectively 93, 97, 97, 93 and 88 feet. These solid logs were just the lower portions of the overall masts; stepped to these for additional height were smaller poles called topmasts. The first four topmasts measured 65 feet in length, while the fifth (the jigger-topmast) spanned 55 feet. Allowing 18 feet of length for each mast standing below deck, since they were stepped to the keel, plus overlap where the two masts were braced together, the five impressive masts of the *David Dows* towered dizzyingly more than 130 feet above the ship's deck. The schooner was gaff-rigged with four sets of yardarms on the foremast, and she could carry five jibs (sails ahead of the foremast). Her regular 18 sails totalled 18,630 square feet of canvas.

The mammoth hull was strapped on the outside with iron for extra strength. The bowsprit measured 37 feet in length. A small steam engine with a donkey boiler resting on deck provided mechanical power to raise and lower the many heavy sails, plus pump out the bilge. An ice and provisions house in midship was considered quite an innovation. The *David Dows'* magnificent figurehead, a construction rarity on Great Lakes ships, attracted much attention, with the Chicago *Inter-Ocean* writing:

The American giant, David Dows.
CRIS KOHL COLLECTION

The largest schooner in the world, the David Dows, *the Great Lakes' only five-master, sailed the inland seas exclusively.* DRAWING BY GEORGE CUTHBERTSON, COURTESY OF THE CANADA STEAMSHIP LINES. Right: *Chicago loved the "Monster Schooner."* CRIS KOHL COLLECTION

...The great vessel's figurehead represents a dragon, and is of large proportions, measuring 24 feet in length from tip to tail, and is handsomely gilded. It is natural enough to be about as repulsive as anything can well be. The scroll work and name on the stern are hewn out by hand. George Back, of Brooklyn, N.Y., did all the carving.

As a whole, the *David Dows* may be pronounced a great, staunch craft and a most important and valuable acquisition to our lake marine. Nothing at all has been neglected in hull or outfit to make her as perfect and complete as a vessel of her class can possibly be, and the builders have succeeded in a most remarkable degree. All success to the *David Dows*.

An equally glowing Buffalo newspaper account stated that the figurehead "represents a dragon, and the head of the animal is a very fine specimen of work," in addition claiming that the artist, "G. E. Buck", lived in their city.

By all accounts, though, the *David Dows* was a noble-looking vessel.

The ship's troubles began immediately. She ran hard aground in Maumee Bay, Lake Erie, on May 5, 1881, and had to be pulled off by a powerful steamer. A collision on June 30, 1881, at Chicago with the schooner *S. Anderson* did significant damage to the smaller ship's rigging, but none at all to the *Dows*. On September 10, 1881, the *David Dows'* inability to maneuver readily caused her to collide with the schooner, *Charles K. Nims,* off Point Pelee in Lake Erie during a race. No lives were lost when the

The David Dows' *sails reportedly took 7,000 yards of canvas, enough, as one Toledo paper wrote, "to furnish clean shirts for a large portion of the Democratic party in Ohio."* FROM A PAINTING BY LOUDEN WILSON, CRIS KOHL COLLECTION

Nims sank, and subsequently the court assigned blame to both ships, but the *Dows'* reputation as a maritime white elephant was solid by the end of her first season afloat.

This huge but impractical sailing ship was like a bull in a china shop in the busy shipping lanes and crowded harbors of the Great Lakes, and collisions ensued, often because the ship required many men doing much work over too brief a period of time to alter her speed or direction. The ship's draft was also too deep, not only eliminating her access to many shallow harbors, but also causing her to strand regularly, particularly when she relied solely upon her sails for propulsion. For these reasons, the *David Dows* was reduced to a towed barge two years after her launching. As a schooner, she required at least a dozen men to handle her, about twice the number for an average-sized Great Lakes schooner. Later, even as a towbarge, she still needed eight.

On Thanksgiving Day, November 28, 1889, the *David Dows,* only eight years old and valued at $60,000, found herself at anchor trying to ride out a furious storm. Towed by the steamer, *Aurora,* along with another enormous towbarge named the *George W. Adams,* the *Dows,* laden with a full cargo of coal, sank the next day apparently after the strong winds and powerful waves broke through her staunch oak construction and tore off her bow section. The eight men on board, including Capt. Thomas Roach of Manitowoc, took to the lifeboats and suffered considerably from the intense cold before the Dunham Towing and Wrecking Company tugs, *Chicago* and *T.T. Mumford,* picked them up, but no

FOUNDERED ON THE LAKE.

The David L. Dows Goes Down—Cost, $100,000.

CHICAGO, Nov. 29.—The largest sailing vessel on the great lakes, the five master, David L. Dows, foundered this afternoon twenty miles southeast of Chicago. Noth-

The sinking of the Great Lakes' largest sailing ship in a violent November storm was reported with varying degrees of accuracy. CRIS KOHL COLLECTION

lives were lost. This same ferocious gale also destroyed the steamer, *Calumet,* off Chicago, and did extensive dock damage elsewhere.

The underwriters (as insurance companies were then called) spent about $30,000 stripping and attempting to raise the *David Dows* before winter finally set in, but were able only to salvage rigging and 1,400 tons of the coal cargo. J. Willis Morse reportedly tried to salvage the *Dows* in April, 1890, but failed. That same year, a hardhat diver who investigated the site reported that the forward 75 feet of the *Dows* was broken clean off the hull, the decks had disappeared, and the midship butts had parted several inches. Further attempts at salvage would be useless. In August, 1908, the lake survey steamer, *Search,* found the wreck to be a hazard to navigation and partially removed it.

The historic wreck of the *David Dows,* relocated by modern Great Lakes scuba divers in 1964, lies in only 40 feet of water. At that shallow depth, the mightiest of the Great Lakes sailing ships ever constructed was soon, for the most part, flattened by time and nature. Regardless, many items of interest remain at this shallow site (see page 141 for color photos). The latter two-thirds of the hull is largely intact, especially a vast centerboard box (This ship was so huge that it had not one, but two centerboards and boxes.) Coal, likely from her final cargo, lies scattered near the centerboard box. The double-planked hull construction is quite visible as the diver swims around the perimeter of the hull. The starboard side has broken away and lies flat upon the lake floor. The broken-off bow section remains missing, despite a report that divers in 1978 tried hard to locate it in their specific quest for the ship's dragon figurehead. This figurehead may have been removed years before the *Dows* sank when the bowsprit and other no-longer-needed sailing features were stripped during the vessel's conversion to a towbarge in 1883.

*   *   *

Five months after the *David Dows* sank, the Canadians, not to be too outdone, launched the largest sailing ship ever built on their side of the Great Lakes on April 26, 1890, and named her the *Minnedosa* (245' x 36'3" x 15'1"). "Minnedosa" is a Sioux word meaning "waters of the rapids." A four-masted schooner, the 1,041-net-ton *Minnedosa*, the largest wooden schooner ever built in Canada, was constructed by master builder James Roney. A special dredge named the *Munson* had been hired to ensure that the water in the launch area at Kingston, Ontario, would be deep enough to receive the new *Minnedosa*. The fact that this dredge sank right after it finished this historic job was seen as a bad omen for the *Minnedosa's* future.

Six thousand people watched the crowded launch of the four-masted wooden schooner, Minnedosa, *the largest sailing vessel ever built on the Canadian side of the Great Lakes, on April 26, 1890, at Kingston, Ontario. A wooden obstruction on the launch-ramp delayed the event.*
CRIS KOHL COLLECTION

The *Minnedosa*, which cost $70,000 to construct, had two decks with doubled deck frames supported by 140 iron hanging knees, each one weighing 400 pounds. The vessel was painted black with two orange stripes on her bulwarks. The ship, given official Canadian number 94884, originally exhibited on her stem

> a graceful cutwater knee and trailboards, culminating in a lifesize half-length figure of Ceres, the Grecian goddess of harvest. Behind her, inverted cornucopiae, or horns of plenty, poured out the bounty ... flowing back in a beautifully carved Greek scroll running along the cheek-knees. On the headrails which braced the figurehead was, at each end, a Canadian beaver with a maple branch [emblems of Canada and also symbols of industry] in

Fully-rigged, the Minnedosa *carried 12 working sails and could make 15 knots in a stiff breeze.*
CRIS KOHL COLLECTION

The Minnedosa *retained all her rigging, even as a barge.* CRIS KOHL COLLECTION

his mouth.... A thousand dollars were spent on goldleaf and painting for this figurehead.... The gilding, all in gold leaf, was done by John Martin. The artist who did the carving was Louis Gourdier, one of the most skilful wood workers in Canada....

Unfortunately, five weeks after her launch, the *Minnedosa's* fantastic figurehead "had to be taken off to enable her to get through the [Welland] canal safely." In her first season, the *Minnedosa* visited Cleveland, where the press wrote that "she probably attracted more attention than any vessel that has been here for many a day and she deserved it all the more, too, even if she was from Canada...." Although the *Minnedosa* retained her topmasts, she was usually towed by steamers, normally the *Glengarry,* until 1903, when the new steel canaller, the *Westmount,* took charge. It was then that the *Minnedosa's* masts were finally cut down to barge size. Again, it

The Canadian giant, **Minnedosa.**
CRIS KOHL COLLECTION

took twelve men to handle her when she was a schooner, but only eight when she was a barge.

The *Minnedosa* sank with all nine hands in Lake Huron, north of Harbor Beach, Michigan, during a devastating storm on October 20, 1905. She had been in tow of the steamer, *Westmount,* along with the barge *Melrose,* bound from Fort William, Ontario, to Kingston with an enormous cargo of 75,000 bushels of wheat at the time of loss. Those lost were Capt. John Phillips of Kingston; his wife, Katie Little Phillips, cook; mate Arthur Waller, Nova Scotia; and seamen James Allen, John Enman, William Hall, George McDermott, William McIntyre and George Smith.

Great Lakes shipwreck hunter, Dave Trotter, from Canton, Michigan, spent 14 years, off and on, searching for the *Minnedosa* before finally locating her on May 30, 1993, several miles from where she reportedly sank.

The *Minnedosa* sits upright in 220 feet of Lake Huron water off Michigan's thumb. See description and color photos on pages 142-143.

Size meant nothing to Mother Nature. The *David Dows* and the *Minnedosa* are prime examples of where "bigger" was not necessarily "better."

NINE HEROES
SLEEP UNDER
THE WATERS

MINNEDOSA'S CREW
MET DEATH BRAVELY

Capt. Milligan's Thrilling Story of
Doomed Ship's Battle With
Storm and Wave.

CUT HAWSER WITH AN AX

Capt. Phillips on Sinking Vessel Gave Order
That Saved Melrose From a Watery
Grave in Lake Huron.

THOSE WHO WENT DOWN WITH THE MINNEDOSA WERE:
Capt. John Phillips, Kingston, Ont.
Mrs. Phillips, the captain's wife.
Arthur Waller, mate, Nova Scotia.
George McDermott, Belleville, Ont.
James Allen, Nova Scotia.
A passenger and three sailors, names unknown to the captain of either Westmount or Melrose, and whose homes are believed to be at Kingston.

Harvey Whipple, Staff Correspondent.

Port Huron, Mich., October 22.—Nine heroes went down with the schooner Minnedosa. The angered, raging wind sent mountainous waves

The Minnedosa's *beautiful, elliptical transom disappeared forever under Lake Huron's ruthless waves during a savage storm on October 20, 1905, with the loss of all nine lives on board. The ship had spent most of her life as a tow-barge because she was too awkward to sail.* Cris Kohl Collection

152

A Tale of
Four Shipwrecks

C ommercial shipping voyages on the Great Lakes more often than
not existed as uneventful activities in which a steamer and the one
or two barges being towed hauled heavy cargoes from one end of
the lakes to the other, then picked up another cargo for the return voyage
home. Often coal or cargoes of manufactured goods steamed from east to
west, while west-to-east freight usually consisted of grain, lumber or iron
ore. A steamship and her tows could make between twenty and thirty or
more round trips in a season, depending upon their destination ports, so
these commercial journeys often became routine and, to some, even
mundane by the time the shipping season drew to a close.

One such trip in late 1891 was anything but uneventful and routine.

*   *   *

H eavy with a coal cargo, the steamer *Nashua* cleared the port of
Ashtabula, Ohio, on Monday, September 28, 1891, towing a string
of three similarly coal-laden and as-old-if-not-older wooden barges
named the *Thomas Parsons*, the *William Young* and the *Newsboy*. All bound
for Racine, Wisconsin, none was destined to reach that port.

Within a couple of hours of departing Ashtabula, the *Thomas Parsons*
sprang a leak off Fairport and sank in 54 feet of water. The towbarges to
which she had been attached had quickly cut the lines when they saw the
Parsons sinking so that none of them would be dragged to the bottom with
her. No lives were lost, but the ship, valued at $4,500, was a complete loss.

In the late 1800's, smoke-belching wooden steamers towing a string of barges (usually former schooners with their rigging and bowsprits cut down), were common sights on the Great Lakes. In this photo, the towing steamer is the Charles H. Bradley *with three unidentified barges, very similar to when the steamer* Nashua *towed the barges* Thomas Parsons, William Young *and* Newsboy *across the lakes in late 1891. The number of towbarges varied. In one famous case in 1880, the powerful tug,* Champion, *towed a string of eight barges up the Detroit and St. Clair Rivers.* CRIS KOHL COLLECTION

The steamer, *Nashua,* and her remaining two tows, the *William Young* and the *Newsboy,* resumed their voyage towards Racine.

In the Straits of Mackinac several days later, a few spectators on shore noticed some unusual activity on the water:

> The steam barge *Nashua,* with a three-masted, black tow barge, was sighted far up the Straits early this afternoon acting strangely. The vessel at first appeared to be drifting away from the *Nashua.* Then it was got alongside and in this way slowly moved down until about in the main channel and headed towards St. Ignace. They separated and drifted about a mile alongside of Mackinaw [sic] Island, when the vessel suddenly sunk [sic] in deep water. No particulars can be obtained as the *Nashua* with all possible haste steamed back up the Straits and was soon out of sight. The vessel's crew is probably safe as the yawl was seen aboard the *Nashua.* It is thought another vessel must be in distress by the *Nashua's* action in hurrying away.
>
> Later -- The barge reported sunk at Mackinaw is probably the *Wm. Young,* which with the schooner *Newsboy* composed the *Nashua's* tow. All the vessels were coal laden. The *Young* was a

The 366-net-ton steamer, Nashua (134'4" x 29'9" x 11'6"), *built by Ira Lafrinier and launched on Saturday, August 8, 1868, carried a Boston-built steam engine capable of 300 horsepower.* RALPH ROBERTS COLLECTION

very old vessel, having been built in 1863. She was owned by
Capt. Richard Millen, who sails the *Nashua*. There was probably
no insurance on the *Young*....

There definitely was no insurance on the old *William Young,* which
rated a low B1 among underwriters and was valued at only $3,500.

The *Young's* crew had salvaged most of their ship's rigging and sails
before she sank, and after the *Nashua* picked them up in their yawlboat --
crew, rigging, sails, yawlboat, all -- the steamer rushed back to take in tow
her surviving barge, the *Newsboy,* at anchor a safe distance away.

The *Nashua* and her remaining tow, the *Newsboy*, resumed their voyage
towards Racine. Now there was but one; towing had become much easier.

The two ships veered into Milwaukee harbor instead of completing
their journey to Racine. Reports remain uncertain as to why. It definitely
had not been a good trip -- the *Nashua* embarrassingly losing two of her
three towbarges on a single run! -- so the journey was cut short in an effort
to end it as soon as possible. No one was told that the *Newsboy* was also
leaking.

The *Newsboy* succumbed the next month. On November 17, 1891, she
stranded in a storm on Fisherman's Shoal off Door County, Wisconsin. Her

The two-masted schooner, Thomas Parsons *(135' x 26' x 13'), built by George Hardison at Charlotte (Rochester), New York and launched on August 18, 1868 with official number 24666, had sunk twice earlier: in the Welland Canal in August, 1874, and off Sarnia after a tragic collision with the schooner,* Clayton Belle, *in April, 1882.*   CRIS KOHL COLLECTION

entire cargo of 54,000 bushels of corn, and very nearly her crew, were lost.

A year later, on October 4, 1892, the steamer, *Nashua*, met with tragedy when it sank in Lake Huron off Goderich, Ontario, with all fifteen hands. The upside-down hull, holed where the boiler broke through, washed ashore, and only one of the bodies -- a woman --was recovered.

At the *Nashua's* 1868 launch in Cleveland, the press declared that "...Extra pains have been taken to make her first class in every particular." Another newspaper announced later that "...She is said to be one of the best boats in the Line.... The boat cost $50,000...." At the time of her loss, the ship plus her lumber cargo were valued at $17,280.

But the *Nashua,* like most vessels on the inland seas, had her share of accidents. In late April, 1874, ice in the Straits of Mackinac punctured the ship's hull, and 150 barrels of flour had to be jettisoned in order to bring the leak level of the ship above water. On June 8, 1876, the *Nashua* reportedly "arrived at Duluth with a broken wheel [propeller]," and on May 8, 1877, she ran into and severely damaged the canal boat, *G. L. Booth* at Chicago.

These four ships were gone. Time went by. A decade passed, then another. Not so much as even one of these vessels made the news again. More time -- fifty years -- elapsed, and from that point, these ships dropped from memory.

NEWSBOY.
S.R. KIRBY BUILDER.

The schooner, Newsboy (152'2" x 31'4" x 12'8"), *built at Saginaw, Michigan, in 1862, official number 18086, collided with and sank the schooner,* E.B. Allen, *in Lake Huron off Alpena, Michigan on November 18, 1871. The* Newsboy *was wrecked 20 years later.* RALPH ROBERTS COLLECTION

*   *   *

On August 15, 2002, the research vessel, *David Boyd,* from the Great Lakes Shipwreck Museum at Whitefish Point, zigzagged in the course of "mowing the lawn" in the Straits of Mackinac, doing volunteer work trying to locate the body of a suicide, a woman who had allegedly jumped off the Mackinac Bridge. Tom Farnquist, the museum's director, kept his eyes glued to the screen of the sidescan sonar unit, hoping that the electronic towfish behind their boat would reveal a body reposing on the bottom of the Straits.

Unfortunately, Tom and his team failed to find any body. However, they did locate a shipwreck. At a distance of only one mile east of the mighty Mackinac Bridge which offers today's mariners a specific and stunningly visual dividing point between Lake Huron and Lake Michigan, the jagged shadow of a rough oval figure sitting at a depth of 118 feet slowly shaped its image onto the monitor. Here, in the midst of this busy, traffic-intense boat and shipping triangle formed by Mackinac Island, St. Ignace and Mackinaw City, lay a shipwreck which no one had ever detected!

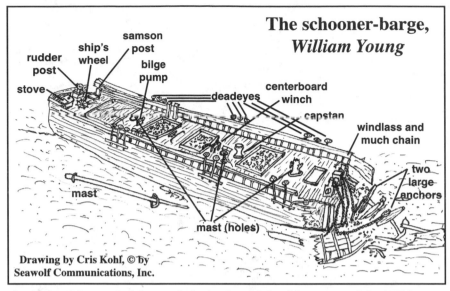

The schooner-barge,
William Young

rudder post
ship's wheel
samson post
stove
bilge pump
deadeyes
centerboard winch
capstan
windlass and much chain
two large anchors
mast
mast (holes)

Drawing by Cris Kohl, © by
Seawolf Communications, Inc.

A virgin shipwreck lying quietly in the thick of human activity! This was indeed a rarity.

This coal-filled schooner-barge must have hit the bottom bow first, as the only damage to the hull appears to be there. Either impact or time dislodged the three masts which lie near the shipwreck. Despite this natural disarray, the wreck retains both wooden-stock bow anchors with considerable chain wrapped around the windlass. In fact, all eighteen lower deadeyes remain in place on the port and starboard sides. The ship's stove sits on the starboard quarter, while the highlight, the ship's wheel, still in its place, graces the deck at the stern. Tons of coal cargo lie below deck. State and provincial laws against artifact removal serve to protect all of the shipwrecks everywhere in the Great Lakes. These nonrenewable underwater treasures, so well-preserved by our cold, fresh waters, belong to no one individual, but to all of us. (For shipwreck photos, please turn to page 144.)

Before long, scuba divers visited this new site and located the important registration numbers carved into the forward beam of the first hatch: 26230. The identification of the wreck as the *William Young* had been made.

The *William Young* (138′6″ x 26′2″ x 11′6″) suffered many accidents during the ship's long career: in November, 1866, she stranded on Bois Blanc Island near the Straits; in May, 1872, she stranded at Door County; in September, 1875, she sank in the Detroit River; in September, 1891, she almost sank off Door County, prompting her captain to flee the old craft. The ship's luck, however, ran out soon after in the Straits of Mackinac.

The *William Young* reminds us all that there are thousands of shipwrecks, or underwater repositories of history, yet to be found in the inland seas.

THE DEAD CAPTAIN'S SECRETS

Howling winds and slashing seas drove the schooner, *George A. Marsh,* out of control north across Lake Ontario. Captain John Wesley Smith, struggling at the wheel, found it impossible to maintain a steady course. The pitch-black night at this midnight hour hid the binnacled compass from his sight except during the occasional crack of a lightning bolt. The blinding rain spurred the aggressive waves to burst beyond any reins by which summer calms normally held them. Never in his 48 years had Captain Smith seen the Great Lakes so wild, choppy and dangerous in August.

Family friend and former sailor, Neil MacLellan, struggled against the powerful wind and waves to assist the captain at the helm, but as the youngest adult male on board, at 42, even he lacked the strength and stamina to subdue Nature. Mate (formerly the cook) Bill Watkins tried as hard as he could to assist at the manual bilge pump, but his short, 66-year-old limbs could not keep up. His partner, sailor William Smith, the captain's 51-year-old brother, pumped desperately in fast body-bending, body-straightening motions at the opposite end of the pump handle. In all the pounding from the heavy seas, the *George A. Marsh* had sprung a leak and was taking on water. Deck hand George Cousins struggled to keep a steam pump and siphons operational, a grueling task for his 59-year-old body.

The summer storm with the unusually fierce winds had begun with 40-mile-an-hour gales at Oswego, New York, on the evening of Tuesday, August 7, 1917. It caught the *George A. Marsh* in the middle of Lake Ontario. To turn around or to proceed was six of one, half dozen of the other.

The only other adults on board the *George A. Marsh* were two young women in their early 20's, Mrs. Neil MacLellan and the captain's wife,

Gertrude Smith. They did all they could to corral and comfort the children on board: the MacLellans' seven-month-old son, Douglas, their four-year-old nephew named Georgie Greaves who was visiting them from Toronto, the Smiths' 18-month-old daughter Lorraine, and four of Captain Smith's six children from an earlier marriage: Clarence who was four, John, Jr., six, Eva, aged eight years, and Greta, who was twelve. All were summoned and told to remain on the heaving, slippery deck in case a hasty departure in the lifeboats became necessary.

Such a wide spectrum of shipboard variety rarely strode the decks of a working schooner. Huddled here on the wet, slippery planks at this forlorn hour were two young women, seven children between the ages of seven months and twelve years, one middle-aged former sailor, and an experienced but aging four-man crew which struggled vainly to keep the 35-year-old vessel from sinking.

The crewmembers numbered among Captain Smith's dearest friends, and they had sailed with him off-and-on for many years. George Cousins, a captain in his own right who had volunteered to work as part of the crew on the *Marsh*, was related to the captain through the latter's earlier marriage. Mate Watkins had left the comparative quiet of his usual job as landlord of the Ferry Hotel in Belleville, Ontario, the ship's home port. He, like everyone else on board at this moment, wished he had never left home.

Normally the Lake Ontario schooner crossing to pick up and return with a bulk cargo, often coal, would be done with only four men besides the captain on board. But Captain Smith saw an opportunity to mix business with pleasure on this particular trip, so he prevailed upon friends and family members to join him for a leisurely sail across the lake. Even though Gertrude was in the process of furnishing their new house, she complied. It would be a relaxing trip for the family and friends, with the usual sailors doing all of the manual labor on board.

Departing Belleville on July 26, 1917, the voyage to Oswego was pleasant and uneventful, perfect on-the-water picnic weather. After lingering in Oswego for several days, crew and passengers boarded the *Marsh* and left that harbor with 450 tons of coal consigned to Seward's Coal Company for Rockwood Hospital in Kingston, Ontario, not too far east of Belleville.

Now, several hours later, with the full fury of the storm now upon them, Captain Smith gave up the idea of reaching the safety of Kingston harbor. He scanned the wet, hazy horizon for the sight of any land onto which he might run his dying ship. His only hope lay in keeping the vessel afloat long enough to reach land -- any land! He had missed Pigeon Island -- a small, uninhabited speck of land which would have served his purpose -- but he could dimly see the lights from Amherst Island ahead. Numerous commercial fishermen and their families lived on that island. Help would be at hand.

Anxiety levels rose. At one point, when water washed over the increasingly submerged deck, Neil MacLellan shouted to William Smith, still working the bilge pump, "Bill, I guess we've had it!"

But the *George A. Marsh* was making surprisingly good headway, and Captain Smith prayed for about another half an hour of time. That was all he needed to strand the ship upon Amherst Island.

Suddenly, with a loud creaking noise and one more rise and dip like a final gasp for breath, the dying schooner slipped beneath the waves.

It was 5:00 A.M., and the ship's holds had reached their fatal combination of coal cargo and flooding waters. The schooner went down two miles off Amherst Island in about 85 feet of water.

The deck disappeared from beneath their feet with such little warning that the men, women and children barely had time to fill the two lifeboats which, with the seas running so high, were impossible to launch properly. Overcrowded, the boats intended to save lives capsized, and most of the people in them drowned. Captain Smith had also equipped the *Marsh* with a large motorboat besides the usual two lifeboats, but the storm thundered with such vehemence that no small boat could survive in those waters.

Neil MacLellan dived in an attempt to rescue his wife, but the waves swept her away from the lifeboats and she disappeared from view forever. George Cousins and one of the little boys were last seen alive clinging to the large provisions box on the *Marsh's* deck. A struggling Captain Smith surfaced momentarily from the churning seas, but then was yanked down by the swirling waters and was seen no more.

Neil MacLellan, Bill Smith and Greta Smith clung to the smooth, slippery underside of one of the overturned lifeboats pounded by the huge waves. For five hours, they clawed tightly to their frail positions. The two men fortified their courage with liberal chaws from a plug of chewing tobacco which Bill had managed to pocket before the *Marsh* sank, but young Greta grew increasingly weak. The men encouraged her to hang on as long as possible, and they themselves held her up for as long as they were physically able. But at 10:30 A.M., Greta Smith, face, arms and legs bumped, scraped and bruised by the waves pounding her against the overturned hull, with a nasty cut marring her right eyebrow, released her weak grip on the lifeboat and was immediately swept away by the still massive waves.

Two commercial fishermen from Amherst Island, Hugh McCartney and Benjamin Wemp, were setting their nets and picked up the two survivors an hour later. Neil MacLellan, rumored to bring nautical misfortune with him wherever he went (he had survived three earlier shipwrecks on the lake!),

VOL. 53.   BELLEVILLE, O

TWELVE LIVES LOST
WHEN SCHOONER SANK

SAD TRAGEDY ON LAKE ONTARIO

SCHOONER GEORGE A. MARSH, OF BELLEVILLE, FOUND-ERED YESTERDAY THIRTY MILES FROM KINGSTON—LIFEBOAT CAPSIZED—TWELVE WERE DROWNED—ONLY TWO SURVIVORS—MARSH WAS OWNED IN BELLEVILLE AND WAS TAKING A CARGO OF COAL TO KINGSTON—SEVEN LITTLE CHILDREN AMONG THE VICTIMS.

(Special to The Intelligencer.)

KINGSTON, Aug. 9.—The Sowards Coal Company, of this ity, has been officially notified of the sinking of the schooner George A. Marsh, of Belleville, between Nine Mile Point and Pidgeon Island, on ake Ontario, yesterday morning. The Marsh had on 450 tons of coal rom Oswego for the Sowards Company. There were fourteen people on oard, and out of that number eleven were drowned and one died from

Twelve out of 14 lives on the George A. Marsh *perished in that sinking. Or was that number inaccurate?* CRIS KOHL COLLECTION

maintained his great personal luck when the *Marsh* sank.

Newspapers across the Great Lakes lamented the tragic loss of 12 of the 14 people on board the *George A. Marsh*: seven children, two women and three men, including the captain. Five of the bodies were recovered and buried: Gertrude Smith, Greta Smith, George Cousins, Bill Watkins and Georgie Greaves. The other bodies were never found. This overpowering tragedy stirred the community of Belleville's fervid compassion for some time after the sinking.

The two oldest Smith children had, fortunately, remained ashore. Seventeen-year-old Horace had procured a job in the mill of the Steel Company of Canada, and was staying with his aunt, Mrs. Bird. Margaret, 15, had not been well and her illness was thought to be too severe for her to face the rugged life on the lake. She was entrusted to the care of a Mrs. Keegan. As it turned out, all five of their younger siblings, as well as their father and their stepmother, tragically perished when the *George A. Marsh* foundered. The shock must have hit the new orphans hard, particularly Margaret when she was asked to help identify the few recovered bodies.

"BUSTER" GREAVES

Left: *Georgie Greaves and six other children died in the sinking.* Above: *The* Marsh's *masts remained above water after the storm.* CRIS KOHL COLLECTION

The tug, *Frontenac,* of the Donnelly Salvage and Wrecking Company, steamed to the wreck of the *George A. Marsh* and began dismantling the vessel. Neither the ship nor its coal cargo was deemed valuable enough to raise. Later the government steamer, *Grenville,* from Kingston, launched an official investigation which concluded that the many deaths were attributable to violent nature, and that, with all three of the *Marsh's* masts protruding above the water, the wreck formed a navigational hazard. In early October, 1917, a hardhat diver named H.E. Poland set dynamite charges on two masts (the third one had toppled over naturally by this time) which removed from sight anything within 27 feet of the water's surface. He also placed a charge of dynamite down the main hatch of the hull which, in his words, "loosened up everything and brought a lot of wreckage to the surface," presumably in a failed attempt to recover any more bodies.

Once that was completed, memories of the catastrophic schooner *George A. Marsh* gradually faded with the passage of time.

*   *   *

Scuba divers Barbara Carson, Edward Donnelly and Ted Symonds found the wreck of the *George A. Marsh* on October 7, 1967, fifty years after the vessel sank, and renewed interest in that ship prompted research into the schooner's history.

Built at Muskegon, Michigan, on the shores of Lake Michigan, in 1882, by the Footlander Drydock and Ship Building Company for Mr. W. B. Ranson of Chicago, this 118-foot-long schooner registered 174 gross tons. Named after Chicago lumber businessman George Andrew Marsh (1834-1888), the ship's maiden voyage was from Muskegon to Chicago with a load of 225,000 feet of lumber. Upon arrival at Chicago, one newspaper claimed "She is a good-looking vessel, barring an ugly stern -- the transom being a straight line." Another newspaper, this one in Cleveland, was kinder when it wrote about the *George A. Marsh* that "She is a three masted craft, and is very neatly and stanchly [sic] constructed. She was built at Muskegon and hails from Marquette. She is sailed by Captain John Solon, and Snow (everybody knows Snow) is mate."

The *Marsh* very nearly came to grief at Chicago in mid-May, 1883, during the same storm which sank the schooner *Wells Burt* with all hands. The end light of Chicago's exterior breakwall was out, and the *Marsh* mistook the middle light for the end light, nearly running upon the rocks.

Although one newspaper announced that the *George A. Marsh* was sold by her namesake to West A. Walker in mid-August, 1883, later reports from 1887 show that the schooner still belonged to the Marsh & Bingham

Lumber Company of Chicago, of which Mr. George A. Marsh was President. During the winter of 1886-1887, the *Marsh* was rebuilt with 17 feet added to her length at a cost of $3,000.

The *George A. Marsh,* in the summer of 1887, played an active role in an incident of international intrigue. Chicago's former Chief of Police, William J. McGarigle, was being questioned at his home about "boodling" (embezzlement of funds) when he went out through his bathroom window. With the help of friends and under the assumed name of "Mr. Williams,"

George A. Marsh, Great Lakes lumber baron after whom two ships were named in his lifetime, died at age 53 in 1888 and was buried in Chicago's Graceland Cemetery. PHOTO BY CRIS KOHL

Above: *The ghostly schooner* George A. Marsh *was photographed one foggy morning in Racine, Wisconsin, docked just ahead of the steamer* William H. Wolf. PHOTO COURTESY OF THE ONTARIO ARCHIVES. Left and below: *The* Marsh, *which spent most of her life in the western Great Lakes, was already more than 30 years old when Canadian buyers moved her to Lake Ontario.* CRIS KOHL COLLECTION

he was secretly put on board the Canadian schooner, *Edward Blake,* on its way from Chicago to Canada as the last ship in a line of four tows. News of the plan was leaked, and soon a tug filled with detectives and journalists went in pursuit of the *Blake*. In the Straits of Mackinac, the *Blake* struck and damaged the *Marsh's* starboard quarter in what witnesses claimed was done purposely to give McGarigle a chance to leap aboard the *Marsh,* so when the police eventually searched the *Blake*, they found nothing. At the St. Clair River, McGarigle was rowed to Point Edwards, Ontario, in the *Marsh's* yawlboat. From Canada, he could not be arrested. Both Captain John Irvin of the *Blake* and Captain John Freer of the *Marsh* pleaded ignorance of the true identity of "Mr. Williams," but their sympathies for McGarigle were known. Capt. John Irwin later mastered the famous *Minnedosa* (see pages 149-152).

In late 1912, the 30-year-old *Marsh* had a very close call. Capt. Herman Olson took on part of a cargo of potatoes at the Lyon dock in Door County, Wisconsin, before proceeding to Washington Island where he loaded another 5,000 bushels, then on to Egg Harbor for another 2,000 bushels. All this was done minus the ship's fore topmast, having lost it in an earlier collision with the *Oak Leaf*. While attempting to sail with this heavy cargo and damaged ship to Chicago, the *George A. Marsh* headed right into the same violent storm which tragically sank with all hands the old schooner, *Rouse Simmons,* already famous as the "Christmas Tree Ship," in Lake Michigan. The press had lost hope in the *Marsh,* reporting under the headline "*George Marsh* Believed to Have Sunk in Lake Michigan" that the ship, "with a crew of seven, [is] believed to have succumbed to the gale." When the *George A. Marsh* finally limped into Chicago harbor in early December, 1912, besides being several days overdue, she was encrusted in ice with her rigging battered and sails torn by the tempest. Captain Olson described it as the worst storm he had encountered in 15 years.

The *George A. Marsh's* last American owner, the Estebrooke Skeele Lumber Company of Chicago, understandably concerned that the schooner would probably not survive another such storm, put the ship on the market in 1913.

Enter Captain John Wesley Smith and a partner, Jonathon J. B. Flint, both of Belleville,

2 SCHOONERS ARE MISSING SINCE GALE

Minerva and George Marsh Believed to Have Sunk in Lake Michigan

HOPE IS ABANDONED FOR ROUSE SIMMONS

Passenger Steamer Easton Is Released and Proceeds to Port Arthur

CHICAGO, Dec. 7.—The schooner Minerva, bound for Milwaukee with a crew of five men, and the schooner George Marsh, with a crew of seven, are believed to have succumbed to the ...

The same storm which sank the schooner, Rouse Simmons, the famous "Christmas Tree Ship," caused concern over the George A. Marsh.

CRIS KOHL COLLECTION

Ontario, who purchased the *George A. Marsh.* Smith and several men went to Chicago and sailed the ship home to Lake Ontario waters. The official change from U.S. to Canadian registry, and from U.S. number 85727 hailing out of Michigan City to Canadian number 133750 out of Toronto, occurred on April 17, 1914. The *Marsh* was one of the many Lake Michigan vessels brought down to Lake Ontario in the early part of the twentieth century for use as coal haulers or stone hookers after a lifetime of usefulness in the western lumber trade. The *Marsh's* final dimensions, as measured for Canadian registry, were 135 feet in length, 27 feet in beam, and 9.3 feet in draught, with a gross tonnage of 220.

The old schooner's name was retained in the firm belief that it is bad luck to change the name of a ship. The vessel was well cared for and had been completely overhauled in the spring of 1917, just a few months prior to the sinking. Despite the extensive care, the aging vessel obviously had found no miraculous fountain to restore her youth, and her creaking, time-worn seams were finally forced open in that severe storm of August 7-8, 1917.

*   *   *

About fifty years later, scuba dive charter boats began taking sub aquatic tourists to the wreck site. What moves most visiting scuba divers, if not yet caught up in the ship's dramatic history, is the integral state of this splendid vessel. The ship rests upright and intact in 85 feet of water, with narrow hatch openings and ladders which sweetly beckon unsuspecting underwater explorers downward into the tight holds. However, even trained, experienced and properly equipped divers must exercise extreme caution if penetrating this silt-laden shipwreck. One fin kick will raise clouds of silt as thick as a Lake Superior fog, making exit impossible for the unprepared. This site is not for the rash or the inexperienced.

Rows of eerie deadeyes hang limply along both port and starboard railings, while the long bowsprit and various chains point with undiminished dignity towards the *Marsh's* ghostly heading.

The ship's wheel marks the focal point of attention at this site, and many a modern romantic has pretended to steer the frozen ship that can be guided today only by a phantom wheelsman on a course into infinity. Nearby, the ship's iron stove displays a teapot, a kettle, and various other galley items, spectral cuisine prepared by a culinary banshee.

Many blocks, tools and belaying pins line the shadowy deck, placed there conspicuously by early divers who wanted to ensure that others who followed would not miss seeing these stately sights.

An underwater tour of a tragic shipwreck. Clockwise from above: *Diver James Taylor at the* George A. Marsh's *wheel; a fallen mast on deck with a block and an axe; Dani Lee and deadeyes; a chain descends into an open hatch; Doug Pettingill at the bowsprit and chains.* PHOTOS BY CRIS KOHL

167

Besides a few bottles and plates which are on exhibit at the Museum of the Great Lakes at Kingston, the only things removed from the wreck by scuba divers, in October, 1971, were the two bow anchors. This was still back in the early days before attitudes and legislation had changed and made such removal a serious crime in the Great Lakes. The cold, fresh and often dark waters of our inland seas maintain the highest possible degree of natural preservation for shipwrecks, and hence these wrecks are unique, obviously non-renewable, and protected by law. It is as illegal to remove anything, even bottles and plates, from one of these ice water museums as it would be to take an artifact out of the Smithsonian.

When I first explored this shipwreck more than twenty years ago, I had not yet done any research on the history of this ship and its sinking. The remains of the *George A. Marsh* impressed me, even in the low visibility which we experienced during our explorations in the early 1980's.

Years later, in 1991, I was introduced to Doug Pettingill, a local diver who had been instrumental in researching and locating several eastern Lake Ontario shipwrecks, and we struck up a friendship.

After another exhilarating dive on the impressive wreck of the *George A. Marsh*, Doug, his voice lowered a bit, asked me, "Have you ever heard anything about the captain of the *Marsh* supposedly surviving the sinking and moving out west someplace after the loss?"

I hadn't, but I mentally filed away that fascinating question before we went diving on more shipwrecks.

I later spent the entire month of August, 1996, exploring the shipwrecks in the Kingston area, including the *George A. Marsh,* all the while staying as a guest of Susan Yankoo and George Wheeler at Duck's Dive Charters and Cabins, my "headquarters" at Point Traverse. Susan and George, besides being famously hospitable hosts, generously introduced me to many people who shared abundant shipwreck information during get-togethers in front of the huge, rustic stone fireplace in their wide open living room. It was they who had introduced me to Doug Pettingill several years earlier.

As part of my research on area shipwrecks, I visited the Belleville Cemetery. Capt. John Smith had purchased a cluster of six cemetery plots for his family (Plot #N, Section #15, Lot #25, Graves #1 through #6) after his first wife, Sarah Ann Bird Smith, died unexpectedly of heart disease at the age of 36 at their home at 54 South George Street on December 18, 1914. She had provided the captain with six children -- three girls and three boys -- all between the ages of one and fourteen, and suddenly motherless.

But much to everyone's surprise, the 46-year-old widower remarried a year later -- and his wife was a 20-year-old resident of nearby Demorestville, Prince Edward County, named Gertrude Manning. Within a year, a baby girl had been added to the family.

The tragedy of the *George A. Marsh* loss filled two more plots in the Belleville Cemetery -- only the bodies of family members Gertrude Manning Smith and Greta Smith had been recovered, and they were interred in graves left unmarked. Apparently there was no money for headstones.

On November 30, 1921, William Bird, the 78-year-old father of the first Mrs. John Smith (Sarah Ann Bird Smith), died and was buried in the fourth of the six plots which the captain had purchased in 1914. At this time, the *George A. Marsh* had been sunk for over four years, and the remaining bodies, including that of Capt. Smith, had never been located or recovered.

> ## DEATH ROLL
>
> **MRS. SARAH ANN SMITH**
>
> Mrs. Sarah A. Smith, wife of Capt. J. W. Smith, passed away suddenly at five o'clock yesterday afternoon at the family residence, 54 South George
>
> *Capt. John Smith's beloved first wife had died suddenly of heart failure just before Christmas, 1914. She was 36.* CRIS KOHL COLLECTION (WITH THANKS TO DOUG PETTINGILL)

In 1996, the office of the Belleville Cemetery listed the contact person for the remaining family plots as Mr. Horace Smith. In September, I attempted telephoning listings for two "Horace Smiths" living in Toronto or in the Toronto area, trying to find out if either one of them was related to the tragic sinking of the *George A. Marsh* in 1917 and would be willing to talk to me about it. One of them indicated that he knew nothing about that story. The other one, however, acted quite differently.

"Don't call me again about this. I don't want to talk about this," was the message that a very gruff-sounding and seemingly chronologically gifted gentleman left on my answering machine. So I did not call him back.

It dawned upon me that this might have been a grandson of the late Capt. John Smith. Only later, after juggling a few dates and numbers in my head, did I realize that this could have been the captain's actual son, who would have been 96 years old. But he clearly did not want to talk about this topic.

A father-and-son relationship can be a very delicate thing, particularly if the father kept the report of his death alive through his silence. Secretly moving far away and never contacting his son would also have resulted in resentment once the truth came out.

I respected this man's right to privacy, whoever he was. I never telephoned him back.

In 1998, during a round of information sharing with Oswego, N.Y., maritime historian Richard Palmer, I brought up the question of Capt. Smith's possible survival. Yes, he had come across some information. He e-mailed me the text of a couple of transcribed newspaper articles from New York state announcing the real death of Captain John Wesley Smith in a small place called Harrah, Oklahoma, TEN YEARS after the *George A. Marsh* sank. That ember of information sparked a bonfire of research, and I located numerous articles in a variety of Great Lakes newspapers which reported the same, plus more and more parts of the story. When I informed Doug Pettingill about them, he found an additional treasure trove of information at Belleville.

Many pieces started to fit together, and by this time, I was wholly absorbed by the tale. Enthusiasm is contagious, and soon my wife, who also has a degree in history and a love of ships and shipwreck exploration, was infected. Joan and I dashed to landlocked Harrah, Oklahoma, in pursuit of a story about a shipwreck 1,500 miles away in the Great Lakes.

*   *   *

I n mid-August, the daily temperatures at Harrah, Oklahoma reached 102 degrees early and stayed up there during most of the day. I had imagined that part of the setting correctly. I could easily picture this agricultural town the way it would have appeared in the summer of 1917, with its population of about 350 people, and its one main road and single railway line, when Captain John Wesley Smith arrived here by train.

Still in a state of grief and shock over the devastating loss of his wife, five children, friends and their children when his ship sank, he might have appeared somewhat bewildered coming here to begin life anew. With its location south of Kansas and north of Texas, it would be difficult to find a place on this continent further away from a maritime setting, the old life that Captain Smith was fleeing forever, than Harrah, Oklahoma.

In the hot summer of 1917, false front buildings, dusty roads and wooden sidewalks obstructed only by the occasional sleeping dog, flies buzzing around his motionless form, probably fit the picture of Harrah. Oklahoma was only eight years into statehood, and it was still the kind of wild west frontier town where an honest man who was willing to work hard could make a good life for himself. Moving to a pioneer state like Oklahoma where people were judged by their present actions was also the closest thing the United States had to joining the Foreign Legion, an ideal future for men with pasts.

The people in today's Harrah, Oklahoma, are rightfully proud of their past. The town's population remained steady at about 700 from 1930 to 1950, but since 1960, it jumped from about 1,000 to nearly 5,000. With this incredible growth came a deep interest in Harrah's beginnings. The town library allowed us to feast upon their local history books and notes, and we consumed a particularly substantial blue-covered book titled *Harrah, Back-*

170

ward and Forward. Assembled in the 1990's and published in 1999, "the blue book" (as we affectionately called it) contained a massive number of stories about the town's history contributed by a small army of local chroniclers, an impressive example of what every community could and should generate. Much to our delight, the book contained information about a "J. Smith" who turned out to be "our man" (as John Wesley Smith had become to us).

But at one point, he was referred to by someone in that book as "Chicken" Smith. We suddenly felt disappointed and frightened that J. Smith had perhaps ended up drifting aimlessly through the rest of his life as a bum, perhaps as the town drunk, salvaging cigar butts from gutters, sleeping in alleyways and wallowing in cheap booze whenever he gathered enough pennies. Our fears were allayed as we uncovered more information about our man.

Smith had arrived in Harrah in August, 1917, with almost nothing, but he surely spied the Masonic emblem on the large building at the top of the small hill a short walk up from the railroad tracks. He was fortunately able

Above: *The main street of Harrah, Oklahoma, with the railroad in the background, in the 1920's when J. Smith lived and worked there.* PHOTO COURTESY OF LINDA PARRISH, HARRAH (OKLAHOMA) HISTORICAL SOCIETY. Right: *Today's view looking down from the former Masonic building on the left towards the railroad tracks.* PHOTO BY CRIS KOHL

to borrow some money from a fellow member of the Masonic Order, a longtime and well-known Harrah man named Walter Wilson. With this grub-stake, Smith set up his one-man, one-horse, one-wagon produce business. The "Chicken" Smith moniker, applied only during his early time in Harrah, was bestowed upon him for his habit of making farm-to-farm purchases of produce and poultry which he sold at a profit in larger markets.

Jack Bartley's story in "the blue book" included information about Smith: "Now, Chicken Smith, I never knew what his other name was, but he went all out through the country and he gathered up chickens, ducks, geese, turkeys, eggs and then if it was Friday, he bought what green produce that he could find and then Saturday he went to Oklahoma City and unloaded. My brother-in-law Tom Donnell worked for him in the summer-time and he had a couple of other people that got together whatever he had to sell."

The Harrah Historical Society, particularly member and contributor Linda Parrish, helped us in our pursuit of information. She met us at the town's old train station, the first edifice in Harrah that J. Smith would have passed after he alighted from the train in 1917. Although damaged in a recent fire, this historic structure is slated for museum restoration. Linda Parrish contacted several longtime, local residents when we told her our story.

Harrah is indeed a friendly town, eager to share, as well as discover more of, its past.

Frank Macarty, born in 1908, remembered "Chicken" Smith very well ninety-five years later. He recalled that Smith, a big, fleshy, tall, big-boned man who got along well with Frank's father, was a bachelor who had no family and seemingly no first name.

"Chicken Smith bought chickens, guineas and other various poultry, and he bought furs from 'us boys,' possum, skunk, raccoons and also the unskinned carcasses of cottontail rabbits, paying 10 to 15 cents each."

Mr. Macarty told a personal tale. "Although not by his own choice, Mr. Smith helped to provide a source of entertainment for the boys on Saturday nights, when another resident tended to drink a little too much and pick a fight with him. The boys enjoyed the excitement of a good fist fight and then moved on to the movie that was located where Jorski Grain Market is now. Mr. Smith didn't start the fights, it was the other man who was the aggressor. In fact, Mr. Smith got along well with the boys and was kind to them." Smith, who held his own if provoked, proved to be no "chicken."

Over several years, Smith worked honestly and hard, repaid his financial debt to Wilson, and quickly expanded his enterprise. By that time, Walter Wilson was more than a benefactor -- he had become Smith's friend, and the two men visited each other often.

Another longtime Harrah resident and contributor to "the blue book," Gwendolyn Wilson Zwick, the 89-year-old daughter of Walter Wilson, the man who had befriended John Smith, remembered Smith vaguely from when she was 12 years old, recalling that he was "very tall, a big man."

Once he arrived in Harrah, the captain named "John Wesley Smith" had been completely replaced by the stranger who went by the name "J. Smith," a man who owned no home, no car and no telephone. He quietly but zealously started his new line of work. Within ten years, he owned a feed and grain business and an ice house alongside the Harrah train tracks and operated a fleet of seven trucks. He donated generously to schools and churches, and was often listed in the local newspaper, particularly in a series of full-page town ads in 1925, among those businessmen who helped build Harrah.

But to everyone, the personal J. Smith still remained a mystery man.

Joan and I drove twenty miles west from Harrah to Oklahoma City and resumed our research in the Oklahoma State Historical Library. While I pored over old newspapers on microfilm, Joan found important census records. On January 20 and 21, 1920, a government census enumerator was busy in Harrah. John Smith, at that time a boarder living among numerous other lodgers who were mostly in their 20's at the hotel run by Lewis and Margaret Woods, gave the following information for the census: male; white; age 45 [he was really 51]; able to speak English -- yes; read/ write -- yes; place of birth -- U.S.; mother's place of birth -- U.S.; father's place of birth -- U.S.; occupation -- merchant/produce store, worker on own account, not salary or wage. John Smith, like his parents, had been born in Canada, so his census information was not exactly truthful, probably an attempt to cover his past. However, every other lodger at the Woods' hotel had named a specific state where they and each of their parents had been born. The Bureau of the Census took no notice of Smith's extreme generalizations in those categories.

Joan wrote a letter to the Masonic Grand Lodge of Oklahoma at Guthrie, OK, explaining the research we were doing and asking if they could provide any information about a possible member named J. Smith of Harrah. Their prompt reply began, "I have searched our files and could not find anyone by the name of John Smith as a member in our Harrah Lodge No. 375, located in Harrah, Oklahoma." The letter, however, did establish that the Harrah Lodge charter was surrendered in 1927, becoming affiliated with Oklahoma City Lodge No. 36 on March 19, 1928, and concluded, in bold letters: "We do not keep any personal information on our members."

In early October, 1926, with his friend, Walter Wilson ill and confined to his house with a severe case of rheumatism, Smith visited him regularly.

Above: *J. Smith regularly advertised his company's ice, flour, cabbage and other produce in the weekly Harrah newspaper.* Lower left: *What really preoccupied J. Smith's mind every Thanksgiving, Christmas and other holidays, when he placed special ads in the local newspaper?* Lower right: *The final advertisement for Harrah Produce House appeared in* The Harrah Herald *on Friday, February 25, 1927 -- offering seeds in anticipation of the coming spring -- the same day that the paper announced the death of proprietor J. Smith on page one.*   CRIS KOHL COLLECTION

But the end of Smith's time neared. In February, 1927, nearly ten years after the *George A. Marsh* sank, J. Smith suffered a ruptured appendix. He had gone several days feeling sick before checking into a hospital in nearby Oklahoma City, where, fearing the worst, he made some revelations to Walter Wilson. Smith told Wilson "some of the secrets of his life," about his two children in Canada, and that he wished for his estate to go to them. Smith also told Wilson the number of his Masonic Lodge in Canada, instructing him to reveal it only in the case of his death.

J. Smith died that night in the early morning hours of Wednesday, February 23, 1927.

Precisely what "secrets of [Smith's] life" were revealed remain a mystery, as his best friend, Walter Wilson, apparently took them with him to his grave two decades later.

Cary W. Townsend, M.D., who certified that he attended the deceased from "2-22-27" until "2-23-27," listed the cause of death as "General Peritonitis." Ben F. Miles, Smith's banker in Harrah, provided the information that the deceased was "age 60" and worked as a "Produce Merchant," but questions about the deceased's birthplace, or about his mother and father, were all assigned the words, "Don't Know."

The Oklahoma City newspaper, the *Daily Oklahoman,* reported the news of Smith's death on February 24th: "J. Smith, 60 years old [he was actually 58], residing at Harrah, died early Wednesday morning at a city hospital. Arrangements will be announced later by the Hahn funeral home."

But Walter Wilson had wasted no time whatsoever in trying to locate Smith's children in Canada. The Belleville, Ontario, *Intelligencer,* on that same date (February 24, 1927) and under the headline "Father is Dead, Fail to Locate Lost Daughter" wrote,

> Two important death messages addressed simply to Miss Margaret Smith, Belleville, are awaiting a claimant at the Canadian National Telegraph office here. So far the officials have been unable to locate the persons for whom they are meant.
>
> The night messages were filed at Harrah, Oklahoma, last night and received here at eight twenty-five and eight thirty-six o'clock this morning. They contain the information that Mr. John Smith the father of Margaret Smith is dead at Harrah and ask for information as to relatives and instructions for burial. The first telegram was signed by Ben F. Miles, President of The First National Bank and the second from Walter Wilson. These men were apparently close friends of the late John Smith.
>
> There is a Miss Margaret Smith in Belleville but she is evidently not the person for whom the telegrams are intended. The police, the acting Mayor and the Chamber of Commerce

have all failed to throw any light on the identity of the person wanted. It is quite probable that Miss Smith has left Belleville and that Smith's friends in Oklahoma were not aware of the change of his daughter's address. The telegraph Company [sic] are advising the senders of the messages of their inability to deliver them. The police would appreciate any information from Belleville citizens which would assist in locating the right Margaret Smith.

The weekly *Harrah Herald* newspaper was published every Friday, and on February 25, 1927, a front-page article, with the headline "John Smith Dies In City Hospital" reported that

> John Smith, 60 years old, owner and manager of the Harrah Produce Company, died in the Rolater Hospital at Oklahoma City Tuesday night. Mr. Smith had been sick several days and had been taken to the hospital Monday. The body is being held at Hahn's undertaking parlor in the city until word can be received from his daughter Miss Margaret Smith, who resides in Belleville, Ontario.
>
> Mr. Smith came to Harrah several years ago and started a wholesale produce business that has proved very successful....

Thus began a flurry of media activity around the Great Lakes in quest of a dead captain's daughter. The two Harrah men named in the article above, Ben Miles and Walter Wilson, soon seemed to merge into one person named Ben Wilson, a careless media error found in many widely-printed articles.

On February 25, 1927, in response to their article seeking a "Margaret Smith," the Belleville newspaper announced that seven Margaret Smiths had been located, and, in a subheading, admitted that "None of Them, However, Prove [sic] to be the Party Wanted." Belleville's City Directory listed 82 Smiths, all of whom were "paged without results." All 26 Smiths, and even Smythes, owning telephones were called, also without results. Surprisingly, "the Masonic books were searched for John Smith but, though it is thought he was a member of that fraternity, his name was not on the local register." But a search had been made of the Belleville Lodge books.

By Saturday, progress had been made. Friends who had once known John Smith to have been associated with the Moira Lodge A.F. & A.M. [Capt. Smith had been initiated into that Masonic order in February, 1913] contacted his son, Horace Smith, now living in Toronto. The son quickly caught a train to Belleville and told reporters that his sister, formerly Miss Margaret Smith, was now married, indicating the reason for their unsuccessful search.

Left: A long series of articles about the 1927 death of "J. Smith" in Oklahoma appeared in the Belleville, Ontario, newspaper. Right: *One Belleville woman claimed to have encountered Capt. John Smith in Toronto just after the George A. Marsh sank in 1917.* CRIS KOHL COLLECTION (WITH THANKS TO DOUG PETTINGILL)

SAW CAPT. SMITH AFTER THE WRECK

Mrs. Luscomb Recognized Him in Toronto But He Avoided Her

"It is the most ridiculous thing I ever heard and it is easy to understand that if came from someone not

News of yet another startling event was about to reach the public: John Smith's daughter, Margaret, in an unexpected and dramatic move, had married Neil MacLellan, one of the *George A. Marsh* shipwreck survivors!

However, the Moira Lodge Masonic records indicated that Capt. John Smith had perished in the sinking of the schooner *George A. Marsh* in 1917, and that his body had never been found. At the same time, word that Smith had "left a considerable amount of money which will go to his two remaining children, Horace and Margaret, if he is proved to be Capt. John Smith formerly of Belleville" reached that Canadian community.

Smith had left no will, and the state of Oklahoma, assuming this Canadian connection to be a case of mistaken identity, was about to pounce on the dead man's estate.

Horace Smith anxiously awaited photographs of the deceased John Smith. He felt that, since the captain's body had never been found, this man could very well turn out to be his long-lost father. The photographs, sent by airmail from Oklahoma to Chicago and regular mail from Chicago to Belleville, would take six days to arrive. Tension mounted.

Complications also arose. One member of the Masonic Lodge in Harrah was convinced that John Smith had been there since 1915, two years before the *Marsh* sank. This turned out to be a memory error, but it was enough

The George A. Marsh *at Belleville, circa 1914, with* (left to right) *Mrs. Smith, Capt. John Smith, Neil MacLellan, Fred Arnott, William Smith, Bill Dingman, Bill Watkins (then cook) and Jack Hunter. Three of these men were not on the* Marsh *at the time of her loss.* CRIS KOHL COLLECTION (WITH THANKS TO DOUG PETTINGILL)

information to give young Horace Smith doubts about this man's identity. He would have to wait until the photographs arrived.

The body of J. Smith, meanwhile, with no instructions having been received, was laid to rest in the Harrah Cemetery two weeks after he died -- Wednesday, March 9, 1927. The Hahn funeral home in Oklahoma City had cared for the body pending word from relatives in Canada. But word never came, presumably because of lack of certainty of identification and a lack of funds. The funeral services were preached by two reverends from the Nazarene church, part of which included speaking the words:

> Mr. Smith was ever willing to lend a helping hand to the churches and schools and to any other needy cause which was for the betterment of the town [of Harrah] and its people. While it is not known that he belonged to any religious organization, his faith in God must have been great. We are not left to be the judge of his destiny, but left to hope that he is prepared ot meet his Maker in the judgment.

Members of the Harrah Masonic Lodge paid their respects by performing the last rites. Before J. Smith's casket was lowered into the earth, the bouquets of beautiful flowers with which it was covered were removed and "the casket was opened to allow the great following of friends to view the corpse for the last time."

By the time J. Smith was buried, news had come back from Canada about events there, and Oklahoma newspapers were reporting for the first time the mystery story of the dead Great Lakes captain.

Finally, keenly anticipated word went out that "good photographs had been secured of the dead man" and that they had reached Belleville. They were mailed to George Dulmadge, who, as the Secretary of the Moira Masonic Lodge to which John W. Smith had belonged, did considerable liaison work and assisted greatly in the search to prove that the Harrah Smith and the Belleville Smith were the same person.

News of J. Smith's burial in March, 1927, clashed with the announcement of Gwendolyn Wilson's 13th birthday party on the same page. Gwendolyn's father, Walter, was Smith's friend and benefactor, and she shared her memories of Smith with the author 76 years later. CRIS KOHL COLLECTION

Friends and relatives, led by Horace Smith, viewed the pictures. Old friend Richard Cornell, the first to view the photos, stared at the images of a face which had become slightly rounded out with mature years, then stated, "I think it is John." James Bird, a brother-in-law of the captain, uncertain at first when he compared the photos to one taken of Smith and two of his children twenty years earlier, studied the facial features in the most recent photos intently and agreed that it was John. James Meehan, who had known John Smith all his life, was assured at first sight that the deceased was Captain Smith. Mrs. Samantha Cousins, an aunt of Captain Smith, stated definitely that the picture was that of her nephew. She displayed a photograph of the captain's grandfather, Captain Henry Smith; side by side, the men in the photographs exhibited a strong family resemblance.

Then the captain's son, Horace, sorrowfully gazed upon the pictures which were taken of the dead man after he had been prepared for burial. They showed a clean-shaven man of straight features, high cheek bones, large nose and high forehead, but rigor mortis had left the face of the dead man expressionless. Horace remembered his father had a thick moustache,

Above, clockwise from upper left: *The Walter Wilson home, built in 1909, and where the stranger in town, J. Smith (formerly Great Lakes Capt. John Wesley Smith) was welcomed upon his arrival in Harrah, OK, in 1917; Harrah Cemetery on the western edge of town (renamed Memory Lane Cemetery in 1948) is where Smith rests with good company, including his kind benefactor Walter Wilson and his wife Della, and Lewis and Margaret Woods, at whose boarding house Smith stayed for a time, including when the 1920 census was taken.* PHOTOS BY CRIS KOHL

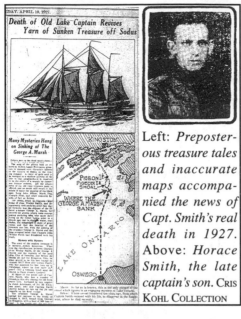

Left: *Preposterous treasure tales and inaccurate maps accompanied the news of Capt. Smith's real death in 1927.* Above: *Horace Smith, the late captain's son.* Cris Kohl Collection

but J. Smith presumably shaved it off "to further assist in his remaining incognito in the States." Horace recognized his father.

A shocking incident from ten years earlier was revealed next. A cousin of Captain Smith disclosed that a Mrs. Luscombe, a Belleville woman visiting in Toronto when the *George A. Marsh* sank, had returned home and told of having seen the captain twice in Toronto just after the loss. On the first occasion, he sat in a restaurant and, when he became aware of this woman looking at him, he dropped his head as if to avoid identification. She later saw him emerge from a hotel, but as she stepped towards him, he disappeared into the crowd. No one then had believed her powers of observation.

Horace Smith announced that he would go to Harrah and take over his father's grain and feed business, but it never transpired. Meanwhile, a sailor proclaimed that Capt. Smith had found long-lost sunken treasure in 1917 and disappeared with it to Oklahoma. This was totally substanceless.

However, the state of Oklahoma was not about to surrender control over the dead Harrah man's estate to a couple of Canadians 1,500 miles away. Both sides produced questionable testimony favorable to their respective interests. Ben Miles, the Harrah banker, stated that J. Smith had first appeared in Harrah and made a deposit in June, 1917 -- two months before the *Marsh* sank! Neil MacLellan testified to a variety of things, first that the captain was not even on board during the *Marsh's* final trip, then that the captain was missing from May to July, 1917 (presumably gone to Harrah to open his bank account), and later that he, Neil, had exchanged letters with John Smith, General Delivery, Oklahoma City, between 1921 and 1927. All of these tales ended up being unverifiable. Ben Miles, who administered Smith's estate, could provide no evidence of J. Smith making any bank transactions before August 17, 1917, nine days after the *George A. Marsh* sank.

On Monday, June 10, 1929, two years after her father's real death, Margaret Smith MacLellan arrived in Harrah, Oklahoma, from Toronto to present evidence that J. Smith was really her father, and that his formidable estate, valued at $3,163 (about four or five years' salary for an average worker in the 1920's) should go to his children and not to the state. Margaret hired attorney Porter H. Morgan, and they argued persuasively enough that the Oklahoma court, on September 10, 1929, awarded the estate to the children, again accompanied by considerable newspaper publicity in two countries.

Surprisingly, when the wreck of the *George A. Marsh* was located by scuba divers in 1967, no one came forward with any of the information about the surprise survival of Captain John Smith which had featured so predominantly in newspapers 40 years earlier. Even George H. Gurren, who had given a ride to the nearest train station to the two *Marsh* survivors on August 8, 1917, and who shared his recollections with local historian Willis Metcalfe after the wreck was found in 1967, did not mention the story of Capt. Smith. Metcalfe himself, who was a young man when Smith died in 1927, never published anything about the captain's survival in any of his later newspaper articles or books.

It seemed that everyone had forgotten that story.

Joan and I stood in front of the massive headstone of "J. Smith, 1868-1927" in Memory Lane Cemetery in Harrah, Oklahoma. Buried near him are some of the people he knew in the final years of his life, among them Lewis and Margaret Woods, at whose Harrah boarding house Smith had stayed for some time, and Walter Wilson, his Masonic benefactor and friend. We had followed his tracks to the very end, but many riddles remained.

The Belleville newspaper, on March 14, 1927, under the subheading "A Mystery," summed up the unanswered questions still with us today:

> Why Captain Smith concealed his identity will probably remain a mystery. Evidently after the wreck in 1917 he made a safe passage to land and ultimately landed in Oklahoma. Why he chose this as his destination is also a mystery as he had neither friends or [sic] relatives in the States.

We know one thing for certain. The remains of a Great Lakes captain lie in a quiet cemetery along the western edge of a small town in Oklahoma, a man who cheated death, but also regretted having survived, and who finally died earlier than he expected.

*　　*　　*

On the morning of Wednesday, August 8th, 1917, a solitary, exhausted figure weakly struggled ashore at Amherst Island and collapsed just out of reach of the storm-tossed waves. Known to be a strong swimmer, the man had just spent three hours struggling in water, swimming more than two miles to save his life. When strength returned to him, he stood up and faced the churning lake. He felt sick with the realization that, while he had been strong enough to survive, his friends and family members had, in all likelihood, lost their lives in these waters during the past few hours. He knew that no lifeboat had been launched, that his wife, his children, his friends -- all had ended up in the merciless, pounding seas.

Soaking wet, exhausted, and all alone along that shoreline, he felt time turn abstract, its meaning and its movement now lost. What would he do now? He weighed his options. Could he return to working on the inland seas. No, a captain was supposed to go down with his ship, not be the only survivor. Should he go home? What would he say to his two oldest children? What could he tell them? That all their siblings and their stepmother were probably dead because of him? Tears of grief and shame stung his eyes. No, he could not go home again. Everything had changed now.

In his pocket he felt a wet wad of money, none the worse for its dunking and tumbling in Lake Ontario. This would be enough to get him someplace far away where he could try to begin life anew. His two remaining children would be taken care of by their grandparents for the short time they might still need assistance. The children would be better off without him. But he could not return, neither to his old life, a wonderful, inherited life as a Great Lakes mariner, nor to his new house, which he had built for his young wife, a place that he would now find difficult even to behold, let alone to live in....

The next day, ex-Captain John Wesley Smith, soon to be known only as "J. Smith" for the remainder of his life, departed Toronto without a trace, like the soon-stilled, gentle wake of a slow schooner, and as evident as the dried track of a spent tear.

Captain John Wesley Smith, 1868-1927
CRIS KOHL COLLECTION (WITH THANKS TO DOUG PETTINGILL)

THE CAPTAIN'S JINX

V isitors to Whitefish Point, Michigan, at the southeastern end of Lake Superior, are always fascinated by the Great Lakes Shipwreck Museum which is housed in the former lighthouse buildings, as well as in several newer dwellings. The exhibits include the stories of dramatic maritime losses in that part of the Great Lakes, shipwrecks such as the *Vienna*, the *Panther*, the *Niagara*, the *John B. Cowle*, the *Superior City* and what is undeniably the most famous shipping loss in the Great Lakes, the *Edmund Fitzgerald*, an enormous steel freighter which sadly sank in a storm on November 10, 1975, with all 29 lives on board. Lying in Canadian waters at a depth of 529 feet, the two broken halves of the wreck of the *Edmund Fitzgerald* are much too deep for the vast majority of scuba divers, although two divers did visit the wreck briefly during a well-planned mixed gas dive in September, 1995, at about the time that family members of the shipwreck's victims requested that the site be declared off limits. Although rather overpowering because of its legendary status and its proximity to Whitefish Point, the *Edmund Fitzgerald* generously shares the museum's exhibit space with many other vessels.

Three other shipwrecks off Whitefish Point have a strong connecting link to one another -- namely a captain allegedly followed by a jinx.

The *Myron* was a wooden steamer (186' x 32'6" x 13') built in 1888 at Grand Haven, Michigan, and initially named the *Mark Hopkins* until it was renamed in 1902. This ship spent more than thirty years towing barges loaded with bulk cargoes around the Great Lakes. The wreck of the *Myron* lies in about 50 feet of water four miles off Whitefish Point, a shallow enough depth and a near-shore location which make it a popular site among visiting scuba divers. These shipwreck remains lie in two clusters. The bow exhibits several anchor chains artistically draped above the rippled, sandy bottom. A spare propeller blade lies on the keel towards the stern near the second cluster of wreckage which includes the engine and the four-bladed propeller, as well as a large boiler off to the port side. The wreck of the *Myron* was located in 1972 by John Steele and Tom Farnquist, the former a well-known Great Lakes shipwreck hunter from 1959 until he retired in 1997, and the latter the driving force behind Whitefish Point's shipwreck museum.

The *Myron's* most regular towbarge was the *Miztec* (194'1" x 34'6" x 14'), a wooden vessel built by J. H. Jenken in Lester's Yard at Marine City, Michigan, along the shores of the St. Clair River, in 1890. The *Miztec* was part of the "tec" fleet (with names ending in "tec") owned by the Marine Transit Company of Marine City, Michigan, two steamers named the *Aztec* and the *Toltec*, and two barges, the *Miztec* and the *Zapotec*. Also lying in about 50 feet of water like the *Myron*, and actually quite close to that wreck, the *Miztec* displays a broken hull, much hardware and many tools. An enormous pile of anchor chain sits near the bow, and a donkey boiler for a cargo engine also proves of interest to visiting scuba divers. The wreck of the *Miztec* was found by a group of divers called the Odyssey Foundation in July, 1983.

At the time of her loss, the *Miztec* was being towed by the steamer, *Zillah* (201'7" x 37' x 13'), which was a wooden vessel originally launched as the *Edward Smith* at West Bay City, Michigan, on March 31, 1890, and renamed in 1901. Again by coincidence, the *Zillah* sank near the *Myron* and the *Miztec* off Whitefish Point, but in much deeper water. At a depth of 250 feet, the *Zillah* sits upright, intact and well-preserved in very cold Lake Superior water. The *Zillah* shipwreck was located in 1975.

Color photos of these shipwrecks can be found on pages 212-216.

The link among these three shipwrecks -- the *Myron*, the *Miztec* and the *Zillah* -- is a man named Captain Walter R. Neal.

*   *   *

He dared not release the grip of both his hands on the floating pilothouse as the icy Lake Superior waves and the sixty-mile-an-hour winds battered, pitched and tossed his frail perch. The electric light in his pocket seemed miles away, out of his reach.

Captain Walter Neal clung to the remains of his steamer, the *Myron*. He had stayed with his ship after he supervised the loading of his 17 crewmen into the two lifeboats, but as the vessel sank, the wooden pilot house broke off while he was inside, and his natural reaction was to climb on top of it and hold on tightly to keep himself above water.

The 54-year-old mariner with 37 years of Great Lakes experience was not going to give up easily. The steamer, *Myron,* had been towing the barge, *Miztec*, both heavily laden with lumber (the *Myron* with 700,000 feet, the *Miztec* with 1,400,000 feet), from Munising, Michigan, towards the locks at Sault Ste. Marie when the ships found themselves in a lashing northwest gale which quickly raged into the worst storm of the year on the inland seas. The date was November 22, 1919, in the month known for harsh conditions, and the two ships were about four miles west of Whitefish Point.

Both vessels had plunged into the teeth of the tempest for an hour before the towline snapped and the barge, *Miztec,* and her crew found themselves unpowered and on their own. They quickly dropped anchor to ride out the storm. The leaking *Myron,* however, sailed into greater distress, unable to make headway in the trough of the seas and caught in the grip of the gales. Before long, the icy waters killed the boiler fire. Crewmembers desperately sounded the steam whistle with what little pressure remained and hoisted distress signals.

Another ship watched the drama. The twelve-year-old, 440-foot steamer, *Adriatic*, which had recognized the 31-year-old *Myron's* troubles, drew up to within a few hundred feet in an effort to break and settle the seas before the wild waters reached the struggling ship, but the unrelenting waves washed over the *Myron's* decks, making her unmanageable. She finally sank at four o'clock in the afternoon, just after the two lifeboats had been launched. Within seconds, the steamer plunged to the lake bottom and the surface was strewn with her wreckage. As it turned out, one of the lifeboats had capsized as the *Myron* disappeared, spilling its human cargo into the freezing, merciless waters. Darkness descended only minutes later, and the final terror began.

Capt. Neal, wearing ordinary sailing clothes with a leather vest, a sweater and a mackinaw coat, held on to the top of the pilot house which floated at a forty-five-degree angle with one end of it about three feet out of the water and the other end submerged.

"It was mighty cold," recalled Capt. Neal later. "I drew my legs up under me on the pilot house until they became stiff from the cold, and then I let them into the water. The water seemed warmer than the air after I had drifted a few hours."

Utilizing all of his strength and presence of mind to keep himself balanced on his emergency float, Neal encountered huge breakers which surged him into the water. He would quickly regain his hold and climb back up onto his raft after it righted itself. A few times he had to work several minutes to turn the pilot house right side up so that he could crawl onto the roof. At times when he felt brave, he held on with one hand and continually beat his legs and body with the other hand to keep his blood circulating.

Neal's hopes for rescue were ignited when he saw the steamer, *Adriatic,* still doing her maneuvers, this time through the *Myron's* wreckage. But the ship apparently did not see him. Neal later learned that the captain claimed that the *Myron* had gone down in only four fathoms (24 feet) of water, much too shallow for them to get close enough to attempt a safe rescue.

Before long, the 12-year-old, 540-foot steamer, *H.P McIntosh,* passed so close to Neal that he could read the name on her bow. He called out to the ship, requesting help.

The steamers, H.P. McIntosh *and* Adriatic, *claimed conditions were too dangerous, and the* Myron *crew too weak, to effect any rescues.* CRIS KOHL COLLECTION

"We will send a tug to pick you up," was the reply as the ship disappeared.

Through superhuman effort and determined endurance, an irate Capt. Neal clung to the pilothouse throughout the entire night until noon the next day, a total of 20 hours, all the while maintaining a tight grip. When he was finally sighted and rescued by the 366-foot, 18-year-old Canadian steamer *W. C. Franz,* under the command of Capt. W. C. Jordan, off Parisian Island, he was almost dead from exposure and exhaustion. His body was stiff and his clothing, which was a mass of ice, had to be cut from his body. But he recovered quickly.

From Fort William, Ontario, where the *Franz* took him, Capt. Neal sent a telegram to O. W. Blodgett, the owner of the *Myron,* in Bay City, letting him

The W.C. Franz *finally rescued Capt. Neal after the* Myron *sank.* CRIS KOHL COLLECTION

know that he was fine. Blodgett, however, knew his employee, and told the press that even if Capt. Neal were dying, he would say he was all right. Neal also sent a wire to his wife:

> Rescued Sunday noon by steamer *W. C. Franz* after 20-hour bath in Lake Superior. I am on board *Franz* at Fort William. Either you or William [their son] meet me at Soo on the way down. Will wire time later. Doing fine. Answer quick.
>
> (Signed) W. R. Neal

The United States submarine chaser 438 and the tug, *Iowa,* searched unsuccessfully for other survivors. The orphaned barge, *Miztec,* and its helpless crew had been picked up on Lake Superior and towed to safety by the steamer, *Argus,* within hours after the *Myron* sank. The steamer, *Calumet,* sighted a waterlogged lifeboat south of Whitefish Point, but it was empty. The lost crewmembers were William Lyons, mate, Marine City; R.B. Buchanan, chief engineer, Conneaut, Ohio; Louis Bastian, second engineer, Saginaw County; Benjamin "Dellie" Deford, watchman, Bay City; Emil Hammerstrom, watchman, Tonawanda; Floyd A. White, chief cook, Buffalo; Timothy Daly, second cook, Tonawanda; Mike Shea and William King, ordinary seamen, Tonawanda; John Wemdish, coal passer, Superior, Wisconsin; _____ Aldrich, coal passer, address unknown; Charles Mayhop, wheelsman, Tonawanda; Walter McCormick, wheelsman, Tonawanda; plus four others who were new to the crew and worked as three firemen and one coal passer, but whose names the captain could not remember.

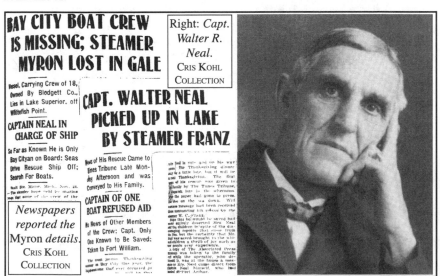

BAY CITY BOAT CREW IS MISSING; STEAMER MYRON LOST IN GALE

Vessel, Carrying Crew of 18, Owned By Blodgett Co.; Lies in Lake Superior, off Whitefish Point.

CAPTAIN NEAL IN CHARGE OF SHIP

So Far as Known He is Only Bay Cityan on Board: Seas Drive Rescue Ship Off; Search For Boats.

CAPT. WALTER NEAL PICKED UP IN LAKE BY STEAMER FRANZ

News of His Rescue Came to Times Tribune Late Monday Afternoon and was Conveyed to His Family.

CAPTAIN OF ONE BOAT REFUSED AID

No News of Other Members of the Crew; Capt. Only One Known to Be Saved; Taken to Fort William.

Right: *Capt. Walter R. Neal.* CRIS KOHL COLLECTION

Newspapers reported the Myron details. CRIS KOHL COLLECTION

Back in his home town of Bay City, Michigan, Capt. Neal described his ordeal:

> I never believed that a man could stand so much exposure and come out of it alive. They tell me that I have the record for all Lake Superior on that score, and if I have, I am perfectly willing to let it stand without any attempt to make a great one. They call me the iron man up at Fort William. Of course I suffered intensely from the cold. I was either in the water up to my knees or it was washing over me for hours and my feet, legs and hands were swollen terribly, but I never even caught a cold. But how good that steam radiator on the *Franz* felt to me! I just clung to that for hours after they took me aboard....
>
> Had I not taken a large chew of tobacco from the wheelsman shortly before the ship sank, it is probable that my jaws would have been paralyzed completely by the cold....
>
> If the *Franz* which picked me up had been equipped with wireless, the news of my rescue would have reached home even before the news of the wreck was sent out, for I was half way across Lake Superior on the way to Fort William when you got the news of the wreck here. *[In fact, the newspaper in Bay City, Capt. Neal's home town, published the sad news that he had written home five days before the* Myron *sank to let everyone know he intended to be there for Thanksgiving, and that he was survived by his wife, one son, William, two daughters, Annetta and Irene, and four sisters.]*
>
> The captain of the *Franz* and the crew treated me fine. They couldn't have done more for any man, and after he had rescued me, the Captain cruised about for some time in hopes of finding some other survivor, but without success. I had drifted miles from the wreck when they found me, and was so close to the lighthouse at Parisian Island that I could distinguish the windows in the dwelling there. It seemed just a short distance, as I looked at it and just as if they ought to have been able to see me, but I found out afterward that I was four miles off shore and of course, they couldn't distinguish a man at that distance.

Capt. Neal felt that the reported rescue efforts of the *Adriatic* and the *H.P. McIntosh* "were colored to fit the occasion."

> The story that we were in only four fathoms of water is all bosh, and I have known of vessel captains who took much greater chances to rescue shipwrecked sailors and succeeded in getting every man off from sinking boats....

When I saw that we were going to sink, I whistled to the *Adriatic* to stand by to rescue us but he never came near enough to help. He could have taken off the entire crew before the *Myron* went to pieces. His story of being covered in ice was all bosh. If ice had been forming in that way, how long do you suppose I could have lived on that pilot house with the water breaking over me for hours?

Then the *McIntosh* came along in the dark but so close to me that I could distinguish its name. I hailed the captain and asked him to take me off. He was only a few feet away *[Neal later estimated 16 feet away]* at the time. He asked where I was and I told him, and then his reply was that he would send a boat after me. But it would take at least four hours for him to reach the Soo and another four hours for a boat to get out to me from the Soo, and in the meantime I wonder what he thought would become of me....

Neal also described his reaction when the *Myron* actually sank:

I was in the pilot house when it parted company with the rest of the boat. The water was up to my knees and it wasn't a very sea-going sort of a craft. At first the pilot house and forward

Seventeen *Myron* crewmembers perished after they took to the two lifeboats; ironically, Captain Walter Neal, who had stayed behind on the sinking ship, became the sole survivor.
CRIS KOHL COLLECTION

cabin floated away together, but it wasn't long before they parted. I had climbed on top of the upper pilot house and at first clung to the ship's bell, but some floating lumber soon knocked that loose and I hung on to the combing. I had a life preserver on, and at times the floating house swung around so as to give some shelter from the wind, and then I would doze off and get a little sleep. Then it would shift so that the wind blew right into my face and wake me up, which was undoubtedly the best thing that could happen to me.... The captain of the _Franz_ happened to have an extra good pair of glasses _[a gift from Mr. W. C. Franz himself! -- Author's note]_ and he had caught sight of my hand as I was waving it when he was nearly four miles away. He headed for me at once and when near by, sent a yawl to take me off. I wasn't unconscious when they got me, as the newspaper reports said. In fact, I helped them to get the yawl along side the pilot house so that I could get into it, but I sure was pretty nearly all in.... Of course, there isn't any hope that any others on the _Myron_ have been saved. If they had been picked up by any other boat they would have been heard from by this time and of course if they had reached shore, they certainly would have been found. I haven't the names of all of the crew. I gave the owners all but three names that I could not remember. The list of the crew together with a letter which I wrote to my daughter Saturday were put into the dispatch box and thrown overboard when I saw that the _Myron_ was doomed. It hasn't been found as yet, but undoubtedly will be unless it was smashed by the floating lumber....

Letters and telephone calls of congratulations on the rescue poured in to the captain's residence. Neal, however, was filled with regret over the death of his crew, some of whom he had known for years and who had joined the _Myron_ at his request. He felt particularly pained about the death of the ship's first cook (also referred to as the steward), Floyd A. White, who had left the _Myron_ on account of illness, but to whom Neal had sent a telegram in Buffalo urging him back to his old position to replace the drunkard who had been working in his place. When Neal fired the besotted first cook at Port Huron, the man responded as he left the _Myron_, "Sometimes these things are for the best." It certainly proved to be the case for him.

For Capt. Neal, his late November survival gave him "more cause to be thankful than any other man in the United States this Thanksgiving Day."

The entire _Myron_ crew, except the Captain, perished in the inky blackness, the mountainous seas, the chaotic turbulence and the zero temperature of November 22, 1919, on Lake Superior.

Six days after the disaster, five bodies, each wearing a life preserver bearing the name *Myron*, were found along the shore encased in ice near Whitefish Point. Myron Blodgett, one of the owners of the vessel, travelled to Sault Ste. Marie to assist with the identification "as soon as the bodies thawed sufficiently." Three were identified as first mate William Lyons, second engineer Louis Bastian and seaman Michael Shea. The two unidentified bodies were of a man about 40 years, with black hair, a gray mustache and a tattooed arm and body, and a man about 25, with Swedish features, in whose clothing was found a cigar cutter with the initials "E.R.D." The fishing launch, *Sea Fox*, had conveyed the bodies, which had been recovered by Charles Gustafson and William Zowaski, to the Soo.

> Frozen and stiff in grotesque and grewsome [sic] forms, some of them covered with ice and snow until it was impossible to see their faces, the bodies were loaded onto the little deck of the fishing launch and were unloaded here before a curious crowd. At the Vanderhook morgue, a roaring fire was maintained all night to thaw out the clothing and bodies so that identification could be made possible....

Two days later, four more *Myron* bodies were located, also near Salt Point and also encased in ice. Men were kept busy digging the frozen forms from the ice, while others chopped out a mile of road through the underbrush so that the bodies could be taken to the Soo through the woods. Two were identified as chief engineer R.B. Buchanan and second cook Timothy Daly.

In the spring of 1920, eight more bodies were chopped out of the shoreline ice and were interred on Mission Hill Cemetery overlooking Iroquois Point. A low, white fence encloses the site, marked with the sign, "Sailors of the Str. Myron." The ship's broken, wooden stern washed ashore in Canada.

Capt. Walter Neal bitterly denounced the captains of the *Adriatic* and the *H.P. McIntosh* for not rescuing the *Myron's* crew. Newspaper reporters and government inspectors to whom Capt. Neal told his story were outraged.

In early April, 1920, both captains, Kenneth McRae from the *Adriatic* and Lawrence Francis of the *H.P. McIntosh,* were tried in Marquette, Michigan, on charges of violating marine statutes for failure to rescue the ill-fated *Myron's* crew. Specifically, the charges were misconduct, neglect and inattention to duty. The captains argued that they had circled the area searching for survivors for hours, that the men on some wreckage were too weak to grasp the lines thrown to them, and that the waters where the *Myron* sank were too shallow for them and would have endangered their own ships.

U.S. Steamboat Inspectors Gooding and Hanson revoked the licenses of both captains, reportedly for life, for "failure to render aid and assistance."

It is unlikely that this verdict remained in effect, and a higher authority likely reversed what many Great Lakes mariners considered to be too harsh.

The ships which perhaps could have rescued the *Myron's* crew carried on long and relatively quiet careers, the 50-year-old *Adriatic* being scrapped in 1962, and the *H.P. McIntosh*, which had been renamed the *Edward S. Kendrick* in 1934, sold for scrap in 1973 at the age of 61. Ironically, the ship which did rescue Capt. Neal, the *W. C. Franz*, sank in Lake Huron after a tragic collision with the steamer, *Edward E. Loomis*, on November 21, 1934.

*   *   *

After the Marquette inquest in April, 1920, the O.W. Blodgett company immediately offered Capt. Walter Neal the position of master on board an old type of lumber boat, the 201-foot steamer, *Charles H. Bradle y*. Almost as soon as he accepted the offer, he ran into difficulties.

On Sunday, July 18, 1920, off Lake Huron's Sturgeon Point, the *Bradley* was towing two barges, the *Miztec* (the *Myron's* old consort) and the *Mary Woolson* (179′1″ x 34′8″ x 13′2″). All three vessels were upbound with cargoes of salt from Port Huron to Duluth. During a summer squall at 4:00 P.M., the *Woolson* unexpectedly rammed the *Bradley's* stern. The steamer was seriously damaged and the *Woolson* began leaking badly from her stoved-in prow. Wireless distress signals attracted the steamer, *Huron*, which removed both barges' crews and made efforts to take the vessels in tow. The *Woolson*, however, sank in deep water at 7:00 A.M., reportedly eight miles northeast of Sturgeon Point, and the *Miztec* was cut loose and abandoned, also reportedly in a sinking condition. Capt. Neal kept the *Bradley's* pumps going and struggled to reach the port of Alpena. With water rising fast in the holds, Neal ordered the *Bradley* beached at the foot of Chisholm Street.

The next day, a tug dispatched to the scene reported the good news that the *Miztec* was still afloat and had been towed into the safety of Thunder Bay River. Capt. Neal procured the services of local barber/hardhat diver George Derry to determine what repairs the *Bradley* would require.

An unusual coincidence occurred that evening. The local press reported:

> The *Zillah,* a sister ship of the *Bradley,* steamed into Thunder Bay at 6 o'clock last evening [Monday, July 19, 1920], towing two barges of exactly the same size and characteristics as those which figured in Sunday's accident. The unit was an exact replica, even to color, of the *Bradley* and its two barges, the *Miztec* and *Woolson.*

192

STEAMER BEACHED TO AVOID SINKING

Captain Neal's Boat More Seriously Damaged Than First Supposed

Diver to Determine Damage Today; One Barge Afloat Rescued from Lake

A wireless dispatch received this morning from a boat passing the scene of Sunday-night's lake accident off Sturgeon Point, in which two

In the summer of 1920, a few months after his ship, the Myron, *sank in Lake Superior, Capt. Neal lost the barge,* Mary Woolson (below), *in Lake Huron -- and nearly lost the other tow-barge,* Miztec, *and the steamer,* Charles H. Bradley *(above right).* CRIS KOHL COLLECTION

JINX FOLLOWING CAPTAIN NEALE

Myron Survivor Loses Two Barges In Severe Storm.

Alpena. July 21.—Buffeted by heavy seas off Thunder Bay the barge Mary Woolson, of the Blodgett fleet, became water-logged and sank after ramming the steam barge C. H. Bradley, which had been towing her. The Bradley was able to make port,

MARY WOOLSON GOES DOWN IN LAKE HURON

The barge Mary Woolson, of the Blodgett fleet, waterlogged and sunk some miles out of Alpena last night. The Woolson was bound from Port Huron for Duluth, in tow of the steam barge C. H. Bradley, and

The *Zillah* had been ordered to pick up the remaining barge, the *Miztec*, which was saved. After a brief conference with those on board the *Bradley,* the visitor weighed anchor and steamed out into the lake, towing its two barges and the *Miztec*.

The Marquette, Michigan newspaper reported this entire story under the headline "Jinx Following Captain Neale [sic]" with no elaboration.

O.W. Blodgett reimbursed the *Mary Woolson's* crew for the loss of all their personal property and provided them with train tickets to any Great Lakes port. The *Charles H. Bradley* was towed to Duluth for complete repairs. Years later, on October 9, 1931, the *Bradley* stranded and burned at the entrance of the Keweenaw Waterway, where it remains to this day.

*   *   *

TELLS OF LAKE WRECK HORROR

Government Employe Says Miztec Went to Pieces Near Whitefish; 7 Missing.

Steamer Zillah, Engine Room in Water, Almost Met Same Fate in Superior Storm.

Sault Ste. Marie, Mich., May 15.

WINTER WEATHER SWEPT PENINSULA

Marquette Fared Better Than Most Places— Blizzard at Soo.

The barge, Miztec *(shown with the steamer,* Aztec, *above), sank with all hands in an unusual May, 1921, blizzard off Whitefish Point.* CRIS KOHL COLLECTION

THE DAILY MINING JOURNAL

THIRTY-SEVENTH YEAR   MARQUETTE, MICH., MONDAY, MAY 16, 1921.   PRICE FIVE CENTS

BARGE AND CREW OF 6 LOST ON LAKE SUPERIOR

SUBSTITUTE IN PLACE OF KNOX PLAN FAVORED

KENTUCKY HILL MEN CONTINUE WAR ON TOWNS

Seven Reported Dead In Train Wreck

IRISH BATTLE TOLL IS OVER DOZEN SLAIN

Dietz, "Defender of Cameron Dam". Will Take Long Rest

MIZTEC BREAKS TOW; IS DASHED TO BITS ON BAR

On May 14, 1921, the salt-loaded barge *Miztec* broke away from her towing steamer, the *Zillah,* during an unseasonable and unprecedented raging snowstorm several miles above Whitefish Point. The entire crew of six men and the woman cook perished. The men were Capt. K. Pederson, Buffalo; mate Robert Campbell, Tonawanda; seamen Erick Johnson and Louis Florence, both of Bay City; John Drecker of Titusville, PA; and "an unknown sailor who shipped from Port Huron" -- he later proved to be a Canadian from Sarnia named Clair Fletcher -- and the cook was Mrs. Florence Pederson, reported as being either the captain's wife or his sister-in-law. On May 20th, an Indian found the body of Florence Pederson on Maple Island in Canada. Five months later, the only other *Miztec* body to be recovered was found by the lightkeeper on Parisian Island. Fittingly, it proved to be the body of Capt. K. Pederson.

Within weeks of the sinking, all traces of the *Miztec* disappeared. By coincidence, the *Miztec* lies very close to her former steamer, the *Myron.* Ironically, Capt. Neal was working as first mate on board the *Zillah* when this tragedy happened. His only comment was, "She's been a Jonah to me, and I guess I have been to her.... God bless her!"

*　　*　　*

On August 29, 1926, the tired, 36-year-old steamer, *Zillah,* heavy with a limestone cargo, opened her seams and sank off Whitefish Point in deep water after the Coast Guard rescued her crew. Captain Walter Neal, who had strong connections to the *Zillah,* was not there for this sinking, which took place close to where the *Myron* and the *Miztec* sank.

STEAMSHIP ZILLAH SUNK IN WHITE FISH BAY; CREW IS SAVED

Bottom of Old Wooden Vessel, Storm Laden, Seemed to Drop Out

Whitefish Point, Mich., Aug. 30 (AP)—The steamer Zillah, a 200-foot freighter, with a cargo of stone, sprang a leak off here yesterday and went down. The crew

The Zillah *sank in deep water on August 29, 1926.* CRIS KOHL COLLECTION

Three dramatic shipwrecks connected to the life of Captain Walter Neal lie together off Whitefish Point, with a fourth awaiting discovery in Lake Huron. Was Capt. Neal cursed by some jinx?

Born on March 1, 1865, in Chatham, Ontario (or rather, Canada West, as that province was called prior to Canadian Confederation on July 1, 1867), Walter Neal moved with his family to Bay City, Michigan, when he was sixteen years of age. A year later, in 1882, he began his sailing career as second cook on board the wooden steamer, *Nelson Mills*. The ship carried lumber and lath from Bay City to Tonawanda at the eastern end of Lake Erie. After ten years, Neal had risen to the rank of first mate.

Capt. Neal's first command was the steamer, *George King*. He worked as master on a number of ships in the early 1900's, including the *Arizona*, the *Curry* and the *Sacramento* before taking over the command of the steamer *Myron*.

Despite his life-threatening experiences during the loss of the *Myron*, Capt. Walter Neal considered the worst storm of his career to have been the one which occurred on Lake Superior in November, 1905. Capt. Neal, at that time master of the wooden steamer, *Arizona*, struggled at the height of the fury to enter the safe confines of Duluth harbor. Three times he tried to guide the *Arizona*, tossing on a seething sea, into the narrow channel leading to calm water. So bad was the storm and its effects upon his ship that Capt. Neal could not get his precise bearings, twice making a run at the channel and twice turning around in the last minute. Finally, aware that he had to either beach his ship along the shoreline, which could have resulted in loss of lives and the vessel, or get it through the narrow cut. On his third attempt, he made it, despite striking a pier and badly damaging his ship's upper works. But no one was hurt, no lives were lost, and the ship was not destroyed.

Capt. Neal died on March 20, 1951 at the age of 86 at his home port of Bay City, Michigan, and was buried there in Elm Lawn Cemetery under the auspices of the Wenona Masonic Lodge. Walter R. Neal had lived a long and busy life, devoting himself almost exclusively to the Great Lakes. Even after he was forced to retire in 1941 at the age of 76, he remained active. He built model ships -- a favored activity among many retired mariners -- but he did not dwell on the ships of his past. His final creation, for example, was a model of the *S.S. South American*, a popular and relatively new Great Lakes cruise ship at the time of Neal's death.

The man born during the waning weeks of the Civil War witnessed spectacular developments during his long lifetime -- the invention of electric lights, telephones, motion pictures, automobiles, airplanes, radio, television and atomic bombs. How completely different the world in his first few years must have been, compared to the one in his final years.

As for the claim that Capt. Walter Neal was a sailor followed by a jinx -- when more than six decades of a man's life are actively preoccupied with one profession, it is only fair to balance all of the events to create one overall picture. Also, the *Myron* had its share of bad luck before Neal became master: On September 27, 1895, the ship sank in the St. Marys River near the Soo after a collision with the steamer *Vanderbilt*, and took nearly two years to be raised, repaired and returned to service. On October 19, 1897, the lumber-laden vessel stranded on Pt. Abino, on Lake Erie, and had to be lightered and rowed off. In late March, 1902, wrecking master Harris W. Baker of Detroit purchased the stranded steamer and successfully released it from the sands of Lake Erie's Long Point. It was Baker who changed the name of the ship from *Mark Hopkins* to *Myron* -- renamed after his only son, six-year-old Myron Baker. On May 31, 1913, the *Myron,* towing two barges towards Duluth, broke her shaft when off Huron Island in Lake Superior -- and all three drifting ships were rescued by the *Zillah!* All these misfortunes happened to the *Myron* long before Capt. Neal took command of the ship.

Captain Walter Neal worked on several vessels prior to the Myron. *The 164-foot steamer,* Nelson Mills, *gave Neal ten years of experience (1882-1892), during which time he advanced from second cook to first mate. The 184-foot steamer,* George King *was Neal's first command. The 201-foot* Arizona *weathered a severe 1905 storm on Lake Superior with Neal at the helm, and the 320-foot steamer,* Sacramento. *For a time, Captain Neal also served as master of the 377-foot* Curry *(not pictured), which was the largest ship on the Great Lakes when launched in 1893.*   CRIS KOHL COLLECTION

After the losses of the Myron, Miztec *and* Zillah, *to which he had connections,* Capt. *Walter Neal worked on many more Great Lakes ships, among them the* Marquette & Bessemer No. 1 (255' x 43' x 21'6"), *the* Liberty (245' x 35'2" x 15'2"), *where he worked from 1928 until 1940, and the* Fleetwood (255' x 41' x 18'), *his last command from 1940 to 1941. During his retirement years from 1941 until his death in 1951, Neal probably often gazed at his old command, the wooden steamer,* Sacramento, *as it lay abandoned in his home port of Bay City.* ALL CRIS KOHL COLLECTION, EXCEPT FOR THE *SACRAMENTO,* WHICH IS FROM THE REV. PETER VAN DER LINDEN COLLECTION

In his 61 years on the lakes, Captain Neal was not a curse to the ships he worked on -- he experienced an enormous amount of good luck, but that fortune was sprinkled with a couple of high profile shakes of calamity over the span of an incredibly long and productive career, one which he was reluctant to surrender towards the end of his life.

The captain's jinx, if anything, was that he could not stay young.

THE CHALLENGE OF
SHIPWRECK IDENTIFICATION

U nidentified shipwrecks are like human beings with amnesia, only they can't talk. They are in the sad position of having no recollection of their past lives, so these interesting pieces of mysterious material history silently beg for human assistance. Fortunately, many unidentified shipwrecks provide clues to their identities so that subaquatic detectives can end their anonymity, research their histories, and present them to the world as new discoveries complete with names, backgrounds and, often, tales of dramatic demises, while simultaneously adding another piece to the jigsaw puzzle of the Great Lakes.

Various shipwreck shows around the Great Lakes offer venues for scuba divers and/or historians to share their shipwreck discoveries and to reveal to an enthralled audience the often painstaking research they did to establish the identity of a shipwreck. Keep in mind that there are over 6,000 shipwrecks lying on the bottom of the Great Lakes, and only about one quarter of these have been found so far, and, for the most part, these have been identified. Many others shall certainly be located and identified in the years to come, but many which stranded and were smashed to pieces, or which were covered by shifting sands, are unlikely ever to be found, let alone identified.

Sometimes when shipwrecks are discovered, they elude all attempts at identification. However, the discoverer's enthusiasm or his determination to proudly proclaim his discovery and ensure a place in maritime history sometimes overrides the lack of a ship's name and history. This puts the sunken nautical stranger into the limelight. It has been to the frustration of several shipwreck show audiences that a still-unidentified wreck has made it past the program directors and onto the auditorium's silver screen. One such unfortunate show in the 1990's one evening offered four shipwreck presentations -- of which three were about unidentified discoveries. The fourth, a segment about the *Judge Hart*, a steel steamer which sank in Lake Superior in 1942, prompted technical diver Matt Turchi, who was co-presenting this topic with his dive buddy Darryl Ertel, to quip, "The shipwreck we're going to tell you about tonight is unique -- we know its name!" As for the other three,... well, unidentified shipwreck presentations get old mighty fast after the first one. Only so many ships can pass in the night before you want to find out more information about them -- like their names!

*   *   *

T his author has been fortunate to have searched for shipwrecks with several well-known Great Lakes shipwreck discoverers, such as Roy Pickering, Dave Trotter, Doug Pettingill, John Steele, Kent Bellrichard, Steve Radovan and others. Each has his own interesting *modus*

Jim and Pat Stayer have found numerous shipwrecks, mostly in Lake Huron. Above, Pat patiently eyes a sidescan sonar monitor on board their boat on Lake Huron.   Photos by Cris Kohl

operandi reflecting various levels of patience, skill and determination. But I have spent most of my shipwreck hunting time with Jim and Pat Stayer of Lexington, Michigan.

In July, 1997, the team of Jim and Pat Stayer, Tim Juhl, David Fritz and I expended several days towing a sidescan sonar unit up and down the middle of Lake Huron, searching for a particular shipwreck. At 4:17 PM, Thursday, July 31st, the sidescan registered a hit. In about 100 feet of fresh, cold, blue water approximately 600 feet on the U.S. side of the international

Left: *Pat Stayer displays a large wrench on the mystery wreck.* Right: *Bolts poke up through the wooden side of the collapsed hull.*　Photos by Cris Kohl

border which divides Lake Huron between Canada and the U.S.A. sat a shipwreck! Actually, it was reclining more than sitting, looking very fatigued. This was not the target we had sought, but it was worth checking out.

The first thing the divers saw after they donned scuba gear and descended to this virgin shipwreck was a huge, four-bladed propeller. This vessel had obviously been a steamship and not a sailing vessel. So far, so good.

Further exploration yielded more wreck characteristics. Enormous slabs of hull timbers had collapsed outward, a common phase in the natural degradation of a shipwreck. The bow stem clearly revealed Roman numeral draft markings, with white paint still clinging to the deep etches. Charred timbers offered strong evidence of a shipboard fire. Upper portions of the

Left: *A collapsed bilge pump lies amidst wire rigging inside the hull.* Right: *The gravel in the hull did not match the lake bottom composition.* Photos by Cris Kohl

hull were either missing or burned. Bands of steel, used to reinforce the hull for added integrity, were molded to the shape of timbers lining the hull, indicating that they were nearly molten from the fire before the ship sank. The rest of the wreck was a maze of broken timbers and stray pipes.

Other than those items, the divers initially found nothing. There were no anchors, no engine, no boiler, no capstan. Some work with tape measures gave the wreck's length as being about 185 feet. The beam would be more difficult to ascertain, since the sides of the hull had fallen outwards.

The divers asked themselves various questions underwater: Did the boiler explode? Was this ship scuttled? Did it burn and sink?

One team member later located a small, wire cage, the type used to protect lightbulbs on board commercial ships. Did that mean that this vessel was constructed after 1887, the first year that a Great Lakes ship, the _Yakima_ (which this same team of shipwreck hunters had located and identified in lower Lake Huron, part of their "Ghost Fleet of the St. Clair River" discoveries in 1993, four years earlier) was equipped with electric lights, or simply that electric lights were added later in this ship's career?

The divers found flattened metal sheets where the boiler and engine once sat. The hull had an inordinate amount of gravel inside it, but it was not the same stuff that the bottom of Lake Huron consists of in this part of the lake. Was that gravel added to the ship as ballast to lower the vessel's center of gravity and thus give it greater stability while underway? Or was this gravel simply used to add weight in the vessel's scuttling?

More searching for clues on the shipwreck yielded a large milk can, a variety of tools such as an enormous wrench, considerable broken china and a few silver spoons and ladles.

At this point, the discovery team had far more questions than answers.

Intense research presented the team with two possible names of this wreck: the burned steamer, _Annie Young_, and the scuttled steamer, _Canisteo_. Records, however, indicated that the _Annie Young_ was only 157 feet in length. Could this sunken vessel have been damaged to the point where it expanded its length by more than 20 feet? The _Annie Young's_ engine and boiler had been salvaged just after that ship burned and sank on October 20, 1890. However, salvaging only the mechanical components of a shipwreck from a relatively deep depth of about 100 feet was not usually done back in those days, particularly for boilers, which were rarely salvaged due to the unlikelihood of their operating efficiently again. Besides, the _Annie Young_ carried a full cargo of coal, and there was very little of that on this shipwreck. If it were the _Canisteo_, it would have been, at a length of 182 feet, close to the measured length, and that ship was reportedly scuttled (purposely sunk) in 1920 to get rid of an unwanted, aging nautical eyesore.

But why did the scuttlers bother to tow it so many miles north of Port Huron? The several scuttled ships which were known to be in lower Lake Huron were sunk about ten miles north into the lake, and this newly-discovered shipwreck was almost twice that distance away. Besides, this wreck displayed obvious signs of having had a fire on board. Again, the questions cried for answers.

Then three things happened in quick succession. I searched through my archival information, having gathered much material in the mid-1980's when I researched and wrote a book, published in 1987, about shipwrecks in the St. Clair River area. Sandwiched in with hundreds of other photocopied newspaper articles from Sarnia, Port Huron, Algonac, Marine City, St. Clair and Detroit was one from the latter place dated October 26, 1920, which told an interesting story originating in nearby Port Huron on October 25th:

> **ABANDONED CANISTEO IS BURNED AND SUNK**
>
> Special to The Free Press.
> Port Huron, Mich., Oct. 25.—Dismantled hull of former sand and gravel carrying steamer Canisteo was towed out into lake early today, set on fire and allowed to sink in deep water out of way of navi-
>
> *This article from 1920 explained the fire damage.* CRIS KOHL COLLECTION

"Dismantled hull of...steamer *Canisteo* was towed out into the lake early today, set on fire and allowed to sink in deep water out of way of navigation...." "Dismantled" meant that the heavy hardware had been removed, hence the absence of anchors, capstans, engine and boiler. But the important connection had been made to explain the fire damage on this sunken hull!

Next, Jim Stayer, consulting with longtime Great Lakes maritime historian Rev. Peter Van der Linden and going over his immense collection of archival photographs, found several of the steamer *Canisteo*, but the one which immediately caught his eye showed the ship's bow clearly displaying the painted words "E. Jacques & Sons, Lake Sand and Gravel, Duluth." The *Canisteo's* last commercial use was as a gravel carrier, first out of Duluth and later from Detroit. That would explain the presence of gravel in the hold!

The information which the Canisteo *displayed on her bow in her waning years became a clue.*
REV. PETER VAN DER LINDEN COLLECTION

Left: *This engine plate clearly named the* Eber Ward *as a Samuel F. Hodge engine recipient.* Right: *The Hodge engine plate located by Pat Stayer on the mystery wreck was badly worn -- but still gave a faint name!* PHOTOS BY CRIS KOHL

Then came the clincher.

Pat Stayer, while exploring various nooks and crannies of the shipwreck, located a brass engine builder's plate, about 15 inches in diameter, mostly buried in silt and debris inside the hull near the stern of the shipwreck. During the removal of the ship's steam engine prior to the scuttling, the engine builder's plate had become dislodged and fallen down to the bottom of the hull. While mildly encrusted with a thin coating of debris, in part fused in place by fire, this brass plate was still readable, particularly around the circumference with the generic, deeply embossed letters of the manufacturer's name and location: "SAMUEL F. HODGE & CO.--- DETROIT, MICH." A slim, rectangular, metal strip near the plate's center with a faint name engraved onto it was more difficult to read, as those letters had just been stamped on lightly instead of being deeply embossed: "CANISTEO."

That cinched it.

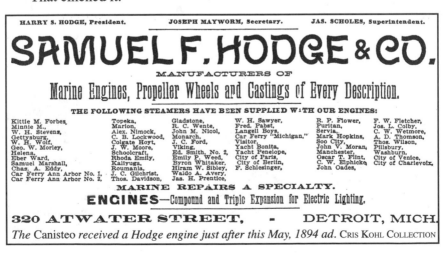

The Canisteo *received a Hodge engine just after this May, 1894 ad.* CRIS KOHL COLLECTION

*   *   *

An unusual fact about the *Canisteo's* sinking is that the scuttlers, instead of simply opening the seacocks and letting the hull fill with water, actually set fire to the ship. The problem with this was that they had not told anyone about their plans. People on shore, seeing distant flames and smoke emanating from the middle of Lake Huron, and fearing that lives were in danger, contacted the Coast Guard, which responded quickly to the alarm. The scuttlers undoubtedly blushed and stammered as they awkwardly explained why they had thought it best to burn the ship instead of sinking it slowly simply by opening the seacocks (without drawing attention to their presence), or why they had towed the hull out to mid-lake instead of abandoning it in one of the many marine graveyards along the St. Clair River south of Port Huron. Whether the Coast Guard people had a sense of humor or not about this incident was not reported.

Little was known about the life of a relatively quiet, wooden steamship named the *Canisteo*, official number 126360. This is not to be confused with an earlier steamer of the same name which sank in the Straits of Mackinac on October 14, 1880, and which is fairly well known because of its known location in one of Michigan's Underwater Preserve areas. The *Canisteo* in our story led such a quiet existence that a spokesperson for the State Historical Commission in Lansing, Michigan, reportedly admitted to a journalist, "We have no record of another [ship] with that name."

The wooden bulk freighter, *Canisteo,* built by the William Dulac Shipyard at Mount Clemens, Michigan, in 1886, had her first enrollment issued at Detroit on July 16th of that year. This 595-gross-ton ship measured 182′2″ x 34′3″ x 12′2″. The ship's original steam power source was replaced in 1894 by a Samuel F. Hodge steeple compound engine from Detroit, capable of producing 350 horsepower. The vessel's boiler remained the original 1886 10-foot-by-16-foot Detroit Dry Dock Engine Works fire box type.

An early photo of the Canisteo *at dock.*
CRIS KOHL COLLECTION

The Canisteo *at the Soo locks in 1909.*   Rev. Peter Van der Linden Collection

The *Canisteo's* four hatches measured six feet by ten feet each, and the compartments had a maximum capacity of 800 gross tons. Early in the ship's career, electric lights were added, replacing the original kerosene lamps.

Initially built for the coal, iron ore and lumber trade for the Tonawanda Barge Line, of Tonawanda, New York, the *Canisteo* later served as a sand and gravel hauler, first in Duluth, then in Detroit. Eli Jacques & Sons of Duluth and Detroit added a large crane or derrick to the *Canisteo's* foredeck in the spring of 1909 when that company purchased the ship from W.J. Clark and others in Toledo for about $15,000. Interestingly, the owners of

The steamer Canisteo *(at right) shared many a crowded lock or harbor.*   Cris Kohl Collection

Russell Island in the St. Clair River successfully took the Jacques company to court in 1912 for removing sand and gravel from the waterway at their feet, a legal decision which likely helped put an end to the *Canisteo's* career.

Two events during the life of the steamer, *Canisteo*, received considerable coverage. On May 14, 1890, the *Canisteo* collided with the large tug, *Wales*, as well as with the vessel being towed by the tug, at Tonawanda Island near Buffalo, New York. The *Wales*

The Canadian tug, Wales, *was later used as a wrecking steamer.* CRIS KOHL COLLECTION

sank in ten feet of water and the towed ship was damaged, while the Canisteo had a hole stove in her bow above the water line. Fortunately there was no loss of life because a passing tug, the *Degraff,* speedily rescued the crew, and the *Wales* was raised within a few days. A subsequent investigation showed that, while the *Canisteo* was considered mostly to blame because she failed to stop when she found her course was not going to bring her short of the *Wales,* had the *Wales* put her helm hard to starboard in good time, the accident might have been avoided. A court decided that the *Canisteo* would pay half of the *Wales'* $8,000.00 damages. The 126-foot tug, *Wales,* built in Sarnia, Ontario, in 1881, was returned to service, but was abandoned years later in 1904.

On November 15, 1893, fears for the safety of the *Canisteo* made headlines in newspapers around the Great Lakes when fishermen and passing steamers in the Straits of Mackinac reported sighting wreckage, such as upper works, cabin doors and hatches, all marked "Canisteo." Much lumber, particularly cedar posts and ties, was scattered along the north shore. William Dulac of Detroit, the *Canisteo's* builder back in 1886 and her managing owner in 1893, waited nervously in Chicago for the arrival of his ship and the two vessels which the *Canisteo* was towing, namely the barges *Pomeroy* and *A. Stewart* (later renamed the *Keuka*). All three of the ships carried lumber cargoes. On November 16th, they all arrived safely at Chicago. The *Canisteo's* aft cabin (with the board bearing the name of the steamer) had been torn away from the ship in a night-time collision with an unidentified, but presumably large, schooner at Mackinac. The *Canisteo* was struck on her starboard side near the stern. The schooner's jibboom pierced the

HAS SHE FOUNDERED?

FEARS FOR THE SAFETY OF THE STEAMER CANISTEO.

WRECKAGE MARKED WITH HER NAME PICKED UP.

It Had Drifted Ashore on Mackinac Island—Marine News.

Chicago, November 14.—Has the steamer Canisteo foundered at the foot of Lake Michigan, near the Straits of Mackinac, and drowned all hands? Dispatches of inquiry to every point around the Straits to-

The three-masted, gaff-rigged schooner, Narragansett, *did the mischief in the Straits of Mackinac.* CRIS KOHL COLLECTION

steamer's cabin, inflicting great damage there. Everything moveable on the stern deck, including part of a deckload of lumber, was swept overboard. This was the wreckage which gave people the impression that the *Canisteo* had met with grief. Fortunately again, no lives were lost in this incident. Four days after the incident occurred, the "mystery schooner" was identified as the 148-foot *Narragansett*, which was but slightly damaged from the collision, but which had that same night experienced an extremely close call from being run down by a larger steamer. Despite the thick fog, lake traffic was obviously heavy. The schooner *Narragansett,* already living on borrowed time, foundered in the middle of Lake Huron in the spring of 1901 when her 40-year-old seams gave out.

Less publicized events in the *Canisteo's* life included the ship's record-breaking round trip in June, 1899, between Manistique, Michigan (on Lake Michigan) and Tonawanda, New York (along the Niagara River), in nine days and eleven hours. The steamer pulled two tows on the way down, and three on the return up, all fully laden. Also, in early October, 1894, a stray shot from a duck hunter named Wycoff took out an eye of the ship's Engineer Ray while the vessel passed through Portage Entry in the Keweenaw Peninsula.

*   *   *

Shipwreck identification is extremely satisfying. Of course, once you have established the identity of a mystery wreck, it becomes easy to research its history -- and that makes for a much better article in the local newspaper about your shipwreck discovery!

PHOTO GALLERY 2

Above: Shipwreck researcher/hunter Doug Pettingill (left) and commercial diver James Taylor head out on Lake Ontario to the wreck of the schooner, *George A. Marsh.* *Left:* James Taylor thinks about the last time this stove on board the *Marsh* was used to prepare a meal. It would have been in August, 1917. *Below:* Doug Pettingill takes a closer look at the deadeyes along the *Marsh's* starboard rail. PHOTOS BY CRIS KOHL

Left: These railroad tracks brought the Great Lakes captain, John Wesley Smith, to the town of Harrah, Oklahoma, in the summer of 1917. Keeping his previous line of work a deep, dark secret, he soon established a grain and feed business near these presentday grain elevators (which were built in the 1930's). The little restaurant named Maggie's Kitchen, *below,* was built nearby in the early 1920's; the ex-captain very likely spent time at Maggie's.

Photos by Cris Kohl

Left: The Great Lakes captain who survived his shipwreck in Lake Ontario kept his survival a secret. He fled as far away from water as he could, living out those final ten years of his life in Oklahoma.

Photo by Cris Kohl

Lumber Tow leaving Soo, Mich.

Above: The wooden steamer, *Mark Hopkins,* later renamed the *Myron*, often carried lumber cargoes while towing barges similarly laden.   CRIS KOHL COLLECTION.
Below, left: Early scuba divers donated numerous *Myron* artifacts to the Great Lakes Shipwreck Museum at Whitefish Point *Below, right, top:* Several *Myron* victims lie buried near the Whitefish Bay shoreline where they were chopped out of the ice in the spring of 1920. *Bottom:* The Michigan Underwater Preserve buoy marking the *Myron*.   PHOTOS BY CRIS KOHL

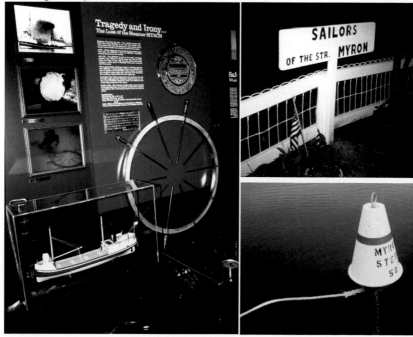

Above: The wreck of the wooden steamer, *Myron,* the first of three eerily related shipwrecks off Whitefish Point, lies in about 50 feet of water. *Left:* Diver Joan Forsberg passes the anchor chains at the bow. *Below:* Joan takes a closer look at a spare propeller blade on the keel.   PHOTOS BY CRIS KOHL

Wreckage of the steamship *Myron, clockwise from above:* bow anchor chains; a fallen rudder; face-to-face with a boiler; between propeller blades.

PHOTOS BY CRIS KOHL

Above: Divers Dean Ziegler, Joyce Hayward and Steve Whitman prepare to explore the barge, *Miztec*. *Right:* Hanging knees grace a large slab of the *Miztec's* hull. *Below:* Steve Whitman follows the anchor chain off the planking. *Inset:* A three-sheave block is one of many interesting items on site.

PHOTOS BY CRIS KOHL

Above: The wreck of the *Zillah*, the *Miztec's* last tow steamer, rests in very deep water. Waterlogged furniture lies inside this open doorway. *Below:* The *Zillah's* engine throttles. VIDEO STILLS COURTESY OF DARRYL ERTEL. *Left:* Technical diver/instructor Darryl Ertel.   PHOTO BY CRIS KOHL

Above: Pat Stayer points to a ship-wreck outline picked up by the sidescan sonar unit. *Below:* Pat passes the submerged buoy on the (then) newly-found wreck of the *Canisteo* in Lake Huron. PHOTOS BY CRIS KOHL. *Right:* Jim Stayer and Cris Kohl emerge from a wreck dive.

PHOTO BY PAT STAYER

A builder's plate, naming the vessel, was usually mounted on the engine, but this sunken steamer was missing its engine. Pat Stayer (*below* at the propeller) found the important plate (held by Jim Stayer at *right*) amidst hull debris like this milk can.   PHOTOS BY CRIS KOHL

Sault Ste Marie, Mich. Whaleback locking up to Lake Superior

Above: Whalebacks were a distinctly Great Lakes ship design of the late 1800's, capable of carrying great loads of bulk cargo. Only 42 of these ships were ever built. The *Henry Cort* is one of eight whalebacks which lie wrecked in the Great Lakes.   CRIS KOHL COLLECTION

Below: Only one whaleback remains above water today, the *Meteor* at Superior, Wisconsin, the most unique ship museum in the Great Lakes, if not the nation.
                                    PHOTO BY CRIS KOHL

Steamer "Tashmoo" Leaving Dock with President Roosevelt on Board,
Detroit, Mich.

Above: The first of many distinctions belonging to the river steamer, *Tashmoo*, is the fact that she was the last ship to be launched on the Great Lakes in the 1800's. In 1985, this vessel, although physically long gone, was inducted into the National Maritime Hall of Fame. In between those years lie more distinctions amidst many memories. The *Tashmoo's* trip with President Theodore Roosevelt on board was certainly one of the more dramatic, as was the vessel's strange sinking in the Detroit River in 1936. The above hand-tinted postcard, printed in Germany, is postmarked July 11, 1914. Cris Kohl Collection. *Bottom:* Moonlight cruises in the summertime on the *Tashmoo* to the St. Clair Flats and Tashmoo Park were popular among city dwellers. Art by and courtesy of Robert McGreevy

Landing, Tashmoo Park, St. Clair Flats.

Left and below: Tashmoo Park's popular dancing pavillion was on an island in the St. Clair River, a stop along the *Tashmoo's* run. (Both cards are postmarked Nov, 1913.)
CRIS KOHL COLLECTION

Dancing Pavillion, Tashmoo Park, St. Clair Flats, Mich.

The steamer, *Tashmoo,* carried millions of passengers in her 36 years; in 1903 alone, more than 224,000 excursionists enjoyed this popular river vessel.

Below: The bustling White Star Line (not at all related, by the way, to the internationally well-known White Star Line from England which owned the *Titanic*) dock at Port Huron, Michigan, in the summertime teemed with passengers exploring town.
CRIS KOHL COLLECTION

Above: The *Success* attracted crowds everywhere, such as here along the St. Lawrence River. COURTESY OF THE RUTHERFORD B. HAYES PRESIDENTIAL CENTER, FREMONT, OHIO. *Below:* Promoters added 50 years to the age of the so-called "oldest ship afloat." CRIS KOHL COLLECTION

THE BRITISH CONVICT SHIP "SUCCESS," OLDEST SHIP AFLOAT, LAUNCHED AT MOULMEIN, BURMAH, 1790.

ENTERING PORT OF BOSTON JULY 18TH 1912, AFTER A 96 DAY VOYAGE ACROSS THE ATLANTIC OCEAN.

THE BRITISH CONVICT SHIP "SUCCESS," OLDEST SHIP AFLOAT, LAUNCHED AT MOULMEIN, BURMAH 1790.

SUCCESS

MELBOURNE

STERN VIEW SHOWING ANTIQUE CARVINGS.

Above: The "prison ship" *Success* was built to cross oceans.
Below: Lurid postcards of (staged) human suffering on board sold well in every port. CRIS KOHL COLLECTION

Having a great time! Wish you were here!

Surely people who purchased prison ship postcards must have had some fun with tongue-in-cheek humor when they wrote those two most popular of all postcard sentences on such cards and mailed them to their friends. With the hundreds of thousands of visitors to the popular ship, *Success,* similar numbers of people "back home" received these morbid souvenirs in the mail. People, however, were unaware that most of the activities depicted on the postcards were never carried out in real life on board this ship.   CRIS KOHL COLLECTION

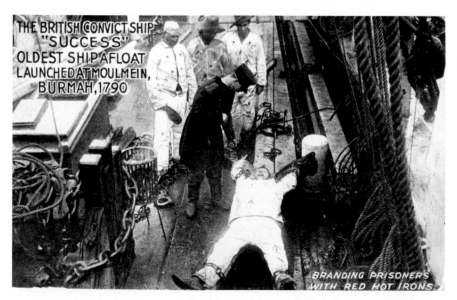

Above: The infamous "iron maiden" was never used on board the *Success*, but it made for good drama and spawned a variety of different souvenir post cards depicting that and other torture devices which one could view on the ship. *Below:* For 1920's prices ranging from 10 to 25 cents, dependent upon the thickness of the item being purchased, tourists could take away a souvenir booklet as a fond remembrance of their visit. CRIS KOHL COLLECTION

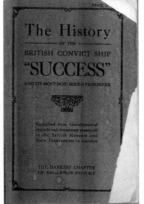

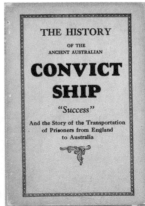

THE HARD LUCK WHALEBACK

N ot often did a ship in the Great Lakes meet with so much misfortune that the press dubbed it a "hard luck" vessel. Not often did such a tainted ship enjoy a productive career spanning 42 years. And no other vessel given the reputation of being a "hard luck" ship was of the unique type called a whaleback.

*   *   *

W halebacks were an easily distinguished and distinctly Great Lakes style of steel ship. Designed by Captain Alexander McDougall in the 1880's at Duluth at the head of Lake Superior, whalebacks received that likely name because their rounded, one-piece hull and deck combination, lacking the usual above-the-waterline corners, resembled whales. But because of their blunt, circular noses, whalebacks quickly attracted an unappealing nickname: "pigboats." The round towrings fastened to the tip of the bow only added to the farm animal appearance of the ships.

Several dozen of the unique and easily recognized whaleback ships were built in the Great Lakes in the late 1800's. DRAWING BY GEORGE CUTHBERTSON, COURTESY OF THE CANADA STEAMSHIP LINES.

Only 44 of these cigar-shaped ships were ever built: 40 on the Great Lakes, two on the East Coast, one on the West Coast, and one in England. Of the 40 built on the Great Lakes by their original designer, 38 were pure whaleback barges or steamers, while of the other two, one was the only whaleback passenger steamer ever constructed, the immensely popular *Christopher Columbus,* and the other was the *Alexander McDougall*, which was the only whaleback to sport a conventional steamer bow design.

Of the 39 whaleback bulk trade workhorses built in the inland seas

Duluth, Minnesota, the birthplace of whalebacks, was proud of these ships. One of the city's newspapers featured a whaleback in its daily "Marine" column artwork. CRIS KOHL COLLECTION

(which includes the *Alexander McDougall),* twenty-three went to the oceans and remained there for the remainder of their careers, seven were scrapped in the freshwater seas, eight sank in the Great Lakes, and one remains as a museum ship at Superior, Wisconsin -- the only whaleback left in the world -- the 366-foot *Meteor* (launched as the *Frank Rockefeller* in 1896 and in 1928 named the *South Park* before being given her final name in 1943).

Captain McDougall enjoyed success with his whaleback designs and production in the 1880's and 1890's, but the much larger 600-foot steel freighters being built in the early 1900's, plus the awkwardness of unloading cargoes through the narrow whaleback hatches, spelled their demise.

Riding on the coattails of the initial success of McDougall's whaleback design, hybrids were developed, like some of the ships built by the Cleveland Shipbuilding Company (such as the *Andaste* and *Choctaw*) and British-built ships working in the Great Lakes (like the *Salvor* and the *Turret Crown).*

Eight whalebacks remain sunk in Great Lakes waters. From this list, *Barge 104, Clifton* and *Barge 129* have not yet been located.:

> 1. *Barge 104* -- Foundered in Lake Erie outside Cleveland on November 11, 1898.
> 2. *Barge 115* -- Stranded on Pic Island and wrecked in northern Lake Superior on December 18, 1899.
> 3. *Thomas Wilson* -- Wrecked in a collision with the steamer, *George G. Hadley*, Duluth, Lake Superior, on June 7, 1902; nine lives lost.

4. *Clifton* (launched as the *Samuel Mather*) -- Wrecked in a Lake Huron storm and lost with all hands, September 22, 1924.

5. *James B. Colgate* -- Wrecked in the "Black Friday" storm of October 20, 1916, Lake Erie; one survivor (the captain).

6. *Sagamore* (barge) -- Wrecked in a collision on Lake Superior on July 29, 1901; two lives lost.

7. *Barge 129* -- Wrecked in a collision with its own towing steamer, *Maunaloa*, on Lake Superior on October 13, 1902.

8. and the *Henry Cort,* the hard luck whaleback.

*　　*　　*

Only one of the eight whaleback ships lost in the Great Lakes, the *Henry Cort,* was shamelessly labeled a "jinx ship" by the newspapers of the day. Certainly the fact that the *Cort* sank a total of four times (and was raised, repaired and returned to service after the first three) and played parts in several maritime accidents, would account for these labels.

Built by Captain McDougall's American Steel Barge Company and launched (along with another whaleback steamer, the *Washburn,* and the tug *Islay,* in the Great Lakes' first-ever triple launching) as the *Pillsbury* (320' x 42' x 25'; rebuilt in 1918-1919 to 315'9" x 42'3" x 24'2"; official number 150587) at West Superior, Wisconsin, on June 25, 1892, this whaleback was the 25th of that design to be constructed since 1888. According to the *Duluth Daily News,* the launching

was witnessed by fully 20,000 people.... Capt. Alex McDougall, minus a coat, waxed the lath which he held in his hand, the ropes holding the blocks at bow and stern were severed with axes, there was a crumbling sound and the first completed package freight whaleback steamer slid down the greased blocks into the slip with amazing rapidity and struck the water with a resounding smack. In spite of the greater weight in the stern, owing to her machinery being in position, the Pillsbury struck fairly and a great wave 30 feet in height burst over the big crowd which was gathered on the opposite dock. The wave caught a pile of planks and timbers on which thirty or forty people were standing and lifted it six feet in the air as though it were tinder. In the mad rush to escape a wetting, a woman and a small boy were caught and carried down by the timbers. Willing hands -- perhaps too many -- soon cleared the debris, so soon that the weight did not have time to seriously injure either woman or child....

No one was to blame for the accident which occurred but those who were injured themselves. All were fully acquainted with the probability of the wave sweeping over the dock, and of the danger invited by standing there. A regiment could not have kept them away when the moment for the launch occurred.

The iced-over steamer, Henry Cort, *one of those unique whalebacks, in the Soo locks.*
CRIS KOHL COLLECTION

Mr. Charles Pillsbury, a director of the Soo Line Railroad Company for whom the ship was built, and the vessel's namesake, was present at the broadside launching. Any comments he might have made about the launching accident -- and whether he considered this occurrence to be an omen -- were not noted.

New owners, the Bessemer Steamship Company, changed the *Pillsbury's* name on June 16, 1896, to the *Henry Cort,* after an 18th century Englishman who was known as "the Father of the Iron Trade" In late May, 1901, the *Henry Cort* struck and damaged the anchored steamer, *C.S. Parnell,* off Lake Huron's Pointe Aux Barques. After this unfortunate incident, Bessemer sold the "jinxed" *Cort* to the Pittsburgh Steamship Company.

However, the first time the *Henry Cort* sank was after a ship collided with her, not vice versa. On December 17, 1917, the *Cort* was rammed by the steamer, *Midvale* (which rescued the *Cort's* crew), and went down in 30 feet of water five miles east of the Detroit River Light. Bad weather delayed salvage, and the *Cort* spent the winter on the bottom of Lake Erie.

The next spring, salvagers could not find the wreck. The *Henry Cort* had moved four miles further east over the winter! Winds, currents and ice movement had all conspired to taunt the salvagers in a game of hide-and-seek. Finally found on April 24, 1918, with seven feet of water over her, the *Cort* was declared a hazard to navigation and three warning buoys were place upon her. Salvage work began immediately, but problems plagued the progress. The *Cort* was finally raised on September 22, 1918, on the fourth attempt, and towed to Toledo and Conneaut for major, and very costly, repairs.

MARINE

CORT SINKS IN RIVER COLLISION

Crew Escapes; How Accident Happened Not Yet Determined.

Detroit, Mich., Dec. 18.—The steamer Henry Cort was sunk off Bar Point, in the lower Detroit river late yesterday afternoon in a collision with the steamer Midvale. Just how the acci-

The wounded whaleback steamer, Henry Cort, *was photographed as she sank amidst ice floes after being struck by the* Midvale *in 1917.* CRIS KOHL COLLECTION

The sale of the *Henry Cort* by the Pittsburgh Steamship Company to Detroit's Lake Ports Shipping and Navigating Company was announced on April 9, 1927. The company added two cranes and enlarged the ship's hatches.

In late August, 1928, the *Cort,* loaded with heavy pig iron and bound from Cleveland to Chicago, seriously stranded on what was described as a rocky bottom at Lake Erie's Colchester Reef near the Canadian shore. The vessel had buckled in two places and was badly damaged. In this, the *Cort's* second sinking, the wreck was out six feet forward and its stern was awash. Wrecking tugs stood by and salvage bids were requested. A salvage contract was quickly awarded, based upon the tough but customary "no cure, no

The Cort *in 1928 with her new "whirly" cranes.* CRIS KOHL COLLECTION

pay" premise (where the salvor received payment only if the shipwreck was completely recovered) and the famous wrecking steamer, *Favorite,* along with the lighter, *Newman,* which would unload the cargo, sped to the scene. It took the lightering of 2,300 tons of cargo before the *Cort* could be patched, pumped out and raised. Within five days, the *Cort* was towed to

Detroit's River Rouge, and immediately went into drydock for repairs.

On December 24, 1933, during the ship's final trip of the season, the *Cort,* loaded with 3,000 tons of pig iron, stove in several bottom plates in the Livingstone Channel near Detroit when she scraped over Ballard Reef. Capt. Charles V. Cox raced the wounded vessel to Detroit and reached the dock at the Nicholson pier with five minutes to spare before the *Cort* sank.

The "ship that refuses to stay wrecked" was pumped out, raised, patched by hardhat divers and refitted for the 1934 season. This had been the *Cort's* third sinking, and 1934 would turn out to be her final year.

At the start of the vessel's second-last haul of the 1934 season, the *Henry Cort* cleared the harbor at Holland, Michigan, at 9:18 A.M., Friday, November 30, heading light for South Chicago to pick up a cargo of pig iron. The ship had traveled 15 miles when the strong winds, pushing hard against the high freeboard of the unloaded vessel, blew the *Cort* around, forcing the 25-man crew to head the ship towards the shelter of Muskegon harbor. But fierce gales drove the ship towards the north breakwater.

The Coast Guard station at Muskegon spotted the distressed *Cort* at 9:30 P.M. and jumped to the rescue. As a crew headed out towards the troubled ship, the *Cort* struck the end of the breakwater about three-quarters of a mile out into Lake Michigan, and launched a distresss flare. Just then, huge waves overturned the 36-foot-long Coast Guard power boat, pitching all five rescuers into the churning seas. Their slogan, "You have to go out, but you don't have to come back," was being severely tested. Four of the five men managed to cling to the

Three different newspapers in one day! A shipwreck was always big news, and the workers at the Muskegon Chronicle *spent Saturday, December 1, 1934, publishing several editions, each containing updated accounts as the drama at their doorstep unfolded. This was during the tail end of newspapers' golden era, and the press had a faithful following, years before television and the internet.* CRIS KOHL COLLECTION

230

When the bow of the Henry Cort *snapped off after stranding along Muskegon's breakwater, it spelled the end for the whaleback. The drenched and frozen crew, warmed up with dry clothes and stoves.* Cris Kohl Collection

boat and were rescued when waves swept it towards shore.

Surfman Jack Dipert, six feet tall and 23 years of age, drowned in the heroic rescue attempt in the darkness of the night as a 60-mile gale pounded the lake waters. He had joined the Coast Guard the previous July. His father had worked for them for 27 years, and was in charge of the station at nearby Point Betsey, although he lived in Pentwater. Jack had been with them for

Capt. Charles Cox mastered the Cort *during her last two sinkings. The Coast Guard cutter,* Escanaba, *stood by to help, but the Coast Guard's newest surfman, Jack Dipert, perished.* Cris Kohl Collection

The beached whale,
Henry Cort.
CRIS KOHL COLLECTION

only four months when he tragically died in the line of duty.

No one doubted the captain's 24 years of experience, the last five years on the *Cort*. Capt. Charles V. Cox, 42, of Detroit, would keep a cool head and do everything possible to ensure his men's survival. After the ship stranded on the rubble breakwall, the crew collected lanterns and, fearing that the boilers at the other end of the ship might explode, assembled in the galley where they repaired the ship's stove, which broke during the crash stranding. With a friendly fire soon blazing, crewmembers enjoyed coffee while the cook distributed Thanksgiving Day leftovers of turkey and mince pie. The rescuers suffered considerably more than the rescuees.

The *Cort's* crew was removed when they slid to safety in a breeches buoy one by one after a line had been shot aboard by Coast Guard members who, lashed together, had walked out on the wave-swept breakwater.

The ship broke in two at a point about one-fifth of the way back from the bow, and mariners knew that the *Cort* could not be salvaged this time.

In 1892, 20,000 spectators had cheered wildly at the birth of the *Henry Cort*. Now, 42 years later, as the stranded whaleback lay dying, 50,000 sightseers quietly paid their last respects. The storm ended, the sun emerged, the waters calmed, and Muskegon's shoreline was crowded with people taking one final look at the unfortunate vessel before she broke up.

Much of the steel from the *Henry Cort* was salvaged during World War II, but the remaining pieces, mainly in two large sections, provide visiting scuba divers with interesting exploration in 55 feet of water off the breakwall.

*   *   *

So, in late 1934, the whaleback, *Henry Cort*, sank for the fourth and final time, taking with her to her grave the nasty reputation of being a "hard luck" ship. That is how most people who recall the vessel at all remember her, and that normally would be the end of the story.

However, there is one more recently uncovered incident in the life of the steamer, *Henry Cort,* which bears examination.

It was 1923, and the *Henry Cort* steamed on a wild ride through a severe storm somewhere in the middle of Lake Superior. Harry Lickfeldt working on board the vessel at that time. Suddenly, and very unexpectedly, he had to plug his ears to stifle the pain of a loud, agonizing, scraping shriek. The steel hull shuddered with steady, violent tremors, as if grinding slowly across some huge object. Finally, when that rugged, grating screech came to a halt, and the frightful, rippling jolts of the hull ceased, Lickfeldt and the other crewmembers quickly examined the *Cort* for signs of damage. Fortunately, there was nothing. The remainder of their trip was uneventful.

The whaleback, *Henry Cort,* had miraculously survived Lake Superior's wild wind and waves pushing the ship over Superior Shoals, which would not be charted for several more years.

In June, 1929, the crew of the U.S. hydrographic survey ship, *Margaret,* were startled to discover hidden mountain peaks in the center of Lake Superior. Halfway between Isle Royale and Michipicoten Island, in the midst of deep, dark waters where their soundings had reached 900 and 1,000 feet, underwater mountains suddenly rose to within a few feet of daylight.

Superior Shoals, about eight miles by five miles in overall surface area, features depths which are considered normal on its fringes, usually 400 to 500 feet -- but rises suddenly and dramatically to 100 or 80 feet. It is the rocky spikes which pop up much higher here and there that have killed ships and mariners. One jagged tip rises to a depth of 42 feet, while 8,000 horizontal feet to the east of it, and across a 600-foot-deep underwater valley, another peak comes to within 39 feet of the surface. A mere 1800 feet away, yet another dangerous finger thrusts up to a depth of only 30 feet. And 3,000 feet north lies the most dangerous submerged peak of them all -- with only 21 feet of water hiding its dangerous head from men and ships.

Not until 1929 was the shallow shoal in the middle of deep Lake Superior surveyed; previous knowledge of its existence had been kept secret! Superior Shoals possibly claimed two French minesweepers in 1918, plus other ships. MAP BY CRIS KOHL

The barely submerged peaks of Superior Shoals came close to sinking the Henry Cort *in 1923. Years later, surveyors found evidence of shipwrecks lying along the submerged slopes and in the valleys. What a remote, but exciting, scuba diving adventure this would be!* CRIS KOHL COLLECTION

On calm days, most freighters would have glided across these submerged peaks without taking notice. But those infamous Lake Superior gales suddenly whip the seas to heights of 15 or 20 feet -- and sometimes higher! -- periodically exposing the summits of Superior Shoals which could impale any ship. Lake captains today know about these shoals and give them a wide berth.

When Chief Engineer Harry Lickfeldt reached the mandatory retirement age of 65 in 1955, one of the highlights of his memorable 48-year Great Lakes career was that incident back in 1923 when the *Henry Cort* miraculously survived the then-unknown Superior Shoals. The ship could easily have gone down with the entire crew perishing -- all within moments -- with no one ever finding out what happened to them.

These shoals were surely responsible for the disappearance of many a ship and crew. In 1930, the lead lines of the Canadian survey vessel, *Bayfield,* snagged into the rigging of a sunken ship there, and later hit the iron deck of another one. Pieces of snagged nets were recovered, suggesting the popularity of these shallows for commercial fishing. As clear a hazard to navigation as these shoals are, they went unreported by commercial fishermen who knew about them. It was later learned that Canadian fishermen, and poachers from the U.S., regularly fished these valuable shoals which they all kept secret.

"Ghost ships" of Lake Superior had disappeared over the years with all hands, leaving nary a trace -- the freighter, *Bannockburn,* in 1902, the built-for-France war ships, *Cerisoles* and *Inkerman,* in 1918, and more. They might have scraped on these barely-submerged mountain peaks, peeled back their bottoms like sardine cans being opened, then plunged fast and furiously down a steep slope to a deep bottom, becoming statistics and memories in Great Lakes maritime history. Indeed, the *Cort* had been one of the very lucky ones to have escaped the grinding grip of the shoals.

So maybe -- just maybe -- the whaleback, *Henry Cort,* was not such a hard luck ship after all.

A QUEEN OF THE RIVERS
HITS BOTTOM

Music danced through the warm, humid night air, as did hundreds of lightharted people on the wooden floor which glided smoothly over the waters of the Detroit River. They danced on board the popular passenger excursion vessel, the *Tashmoo*, which had just started her 37th season. The Pals Club from the Detroit suburb of Hamtramck had chartered the ship, and this organization of about 200 young men had no trouble filling the *Tashmoo* with over 1,400 people for this romantic moonlight cruise. While many passengers thrilled to the music on the ship's decks, others, mostly couples, drifted to the edges so they could lean over the vessel's rails and watch the moonbeams play upon the gently-ruffled waters. It had been an excellent evening, and the *Tashmoo* was returning to Detroit after a 25-mile run down to Sugar Island. It was the night of Thursday, June 18, 1936, and the many people who began their weekend a day early also celebrated the arrival of another enchanting summer on this lively river.

Only Captain Donald McAlpine and a few of his crew knew that the ship was sinking. His greatest trial of seamanship had arrived.

While his passengers laughed, danced and caroused, the worried captain raced against time to reach the nearest pier, the Bruner-Mond dock at Amherstburg on the Canadian side about a mile away. On board, he had 1,419 passengers and 120 crewmembers, all of whose lives were in his keeping.

He had felt the ship's hull strike something at 11:45 P.M., and he soon received a report from the engine room that water was gushing in at an alarming rate. A flash of some disaster shot through his mind -- an image of the *Eastland* tragedy from 20 years earlier, when over 800 lives were lost

Many of the 1,400 young roisterers on board the Tashmoo *posed happily for photos after their ship sank.*
CRIS KOHL COLLECTION

within minutes after the steel-hulled excursion steamer capsized in the Chicago River. At that time, Captain McAlpine was second mate on the Detroit River excursion steamer, *Greyhound,* and he heard experienced sailors conjecture about how something like the *Eastland* disaster could happen just as easily on their river.

But it would not happen tonight, not this night, he kept telling himself. Panic among so many passengers would inevitably create disaster. It was best not to let them know. Not yet. He arranged for the band to keep playing and had his crew spread the word that the ship had to make a stop at nearby Amherstburg for a quick engine repair. Any fears had by the passengers who had felt or noticed the minor collision with what was presumed to have been a submerged boulder in the river were allayed by the ship's crew. Most of the lively crowd of passengers maintained a rhythmic revelry and made merry, none the worse for its ignorance of what really happened.

As the *Tashmoo* ploughed full speed ahead for Amherstburg, its search light aimed strong and steady at its riverside destination, a nearby Coast Guard boat, summoned by wireless, escorted the stricken vessel.

The *Tashmoo's* clocks all struck midnight when a small, makeshift gangway was dropped and the many passengers, thrilled by this adventure, were slowly discharged. Then the ship settled to the bottom of the river.

Headlines blared the good and the bad Tashmoo *news.* CRIS KOHL COLLECTION

The steamer, Tashmoo, *settled in 18 feet of water at Amherstburg, Ontario, after striking an object while underway.* REV. PETER VAN DER LINDEN COLLECTION

This crowd of roisterers was just the right bunch to have had on board for a sinking. There had been no panic, no injuries and no deaths. Capt. McAlpine breathed a deep sigh of relief. His engine crew left their posts only when the water was waist deep, and it became clear that the boiler fires would soon be extinguished. The entire crew, too, left the *Tashmoo* uninjured.

Charles F. Bielman, Jr., the general manager of the Tashmoo Transit Company which owned the ship, left his home in Detroit at once for Amherstburg to arrange transportation for the stranded passengers. Despite the best efforts of steamship officials to get them home quickly, the

Many ships had been recovered after a shallow sinking. CRIS KOHL COLLECTION

passengers spent several of the night-time and early morning hours waiting.

"From what the captain and the officers have told me, there was no irregularity on the boat," said Bielman. "I am proud of the crew and the way they behaved."

"From the time the ship's lights went out and the emergency lights were turned on, until all the passengers were off the ship, the band played continuously," stated ship's purser J. M. Christie, who praised the self-control of Jean Calloway and her band, a Negro organization from Baltimore. "They showed a lot of spirit and worked hard to help us out," he added.

The stranded merrymaking passengers made the most of their predicament. They stood on the shore near the dock, dancing, singing and relaxing. A few built several small fires which soon attracted large crowds of light-hearted carousers.

"I never saw passengers like those," commented Lorne Helpel, cabin watchman. "They didn't seem to care whether the boat sank or not, as long as there was music."

Three trolley cars from Windsor were dispatched to Amherstburg, where they collected 300 of the marooned passengers and conveyed them to Windsor, from where they caught busses to Detroit (both the Detroit-Windsor Tunnel and the Ambassador Bridge had been built by this time). Another excursion steamer, the *Columbia* (one of the two Bob-Lo Island Amusement Park boats), steamed down from Detroit, picked up the remaining passengers, and took them home.

This art-deco style newspaper ad for the Tashmoo *appeared on June 10, 1936, a week before the ship sank. The $25,000 worth of new furnishings was rescued by the crew.* CRIS KOHL COLLECTION

The *Tashmoo's* crew, working swiftly, saved $25,000 worth of new furniture which had just been installed for the 1936 season.

Efforts were made to float the *Tashmoo*. Captain J. Earl McQueen, an Amherstburg salvage man, brought pumps alongside on board his tug, the *Progresso*, but this failed. The large, jagged hole which had been ripped in the keel on the starboard side could not be plugged.

It was reasonable to assume that the *Tashmoo* could be raised, repaired and returned to service after this accident. Similar grief had occurred two years earlier, on August

3, 1934, when near-hurricane-force winds drove the ship hard aground on the Canadian shore opposite Tashmoo Park in the St. Clair River. No one was injured, but the picnickers were marooned on rain-soaked Harsens Island for hours until another steamer, the *Put-in-Bay*, took them off. The *Tashmoo* was floated the next day, her left paddle wheel broken.

Tom Reid of the famous Reid Towing and Wrecking Company in Sarnia warned the press that, in all likelihood, the *Tashmoo* would never run again.

He was right. The *Tashmoo* had settled on the river bottom with her bow and stern lower than the middle, and the pressure broke the ship's back. It would take $40,000 to raise and recondition the hull of this 37-year-old ship as she lay, with a heavy added expense for refurnishing much of the interior. The owners opted to ask for tenders on salvage and disposal of the ship's hull. Wreckers planned to strip the ship and scuttle her remains in Lake Erie. In 1936, scuttling -- towing a vessel into deep water and sinking it on purpose -- was still the easiest, the cheapest and the accepted method of getting rid of an old, unwanted ship. But in the end, the raised and dismantled hulk of the once proud and mighty *Tashmoo* was cut up by the scrappers' torches.

At the investigation, the *Tashmoo's* officers all stated that a rock caused the accident. The channel off Sugar Island was swept, but the rock which had endangered the lives of more than 1,500 people was not found. Captain McAlpine, claiming to have been on the usual course and that he had passed over the same spot on the outgoing trip earlier that evening, testified:

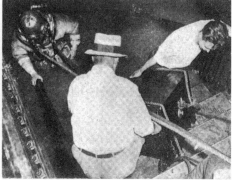

Left: *Capt. Donald McAlpine, of Windsor, and Walter Webster, first officer.* Above: *Amherstburg hardhat diver W. J. Atchison raised the* Tashmoo's *safe containing company papers and $2,000. This work was directed by Capt. McQueen.*

CRIS KOHL COLLECTION

The only way I can explain what happened is that a big boulder must have been washed into the channel by freighters. We had just left Sugar Island and were about opposite the Livingstone Light when we felt a slight jar. The paddle wheels quite often strike objects in the water, and at first we didn't think anything was wrong. Then I called the engine room and they told me that a hole had been punched in the bottom and that we were taking water. The power pumps were started and we headed for the nearest dock.,,, There was not the slightest sign of a panic. Even after we docked, the passengers didn't want to leave the ship.

At the requst of C.F. Bielman, Jr., a telegram from the Director of Marine Inspection and Navigation was read into the record at the federal hearing:

Capt. Donald McAlpine and Crew: Reports of your successful efforts in safely landing passengers and crew from steamer *Tashmoo* on night of June 18 most highly commended.
(signed) Joseph B. Weaver

W. Adamek, the wheelsman who had 14 years of river experience, the last seven of them on the *Tashmoo*, substantiated that the ship was on her course at the time of impact, but he was unable to account for the accident.

It was suggested that the *Tashmoo* may have struck a drifting or partially submerged log or tree (a "deadhead"), or she hit a rock dumped by a dredging crew eager to get home, or that one of her newly-added buoyancy stabilizing "sponsons" somehow pushed itself into and through her hull.

Tashmoo Park remained open to the public, but without steamer access, as a replacement for the *Tashmoo* could not be found. People could drive one mile south of Algonac and take the car ferry a short distance over to

Tashmoo Started for the Junk Heap

Hull Found Broken, Ending Hope of Raising Ship

Wreckers began Tuesday to dismantle the excursion steamer Tashmoo, which sank on the Amherstburg shore June 19 after striking an obstruction in the Sugar Island Channel.

The plan to raise the thirty-six-year-old steamer was abandoned

A broken keel fated the Tashmoo *to the scrapyard shortly after sinking in the Detroit River.*
CRIS KOHL COLLECTION

Harsens Island, the home of Tashmoo Park. The loss of the steamer gave a huge boost to the excursion company's chief competition: the automobile.

By July 15, 1936, realizing that salvage was hopeless, wrecking company Pyke & Sons of Kingston, Ontario, which had constructed a $13,000 cofferdam around the *Tashmoo* for a closer examination, began dismantling the ship. They quickly sold the lifeboats, chairs and other furniture, estimating another three weeks to remove the upper works and salvage the machinery.

The *Tashmoo's* pilothouse outlived its ship. C. F. Bielman, aware of Capt. J. Earl McQueen's admiration for the *Tashmoo,* invited him to remove parts of the ship for himself after the inspection sealed the ship's fate. McQueen purchased the entire wreck outrightly. He removed the wheel house, planning to use it as a den in the summer home he expected to build at Amherstburg, while the wood from the *Tashmoo's* observation room and the smoking rooms would form the main section of the summer house. For some reason, these plans never materialized, for in June, 1937, Capt. McQueen sold the pilothouse, card room and a portion of the former dance cabin to Capt. J. A. McKenty of Chatham, Ontario, who transported this large section on a barge to a lot he owned on the Snye Channel (Chenal Écarte), west of Wallaceburg, and turned it into a cottage. Flames destroyed it on June 10, 1951.

A suggestion to use the *Tashmoo's* hull as the base of a dancing pavilion at Bob-Lo Island Amusement Park in the Detroit River fell through.

Eight years after the *Tashmoo's* loss, Capt. Donald McAlpine passed away on Saturday, January 1, 1944, at Grace Hospital in his home port of Windsor, Ontario, after a lengthy illness. The man who had succeeded in saving 1,539 people that June night on the Detroit River was remembered by many, and the press served sizable obituaries as reminders to the others.

*   *   *

Tashmoo Admirer Gets Wheel House

Owner Provides Material for a Summer Den

Capt. J. Earl McQueen, of Amherstburg, Ont., admired the steamer Tashmoo. He admired her trim lines, her furnishings, and everything about the excursion steamer which had taken so many thousands of pleasure-seeking folks

The pilothouse of the wrecked steamer, Tashmoo, *converted to a cottage, burned on June 10, 1951.*

CRIS KOHL COLLECTION

A 320-Foot Side Wheel Steamer for the Detroit, Toledo and Port Huron Route

Built for the excursion trade from Detroit to Port Huron and Toledo, the steamer, Tashmoo *(302'9" x 37'6" x 13'6") was designed by Detroit's famous Frank E. Kirby to carry 4,000 people, but the company limited the number to 2,800 for comfort. The Detroit Ship Building Company constructed the 2,500 horsepower inclined triple expansion steam engine and the five boilers which powered her.*   CRIS KOHL COLLECTION

The luxury steamer, *Tashmoo,* designed by Frank E. Kirby in 1898, was launched at Wyandotte, Michigan, on December 30, 1899 -- the last Great Lakes ship from the "Gay Nineties" and the 19th century.

The 1,344-gross-ton *Tashmoo,* named after the 1897 island park and purportedly meaning "tall and noble" after the son of a Chippewa chief, was soon nicknamed "The Glass Hack" because of the many lights at night emanating from the vessel's more than 600 windows. The ship's day trips from Detroit to Port Huron and back within a 12-hour span were the most popular of the river excursions. At "The Flats," the St. Clair River split into seven main streams which wound past splendid cottages and pleasure resorts into Lake St. Clair. The *Tashmoo* regularly made quick and punctual pinpoint stops at ten different resorts in "The Flats" within one hour to discharge or to collect passengers.

Above: *The golden era of excursion steamers embellished the first two decades of the 1900's. The Detroit waterfront buzzed with crowds (men wore bowlers or straw hats, women, all Gibson girl types, carried rainbow-hued parasols), ships and activity when river steamers such as the* Tashmoo *and the* Idlewild *loaded for day trips to Port Huron or Toledo. Promptly at 9:00 A.M. every summer day, the magnificent steamer,* Tashmoo, *swung out from her dock at the foot of Griswold Street for the 61-mile trip to Port Huron. Below, left: The* Tashmoo's *grand salon, paneled in mahogany, featured two ornately carved grand pianos in its center, surrounded by an audience of wicker rocking, and other, chairs. The* Tashmoo *lacked a ballroom, but in later years, the grand salon served that purpose. A mahogany-paneled dining room was featured aft on the main deck. Below, right: The* Tashmoo's *beer garden was situated below deck near the bow, as indicated by the low ceiling and walls narrowing towards the bar. The bar itself was finished in oak. One level above the beer garden was the smoking room.* Cris Kohl Collection

A century ago, just like today, people wanted to go faster than everyone else. Many races, mostly informal, took place on the Great Lakes, but one of the most publicized and anticipated was the one between the Tashmoo *and the* City of Erie *on June 4, 1901. The course covered 94 miles between Cleveland, OH, and Erie, PA. The larger* Erie *won by 45 seconds, an extremely close race considering that the distance took four hours and twenty minutes to run. The* Tashmoo *lost the race, but not her esteem.* CRIS KOHL COLLECTION

CITY OF ERIE WON BIG RACE BY ONLY 45 SECONDS

THE CITY OF ERIE.

Greatest Steamboat Contest in History of American Navigation Captured by C. & B. Line Boat From Detroit's Flyer, the Tashmoo, After 100 Miles of Running at Top Speed From Cleveland to Erie—$100,000 Changed Hands—Close Finish Shows Little Choice Between the Two Freshwater Greyhounds.

The luxurious Tashmoo *hosted a number of dignitaries early in the ship's career. Admiral George Dewey (1837-1917), the national hero who had just conquered Manila and the rest of the Philippines in the Spanish-American War, sailed on her from Cleveland to Detroit on June 9, 1900, two days before the vessel officially started her public service.*

However, the most famous of the steamer Tashmoo's *many passengers was Theodore Roosevelt (1858-1919), author, explorer, colorful leader of the "Rough Riders" in Cuba and 26th president of the United States. On Monday, September 22, 1902, Roosevelt, in Detroit to address a national convention of the United Spanish War Veterans, enjoyed a nautical sightseeing tour past the city's skyline. Detroit was eager to impress "T. R." on his first visit after becoming president, so the relatively new and lavishly appointed* Tashmoo *was selected. Roosevelt and*

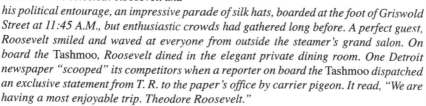

his political entourage, an impressive parade of silk hats, boarded at the foot of Griswold Street at 11:45 A.M., but enthusiastic crowds had gathered long before. A perfect guest, Roosevelt smiled and waved at everyone from outside the steamer's grand salon. On board the Tashmoo, *Roosevelt dined in the elegant private dining room. One Detroit newspaper "scooped" its competitors when a reporter on board the* Tashmoo *dispatched an exclusive statement from T. R. to the paper's office by carrier pigeon. It read, "We are having a most enjoyable trip. Theodore Roosevelt."*

This was the only time that the Tashmoo *left its Detroit dock proudly flying the blue and gold ensign of the President of the United States.*   CRIS KOHL COLLECTION

245

Creating newspaper advertising for the Tashmoo *was a seasonal cottage industry unto itself.* Upper left: *On June 2, 1927, this ad announced the beginning of the river excursions season.* Upper right: *A September 1, 1933 ad offered the season's final moonlight cruise.* Left: *Free dancing was featured in this June 10, 1927 ad.* Below: *The season ended early with this September 6, 1924 ad (note the whaleback).*

CRIS KOHL COLLECTION

Reflecting the Indian origins of the name "Tashmoo," above, that ship annually ran trips to the "Great Indian Fair" at Walpole Island (August 22, 1933) and, right, invited excursionists to sail with them "through the old land of the Chippewas" (August 7, 1926). CRIS KOHL COLLECTION

The steamer, Tashmoo, made stops at many of the island resorts along the St. Clair River between Detroit and Port Huron, where passengers could spend a day, or overnight in splendid lodgings. The establishments included the River-side Hotel (upper left), *the Mervin Club* (upper right), *and the "Old Club"* (left).
CRIS KOHL COLLECTION

At the time of the *Tashmoo's* fatal accident in 1936, newspapers editorialized over the importance of the ship. The Port Huron paper wrote:

> ...the *Tashmoo* has long been a popular means of summer transportation up and down the St. Clair River. It has been every year the scene of many midsummer festivities..., and the suggestion that it might never be put to service on the river again has caused much regret. Although the automobile and the desire for speed have cut heavily into steamboat patronage in recent years, the advent of the *Tashmoo* at the opening of the summer season, with the opportunity it has offered for river trips and moonlight excursions, has been anticipated annually with pleasure by hundreds of people, for whom its retirement would be almost like the loss of an old friend.

Another editorial from June, 1936 stated, "The *Tashmoo* was more than a boat. She had come to be an institution in the life of Detroit."

On May 18, 1985 (Maritime Day), the steamer *Tashmoo* was selected to enter the National Maritime Hall of Fame at King's Point, New York.

The *Tashmoo,* the Queen of the Rivers, was enjoyed by an estimated 12,000,000 excursionists between 1900 and 1936, and left a legacy of hundreds of photos, thousands of words, and millions of memories for those who knew her. Other "floating palaces" have been forgotten by comparison.

The *City of Erie* won that competition for speed back in 1901, but the *Tashmoo's* midnight race to port, flying to save the lives of more than 1,500 passengers and crew while she herself was dying, has become a river epic.

Farewell, Tashmoo!

CRIS KOHL COLLECTION

FLAUNTING "SUCCESS"

Mutiny and violence threatened to erupt several times during the Atlantic Ocean crossing of an ancient Australian "Convict Ship" in 1912. The crew, mostly Russians and Finns who spoke no English, coal operators thrown out of work by recent strikes, had developed nervous feelings about the vessel. For one thing, the ship sailed very slowly and the crossing was taking much longer than anticipated. Food was running low, and the men were on short rations, namely a biscuit, a small piece of ham and a mug of water a day. Adding to that difficulty, the men were

The three-masted convict ship, Success *(135' x 30' x 14'),* spent her early years in the East Indies and Australia.   ART BY AND COURTESY OF JAMES A. ANDREWS

The Boston Daily Globe.

BOSTON. FRIDAY MORNING. JULY 19. 1912=SIXTEEN PAGES.

D **AR"**

Party **l.**

CASEY RETIRED BY COMMISSION

Used City Auto for His Own Purposes.

Executive Clerk of Shhoolhouse Department Since 1902.

Action on Recommendation of Finance Board.

MUTINY NEAR THREE TIMES ON BOARD CONVICT SHIP

Old Success Towed Into Boston After Hard-Luck Passage of 95 Days Across the Atlantic.

THE CONVICT SHIP Success

CAPT. JOHN SCOTT

ASK **W|**

Carme At Gre

Vahey With

Pelletier Tak

CROWD F

The controversial arrival of the Australian "Convict Ship," the Success, *at Boston in the summer of 1912 made front page news there.* CRIS KOHL COLLECTION

hearing strange sounds besides those made by their rumbling stomachs. Once at sea, they had found out about the ship's past and its former purpose (even though they could not understand the words "Convict Ship" in large, black letters on the ship's hull), and the men fell prey to superstitions. Claiming that the restless ghosts of former prisoners who had died on the vessel still resided there, the crew swore to having heard unusual sounds and witnessed inexplicable happenings on board. The large collection of unusual and unnerving instruments of torture, such as the handcuffs, leg irons, an "iron maiden," branding irons, iron straitjackets, a whipping triangle, and more, on the ship clanged and clinked together for no apparent reason, and the men saw blue lights emanating from a former solitary confinement cell -- the "Devil's Den," as the they called it. Initially quartered in the damp, dark and dismal cells, the crew refused to bunk below deck, preferring the open deck to conditions below. Only five men on the ship spoke English: the captain, mate, wireless operator and two seamen. Somehow the captain quelled the three increasingly onerous uprisings from the foreign sailors. In his dealings with a mutinous crew, haunted cells and an old ship which sailed, as he put it, "like a bale of hay," Captain Scott had aspired to the name of his command -- *Success*.

Solid but old, the Success *had sailed first from Australia to England in 1895 and then across the Atlantic Ocean to the United States in 1912. The new American owner, Captain David H. Smith (inset), spent $30,000 on rerigging the ship as a barkentine before the ocean crossing. He declared that the ship was "still capable of going to any port in the world under her own canvas," yet he was not on board when she seemingly took forever to sail across the Atlantic. This floating museum was an arsenal of torture equipment -- none of which was actually ever used on board this ship.*

COURTESY OF THE RUTHERFORD B. HAYES PRESIDENTIAL CENTER, FREMONT, OHIO

Two ships left England on April 10, 1912: *Titanic*, the newest ship in the world, and the *Success*, touted as the oldest working vessel on the planet. Only one of them made it across the ocean: the *Success* took a total of 99 days to reach Boston, but at least it arrived. The master of the new *Titanic* was a man named Captain Edward Smith, while the *Success'* new owner was similarly named Captain David H. Smith (although he himself did not sail across the Atlantic on his newly-purchased vessel).

Surprisingly, for the time (i.e. <u>before</u> *Titanic* sank), the *Success* had been equipped with wireless radio equipment prior to departing England. This was very fortunate, for, several days out, the foremast broke, and the officers were able to call for a tugboat to rescue them. The *Success* was towed to Ireland for a three-week delay while having a new mast installed. During this time, several of the crew deserted and had to be replaced.

While in Ireland, the men aboard the *Success* heard about the sinking of *Titanic*, with its tragic loss of life, and they knew that they would be sailing through those same waters within weeks. When the *Success* passed the spot on June 10, 1912, where *Titanic* had gone down, icebergs were sighted, an event written down in the ship's log. The last mention of icebergs in the ship's log was on June 16th.

Upon arrival off the coast of the United States on July 17, 1912, the *Success'* wireless was again used to call for a tow, with an additional request for food and water as well. However, it took the harbor tug, *Charles T. Gallagher*, with David H. Smith, the owner of the *Success*, growing increasingly restless on board, thirteen hours of searching in the fog before picking up the ship seven miles off Baker's Island. A large supply of bread and fresh meat was transferred to the *Success*, and she was towed to an anchorage off the East Boston Flats. The local waterfront took its hat off to the seamanship and daring of old Capt. John Scott -- at 65, himself almost as ancient as the ship he commanded -- and his crew, while the harbor's watering holes paid them similar tribute. The *Boston Post* described the unusual ship like this:

> ...The square sails on the *Success'* foremast and the sails on the other two masts are decorated with black arrows and the sides of the vessel are also marked with arrows. Those on the craft declared that in the olden days, convict ships and some of the naval vessels were marked by the black arrows.
>
> A beautiful figurehead of a woman stands out conspicuously, and the whole vessel seems to rise high out of the water. The main and mizzenmasts are the same that were stepped into the *Success* when she was built about 1790. They are of teak wood and seem to be in perfect condition.

Below the main deck are two tiers of cells and dark rooms. The lowest row of cells are in the bottom of the barkentine, where not a ray of sunlight can possibly enter. In these small cells, with heavily barred doors, scores of men, confined for having committed misdemeanors, have perished from abuse or contracted disease from close confinement and lack of fresh air.

Thousands of people in Boston in 1912 paid the nominal fee to visit the convict ship, _Success,_ a vessel claiming to be even older (by seven years) than "Old Ironsides," the beloved _U.S.S. Constitution,_ reposing quietly at a dock in Boston harbor. The line-ups to board the _Success_ proved to be the beginning of the longest and most successful nautical hoax in North America.

* * *

The _Success,_ a 135-foot, 1,100-ton barkentine, was built in 1840 (not in 1790 as claimed by promoters). The records of Lloyd's of London give us an accurate history of the vessel. For one thing, the _Success_ was never used in the notorious transport of convicts from England to far-flung Australia, Britain's method of removing undesirables from the mother land. Out of sight was out of mind, and distant Australia served the purpose well. It was England's version of Alcatraz Island, only larger and further away. Most convicts sent there for comparatively small crimes and short terms of five or ten years never made it back to England. They remained in their new land, beginning life anew, and a large percentage of modern Australians are there because of their convict ancestors. A reason for shame until a few decades ago, Australians with convict ancestry today have more than come to terms with it. Now a matter of national pride rather than private shame, government publications and agencies exist to assist in the research of convict genealogies. Australians' relations with the mother country, however, remain, literally and figuratively, distant.

The following facts about the _Success_ have been proven:

The ship was built at Moulmein, Burma, in 1840 and was used in the immigrant, not convict, traffic between England and Australia until 1852. On June 1st of that year, upon hearing news of the big gold rush going on at Ballarat, the crew deserted the _Success_ when it arrived at Geelong and headed for the gold fields to get rich quick. This resulted in the _Success_ being purchased by the Victorian (then a separate British colony, but now the Australian state of Victoria) government for use as a prison ship. It was no secret in Victoria that the government's plans to build a prison there had been delayed because laborers could not be found -- they were all in the

253

The Success *posed for this early photograph while quietly at anchor in Sydney, Australia's, Wooloomooloo Bay in 1870. The ship was a storehouse for explosives at this time.*

COURTESY OF THE RUTHERFORD B. HAYES PRESIDENTIAL CENTER, FREMONT, OHIO

gold fields. So the *Success* became a floating holding tank for punishable people. It was six or seven years before enough manpower returned, disappointed and hungry, from the gold fields to take on the job of constructing the prison. All the male prisoners from the *Success* were transferred to *terra firma* incarceration. The problem now was what to do with the female convicts. There were not enough of them to warrant the construction of their own prison, so they were confined on board the *Success*. Between 1860 and 1869, the ship held imprisoned women, with one section of cells utilized for wayward boys. In a general sense, then, the *Success* did indeed serve as a convict ship, but not in the transport trade as advertised in the ship's promotional publications.

For fifteen years (from 1869 until 1884), the *Success* sat at anchor as a storehouse for explosives at Wooloomooloo Bay near Sydney.

In 1885, a man named Alexander Phillips bought the *Success*. In his own words, "I purchased her for to convert into a cargo lighter, but changed my mind and fitted her out for exhibition." However, the *Success* was sunk in Sydney Harbor for five years from 1885 until 1890, some say to appease angry Australians at a time when all the ships which had connections to the nasty transport of criminals business were being destroyed. The *Success*, built of Burma teak, did not corrode during her five years in 72 feet of water. The ship was raised at considerable expense in 1890 and very quickly restored, as she was put on exhibition attracting crowds in Melbourne in 1891 and Sydney in 1892. However, the ship sank again, apparently from a leak, this time in Kerosene Bay at Port Jackson on June 17, 1892. Sold in "as is" condition for the sum of twenty pounds, the wreck of the *Success* was purchased by a Melbourne business concern named "The Prison Hulk *Success* Co. Ltd." at the time it formed on February 27, 1893. That group clearly intended to make money from the exhibition of the raised, restored and refitted "convict ship." They also furnished the notorious vessel with wax figures of guards and prisoners. In 1894, after sailing to, and exhibiting at, Brisbane, the *Success* journeyed to Hobart on the island of Tasmania (the most southern of Australia's states), where the ship received a certificate of seaworthiness from Lloyd's before departing for Adelaide.

Between March 30 and September 12, 1895, the *Success* sailed from Adelaide, west past the treacherous, endless southern rim of Australia, across the Indian Ocean, through the Suez Canal and across the Mediterranean Sea to London, England.

The misinformation about the history of the *Success* came from a booklet written in 1895 by Joseph C. Harvie, who had been appointed advance agent and lecturer for the British tour by the owning company. He essentially

The old ship's "safe," claimed to have been made in England in 1772, lay scuttled with the Success *in Sydney Harbor for five years and, when raised and opened, reportedly contained old documents, handcuffs, ankle-locks, and keys.*
COURTESY OF THE RUTHERFORD B. HAYES PRESIDENTIAL CENTER, FREMONT, OHIO

Another attraction exhibited on board the convict ship, Success, *was the armor reputedly made and worn by the notorious Australian outlaw, Ned Kelly, whose gang had the same reputation in the land down under as did the Jesse James gang in the American West. In a famous stand-off, Kelly was shot to death by Australian troopers.*
COURTESY OF THE RUTHERFORD B. HAYES PRESIDENTIAL CENTER, FREMONT, OHIO

was placed in charge of the *Success* from 1895 until 1908, during which time the vessel toured England and Ireland as the convict ship with lucrative results. He possessed the mind of an imaginative novelist crossed with the marketing ability of a circus barker. Harvie's fanciful and inaccurate story of the *Success* was published as the exhibition ship's official souvenir booklet, which sold by the thousands.

In this British booklet (later reprinted in the U.S.A. for the benefit of equally enthralled and fascinated American tourists there), Harvie claimed that the *Success* was built in 1790, which would have placed the ship at an astounding 122 years of age when she crossed the Atlantic in 1912!

Harvie "retired" in 1908, and with him went the driving force behind the success of the *Success* in England. After his departure, the owners encountered financial difficulties, so they did not hesitate to sell the aging ship in 1912 to Captain David H. Smith, who had the vessel brought to America.

From the time the *Success* left Engand in 1912 until her ultimate demise years later, she toured extensively, visiting many ports. In 1924, at Toledo, Ohio, (where "every day since its arrival here it has been visited by good-sized crowds"), the reported long-range plans for the *Success* were to return to the U.S. East Coast after completing her tour of the Great Lakes, pass through the Panama Canal and visit Pacific Coast ports once again, then sail across the Pacific Ocean to become a permanent museum in Australia.

But for nearly 30 years, the *Success* toured the coasts, the rivers and the Great Lakes as the popular "Convict Ship" exhibit. Whenever this remarkable throwback to another long-gone era made harbor, dropped anchor or tied up at the town wharf, she attracted journalists. The arrival of a sailing vessel not only bearing such a striking appearance but also claiming so notorious a history was good copy, certain to help sell newspapers. The owner of the *Success* never rejected free promotional articles about his floating exhibit.

A 1924 account stated that "Since she has been placed on public exhibition, the convict ship has been shown throughout Australia, the United Kingdom and the United States, and it is calculated that more than twenty million visitors trod her decks...."

During 1913 and 1914, the *Success* toured East Coast harbors such as New York, Coney Island, Newark, Baltimore and Philadelphia, and in 1915, made the ambitious sail to San Francisco by means of the Panama Canal for exhibition at the Panama-Pacific International Exposition. West Coast ports hosted the *Success* in 1915 and most of 1916. The ship again passed through the Canal into the Gulf of Mexico and spent 1917 touring cities like Mobile, New Orleans and Baton Rouge before heading up the

Mississippi River system to Vicksburg, Memphis, St. Louis and Louisville. The years 1918 and 1919 saw the *Success* enjoy the river waters of Cincinnati, Wheeling and Pittsburgh. In 1920, 1921 and 1922, the ship again visited the Northeast coast before entering the Great Lakes for the first time in 1923, where she toured for five years. Between late 1928 and early 1933, she tasted her last saltwater travels, again in the Northeast, before returning to Chicago and the inland seas for her final years.

By the 1920's, the *Success* rarely moved under her own sail power any more due to the scarcity of experienced, old-style sailors and the fact that a towing tug would be needed at both the harbors of departure and arrival anyway, so hiring one tug to tow the *Success* the entire length of the trip made it a more practical operation which was not that much more expensive, considering the usually short distances between exhibition ports. For example, the tug, *Favorite,* towed the *Success* through the Straits of Mackinac on Monday, July 18, 1927, from Charlevoix, Michigan, to Mackinac Island, a distance of 65 miles.

A full-page announcement would be placed in the newspapers of larger harbor cities in the Great Lakes, advertising the fact that this unique member of Britain's notorious "felon fleet," the convict ship, *Success,* had arrived:

This wonderful vessel has made history through three centuries [the subheading would blare]. She is the oldest ship in the world

Quite a public amusement herself, the Success *spent a fair amount of time docked at Cedar Point, Ohio's famous amusement park.*   CRIS KOHL COLLECTION

257

and the only convict ship left afloat out of that dreadful fleet of ocean hells which sailed the Seven Seas in 1790 A. D.

She is unchanged after all these years, nothing being omitted but her human freight and their suffering from the cruelties and barbarities practiced upon them.

Aboard her are now shown, in their original state, all the airless dungeons and condemned cells, the whipping posts, the manacles, the branding irons, the punishment balls, the leaden-tipped cat o' nine tails, the coffin bath and the other fiendish inventions of man's brutality to his fellow man.

She has held lurid horrors and dreadful iniquities beside

167,000 men, women and children were transported from Great Britain to Australia, in the early part of the 18th Century. It was a voyage of 16,000 miles and took eight to nine months. Today, you can inspect the last of the terror-fleet engaged in the traffic. Aboard her remain all the original methods of torture, nothing being omitted but her human freight and their suffering from the cruelties and barbarities practised upon them. She is the

CONVICT SHIP

Now on Public Exhibition
FOOT OF JEFFERSON AVENUE
Open Every Day from 10 A. M. to 11 P. M.
(Last Lecture Starts at 10:20 P. M.)

PRIZES WILL BE GIVEN FOR A COMPLETE SERIES OF THESE ADS. SAVE THEM DAILY—NO. 2

"For the Term of His Natural Life"

Men, women and even . . . . en were transported, often for minor offenses, from their English homes to far-away Australia, where they were treated worse than we would treat cattle today. The oldest ship afloat is one of the vessels used in this nefarious transportation traffic. Now she is in this city with hundreds of old-time prison exhibits aboard her. You will realize the terrible tragedy of the lives of these unfortunates when you visit the infamous old Australian

CONVICT SHIP

MADISON STREET BRIDGE
Open Daily 10 A. M. to 11 P. M.
Admission, 50 Cents; Children Under 10, Half Price

"For Stealing A Yard Of Linen"

Women and even children of tender age were sentenced to transportation and hard labor for seven years for such trivial offenses. One cannot realize what this meant without visiting the scenes of their suffering and the hundreds of exhibits aboard the famous old Australian

CONVICT SHIP

NOW ON PUBLIC EXHIBITION
Belle Isle Bridge (GRANADA PARK)
OPEN EVERY DAY FROM 10 A. M. TO MIDNIGHT

"Flog Me Fair"

Was the only appeal which the agony of 300 lashes with a leaden tipped cat o'nine tails could wring from the more hardy unfortunates transported to Botany Bay. Her decks no longer resound with this strange prayer for pity, but the flogging frames, the cat o' nine tails, and the other implements used to impress upon the minds of convicted felons the might of Britain's majesty may still be seen aboard the old

CONVICT SHIP

NOW ON PUBLIC EXHIBITION
Belle Isle Bridge (GRANADA PARK)
OPEN EVERY DAY FROM 10 A. M. TO MIDNIGHT

which even the terrible stories of the Black Hole of Calcutta and the Spanish Inquisition pale into insignificance.

She marked the beginning and the end of England's monstrous penal system.

From keel to topmast, she cries aloud the greatest lesson the world has ever known in the history of human progress.

Drama and melodrama found their place into these advertisements, and they worked. People swarmed in huge numbers to see the convict ship. A portion of large advertisements for the *Success* were aimed at people's sense

of history, a stronger trait in the 1920's than it is today:

> Do You Realize That When the Convict Ship Was Launched
> in Far Away India in 1790 ---
> 1--George Washington was serving his first term as President of the
> United States?
> 2--Toledo didn't exist?
> 3 Buffalo was the western frontier of America?
> 4--The Battle of Waterloo was still 25 years in the future?
> 5--There were 145 offenses punishable by death in England?

"All work and no play"—was the lot of the felons shipped from England in the olden days. Their only exercise, their only chance to breathe fresh air, the only sight of the changing sea was when during one hour a day they dragged a heavy punishment ball up and down the deck. They and their sufferings are gone. But the original punishment balls—and the grooves they wore in the heavy decks can be seen today among the hundreds of exhibits aboard the famous old

CONVICT SHIP
NOW ON PUBLIC EXHIBITION
Belle Isle Bridge GRANADA PARK
OPEN EVERY DAY FROM 10 A. M. TO MIDNIGHT

Could make pleasant a dip in the compulsory baths aboard the old convict transports. Prisoners were dipped there to stop the flow of blood after being whipped. So many died or committed suicide there these tubs were called "coffin baths." One of the original ones—the only one extant—may be seen today among the hundreds of exhibits aboard the famous old

CONVICT SHIP
Now on Public Exhibition Foot of Jefferson Ave.
Open Every Day From 10 A. M. to 11 P. M.

Start Saving This Series of Ads Today. 25c Will Buy a 50c Ticket When Accompanied by Eleven Consecutive Ads Starting from Any Number. No. 11 Prizes will be announced later for a Collection of the Full Series.

Started the old-time sailors on a four-hour job in the romantic days of yore. The only such windlass, still in working order, over which a dozen men worked while singing their chanties, is today among the hundreds of interesting exhibits and in actual use aboard the famous old

CONVICT SHIP
Madison Street Bridge
OPEN EVERY DAY FROM 10 A. M. TO 11 P. M.
ADMISSION—50 CENTS; CHILDREN UNDER 10 HALF PRICE.

Start Saving This Series of Ads Today. 25c Will Buy a 50c Ticket When Accompanied by Eleven Consecutive Ads Starting from Any Number. No. 12 Prizes will be announced later for a Collection of the Full Series.

How many unfortunates chained to giant stones in the wilderness that was Australia in the last century must have repeated De Foe's words. One of these giant blue granite silent guards which kept men prisoners in the awful bleakness of a desert world may be seen among the hundreds of exhibits aboard the famous old

CONVICT SHIP
Madison Street Bridge
OPEN EVERY DAY FROM 10 A. M. TO 11 P. M.
ADMISSION—50 CENTS; CHILDREN UNDER 10 HALF PRICE.

A series of graphic illustrations highlighting the horrors of the convict ship formed an effective newspaper advertising campaign. Children collected all thirteen (an unlikely 14th, featuring pirates, sometimes appeared). CRIS KOHL COLLECTION

The Success _was regularly drydocked, recaulked and repainted, showing off her immensely high freeboard._

COURTESY OF THE RUTHERFORD B. HAYES PRESIDENTIAL CENTER, FREMONT, OHIO

Having Survived the Terrors of the Black Hole of the

CONVICT SHIP

FOR TWENTY-SEVEN HOURS

Thereby Breaking the World's Endurance Record,
the Bravest Woman in Detroit

MISS ANNA CASE   **22-Year Old Diana**

Has Been Specially Engaged for One
Week Only to Answer All Questions in
Relation to Her Astounding Feat.

Miss Case Will Be Aboard the

CONVICT SHIP, Belle Isle Bridge (Granada Park)

Daily From 10 A. M. to Midnight.

Contests were held to determine courage and stamina plus, indirectly, to give contestants some prize money and an idea of the horrors of windowless confinement on board the dark, damp ship with only bread and water for nourishment, and, directly, to attract more paying customers to the exhibition ship. It was a successful marketing ploy, as attendance figures rose after each contest held. In 1924, Detroit's Anna Case (pictured below before her attempt) *set the record, and received the publicity and prize money (and* above right, *a free lift out of the cell after fainting from her ordeal), while, a year later, Miss Mary Martin was proclaimed "Chicago's Bravest Girl" for lasting 28 hours in the Success' "Black Hole," thereby establishing a new "world's record." Miss Case said, "The experience was much worse than I would have believed possible. I need money pretty badly, but I wouldn't repeat this experience for a million dollars."*   CRIS KOHL COLLECTION

Twenty-two-year-old Joyce Haller toured the convict ship, Success, *at Erie, Pennsylvania, in October, 1923, as part of group when she met Walter H. Munyon, the youngest lecturer and guide with the ship. Munyon toured the group through the vessel, explaining as he went along. But his attention kept straying to Miss Haller, and for the first time in his life, he forgot his lines. Their meeting began a romance which culminated in the couple's marrying in May, 1924, after the ship had moved to Toledo, Ohio. For some reason, the couple was married in St. Paul's Lutheran Church in that city rather than on board the ship where they had met.* CRIS KOHL COLLECTION

The caption to this photo (right) *indicates only that this unidentified couple getting married in the condemned cell on board the* Success *received a $200 prize. The stunt-driven 1920's witnessed many unusual events, among them dozens of marriages being performed in one of the dark prison cells on the* Success. *It would certainly be interesting to find out how those marriages fared! (To find out how one of them ended up, read the next page).*
COURTESY OF THE RUTHERFORD B. HAYES PRESIDENTIAL CENTER, FREMONT, OHIO

Requests for marriages to be performed on board the Success *became so numerous that a lottery system was devised. Detroiter Louise Quinn, 29, drew number 13 (from her point of view, "lucky" number 13) from a hat, winning for her not only $100 (which was presented to her by Capt. D. H. Smith in the form of 13 gold coins -- seven ten-dollar pieces and six five-dollar coins), but also the right to be married to her fiancée, shingler Thomas L. Boyce, 30, on Friday, June 13, 1924, in condemned cell Number 13 on board the convict ship while it was lying off the Belle Isle Bridge in the Detroit River. The ceremony would be performed at 13 minutes past the 13th hour, with 13 witnesses and a black cat which Boyce agreed to bring. The couple said they would smash mirrors immediately before the ceremony. The non-superstitious couple was elated! One newspaper described the marriage as taking place "under the weirdest circumstances ever known in Detroit." As it turned out, two of the 13 witnesses had been born on Friday the 13th, facts which surely helped bring more joy than one can imagine to the bride and groom. The bride carried the black cat in one arm and a bouquet of flowers in the other during the ceremony. The groom kissed his new bride 13 times, and after the ceremony, 13 bags of rice were thrown. This is also the ideal story to end up in the 13th chapter of a book! Keep reading to find out how our blissfully wedded couple fared.* CRIS KOHL COLLECTION

Convict Ship Husband Out of Luck Friday

On September 5, 1924, several Fridays after he was married, Thomas Boyce was charged with the murder of Clyde Keller, 45, in Detroit. Boyce, with Keller, a 30-year-old divorcée and another married woman, had been drinking at the divorcée's apartment. Keller was found the next morning with his head crushed in a moving van outside the apartment. The three said that Keller had fallen, and was last seen limping towards his van. They claimed to know nothing about the hammer beside Keller's body, which police claimed killed him. The charge against Boyce was later dropped.

PRISON VESSEL BRIDE DIVORCED

Louise Boyce was granted a divorce on August 6, 1928 on grounds of "cruelty." Tom had taken up a naval career operating a boat between Canada and the U.S.A. As this was during Prohibition, Mr. Boyce and goverment officials soon had a conference, and Mr. Boyce was consigned to Leavenworth penitentiary for nearly a year. Louise later took him to court for the $1,500 he owed her as a financial settlement. Louise was later arrested for carrying a concealed weapon after she allegedly threatened another woman's life. The Boyces were quite the unlucky couple!

WED ON CONVICT SHIP; THREAT CAUSES ARREST

Mrs. Louise Boyce, 1238 LeMay avenue, who was married in the Convict Ship about two years ago, was arrested last night, charged

Referred to as the "Australian Bastille," the Convict Ship, Success, _displayed on her sails and hull very attention-grabbing, upward-pointing arrows (below), the British prison sign which marked every convict ship in the days of the penal colonies. Prisoners' clothing was also marked with this sign, a strong giveaway for identifying escapees. At the end of the_ Success' _stay at a particular harbor, market-savvy exhibit organizers placed an advertisement in the local newspaper indicating that "when she leaves, she will never return" or "positively last day tomorrow, she will never return..." as a means of attracting a good-sized farewell crowd. In the case of Cleveland and Toledo, the_ Success _did return -- several times!_ CRIS KOHL COLLECTION

Now in **Cleveland** E. 9th ST. PIER

At C & B Boat Landing

Open Daily -- 10 A. M. to 11 P. M.

Visit the Ancient, Famous and Infamous

Convict Ship

Oldest and Most Historic Ship Afloat

When She Leaves She Will Never Return

CONVICT SHIP

POSITIVELY LAST DAY TOMORROW

She Will Never Return to TOLEDO

Until Sunday Night Open Daily 10 A. M. to 11 P. M. Foot Jefferson Avenue.

The *Success* Tour -- Many Years, Miles and Millions!

The Convict Ship, *Success,* after leaving Australia in 1895 and England in 1912, arrived in the United States and toured the nation and Canada -- both East and West Coasts, the Gulf of Mexico, up the Mississippi and Ohio Rivers, and ultimately into the Great Lakes -- an unusual floating exhibition which attracted and fascinated millions. A collection of all of the newspaper clippings about the *Success* would fill a ridiculously huge scrapbook!

1912 --	Boston, Massachusetts		Trenton, New Jersey		Atlantic City, New Jersey
	Providence, Rhode Island	1921 --	Chester, Pennsylvania		Newark, New Jersey
1913 --	New London, Connecticut		Newark, New Jersey		Albany, New York
			Elizabeth Port, New Jersey		Kingston, Ontario
	New York City (96th Street)		Albany, New York		
			New York City (125th St.)	1931 --	Poughkeepsie, N.Y.
	Coney Island	1922 --	New York City (Battery Park)		New York City (79th Street)
	Newark, New Jersey		Boston, Massachusetts		Newport, Rhode Island
	Norfolk, Virginia	1923 --	Providence, Rhode Island		
	Richmond, Virginia		New Bedford, Massachusetts		Fall River, Massachusetts
1914 --	Washington, D.C.		Cleveland, Ohio		Providence, Rhode Island
	Baltimore, Maryland		Buffalo, New York		
	Wilmington, Delaware		Erie, Pennsylvania	1932 --	Boston, Massachusetts
	Philadelphia, Pennsylvania	1924 --	Toledo, Ohio		Portsmouth, New Hampshire
1915 --	San Francisco, California (Exposition)		Detroit, Michigan		Portland, Maine
			Port Huron, Michigan		
	Oakland, California		Bay City, Michigan	1933 --	Sarnia, Ontario
	Portland, Oregon		Milwaukee, Wisconsin		Chicago, Illinois
	Astoria, Oregon (one day)	1925 --	Racine, Wisconsin	1934 --	(Did not operate)
			Chicago, Illinois	1935 --	(Did not operate)
	Seattle, Washington	1926 --	Chicago, Illinois (Madison Street)	1936 --	Cleveland, Ohio
	Tacoma, Washington				Racine, Wisconsin
	Everett, Washington		Michigan City, Indiana		Kenosha, Wisconsin
1916 --	Bellingham, Washington		St. Joseph, Michigan		Benton Harbor, Michigan
	Ana Cortes, Washington		South Haven, Michigan		
	Port Angeles, Washington		Holland, Michigan	1937 --	Muskegon, Michigan
			Muskegon, Michigan		Manistee, Michigan
	Port Townsend, Washington	1927 --	Manistee, Michigan		Charlevoix, Michigan
			Manitowoc, Wisconsin		Saginaw, Michigan
	Aberdeen, Washington		Sheboygan, Wisconsin		
	Hoquam, Washington		Green Bay, Wisconsin	1938 --	Bay City, Michigan
	South Bend, Oregon		Charlevoix, Michigan		Port Huron, Michigan
	North Bend, Oregon		Mackinac Island, Michigan		Wyandotte, Michigan
	Marshfield, Oregon				Sandusky, Ohio
	Eureka, California		Detroit, Michigan	1939 --	Lorain, Ohio
	Port Coste, California		Toledo, Ohio		Cleveland, Ohio
	Pensacola, Florida	1928 --	Lorain, Ohio	1940 --	Cleveland, Ohio
1917 --	Mobile, Alabama		Cleveland, Ohio	1941 --	Cleveland, Ohio
	New Orleans, Louisiana		Charlotte (Rochester), New York	1942 --	Cleveland, Ohio
	Baton Rouge, Louisiana				Sandusky, Ohio
	Vicksburg, Mississippi		Oswego, New York	1943 --	Sandusky, Ohio
	Memphis, Tennessee		Alexandria Bay, N.Y.	1944 --	Sandusky, Ohio
	Cairo, Illinois		New Haven, Connecticut	1945 --	Sandusky, Ohio
	St. Louis, Missouri	1929 --	Bridgeport, Connecticut		Towed to Port Clinton, Ohio, in the fall
	Evansville, Indiana		South Norwalk, Conn.		
	Louisville, Kentucky		Hartford, Connecticut		
1918 --	Cincinnati, Ohio		New London, Conn.	1946 --	Port Clinton, Ohio
	Pomeroy, Ohio		Port Chester, New York		
	Wheeling, West Virginia		Yonkers, New York		
1919 --	Pittsburgh, Pennsylvania		Baltimore, Maryland		
1920 --	Atlantic City, New Jersey		Richmond, Virginia		
	Philadelphia, PA	1930 --	Washington, D.C.		

The owner of the *Success*, Capt. David H. Smith, reportedly in 1925 (thirteen years after he had purchased the ship in England) stated in Chicago that his exhibition ship "was a tremendous paying game." A conservative estimate of the ship's annual income in the middle of the "Roaring '20's" was $450,000 a year, from which Smith paid his crew of 21 about $40,000 total, advertising fees of $30,000, variable towing fees of about $35,000 and variable dockage fees of about $40,000. Even with leeway for other overhead and maintenance expenses, this left a considerable profit well into the six figures--incredibly high for the times.

Sometimes the promoters of the Success *managed to tie in an appropriate guest to attract tourists. René Belbenoit, an educated inmate of the notorious French prison on Devil's Island, escaped five times and wrote a bestselling book about his experiences.*
CRIS KOHL COLLECTION

"Captain John" of Manistique, Michigan, became so enthusiastic about what could be learned from the Success *that he had this postcard of himself and a model of the convict ship printed in Milwaukee. His message on the back included the admonition to "come forward and help save the children of today from crime, sin and careless accidents, that we may not have a repetition of such days as that of the Convict Ship. Crime Does Not Pay."* CRIS KOHL COLLECTION

Enticing newspaper ads with a penchant for the dark side of human nature prompted millions of people to visit the notorious "convict ship" all around North America. Contests were held to see which young lady could stay in the dark hold in solitary confinement the longest, and every port had a winner. For some macabre reason, many young couples in the 1920's flocked to get married at the infamous Cell 13. Many of these marriages worked out fine, but some ended up very publicly messy when divorce details were published in the newspapers. Prize money was also offered for students writing the best essay about the *Success;* in 1925 in Chicago, the awards were $50 for first prize, $25 for second, $10 for third, and fifteen prizes of one dollar each. Participation was plentiful and enthusiastic.

A report in Halifax on October 5, 1928, stated that the *Success* had been sold to the Australian government for use as a museum, and that the ship would soon sail back to her old waters. When the Great Depression began suddenly in late 1929, the *Success,* on the East Coast again, found itself in a quandary; with the economy so bad, now was not the time to begin a cruise halfway around the world. During the worst years of the Depression (1930, 1931 and 1932), the *Success* wandered randomly among Atlantic harbors in the northeast. Hoping to find some semblance remaining of her best financial years, the *Success* returned to the Great Lakes, specifically to Chicago by early June for the 1933 World's Fair. However, this turned out to be a hollow event, and the glory days of the "Roaring

By the late 1920's the Success *fell into disrepair. The distinctive figurehead, however, kept its chin up, until cut down by vandals. Most reports indicate that the figurehead had been removed before the fire.* CRIS KOHL COLLECTION

'20's" were nowhere to be found. In 1934 and 1935, the *Success* did not operate.

Eventually, accounts of this Australian convict ship which had met with such huge financial success earlier in the United States reached Australia, where a thorough investigation of records, official and otherwise, was made in the early 1930's. Efforts to set the record straight met with failure, since the promoters' longtime published rendition remained a more exciting history of the *Success*, and particularly since this was the 1930's during the Depression, when people craved escapism, i.e. opportunities to be whisked away to exciting times and places far different from their day-to-day misery. The world's oldest vessel, a convict ship from exotic Australia, fit the bill. The fictional history of the *Success* remained the accepted, indeed the embraced, chronicle of the ship.

By the late 1930's, the *Success* remained in Lake Erie ports, slowly falling out of popularity and into disrepair.

Finally, on the Fourth of July, 1946, vandals in a small power boat set fire to the *Success* off Port Clinton, Ohio, making this one of the newest shipwrecks of one of the oldest ships in the Great Lakes. The restless bones of *Success* found a permanent home in the shallow waters of Lake Erie.

*　　　*　　　*

At Sandusky in 1942, the Success *rested on the lake bottom.* CRIS KOHL COLLECTION

269

T he ship which sailed smoothly, if slowly, across thousands of miles on the Seven Seas ironically met a violent demise on a relatively small, shallow freshwater lake near the middle of the North American continent. Had the *Success* truly been a relentless convict ship upon which hundreds of prisoners succumbed to torturous deaths over several decades, one could argue that avenging ghosts had cursed the vessel. But that did not destroy the ship.

By 1946, scores of the nineteenth century wooden vessels between 100 and 200 feet in length, surpassed during the previous forty years in size and cargo capability by steel ships over 600 feet long, had, mostly in the 1920's and 1930's, been consigned to maritime gulags around the Great Lakes, scuttled in ships' graveyards such as those off Kingston in Lake Ontario; north of Port Huron and Sarnia in Lake Huron; off Chicago and in Sturgeon Bay in Lake Michigan; and in the Keweenaw Waterway and off Ontario's city of Thunder Bay in Lake Superior.

Dozens more old ships had met fiery deaths as public spectacles, set ablaze for bored landlubbers willing to pay the viewing fee. Victims of these modern nautical witch hunts included the 61-year-old schooner, *Lyman M. Davis,* burned at Toronto's Sunnyside Amusement Park on June 29, 1934, and the 42-year-old steamer, *Robert Fryer,* incinerated at the Welcome Islands off Thunder Bay, Ontario, on July 29, 1930, while many patrons on several ships paid $1.00 each to be ferried out there to view the fun. Such "fun" did not end with the burning of the *Success* in 1946 -- the beloved St. Clair River excursion steamer, *Put-in-Bay,* 42 years old, was torched on Lake St. Clair on October 3, 1953, and the historic 65-year-old former "Gospel Ship" once named the *Glad Tidings* had an enthusiastic audience off Mackinac Island on May 16, 1954, when it was ignited and sent to the bottom in 90 feet of water.

The message -- old ships are eyesores which must be removed, and fire can be fun -- had been clearly received all around the Great Lakes, as vandals ignited a number of derelict vessels lying close to shore on the edge of harbors.

The 106-year-old *Success,* for years already a victim of an unhappy old age, also fell victim to the modern age -- a world which felt that it had neither need, nor room, for the old-fashioned ships of its fathers. So vandals set the ship on fire for some post-World War II Independence Day fun.

Today, scuba divers explore the teakwood pieces of the historic *Success* in fifteen feet of Lake Erie water, and as they swim along those exotic timbers which once saw so much life -- from sailors and passengers to convicts and tourists -- they sigh longingly, "Oh, if only she could sail again."

But then, every Great Lakes shipwreck has heard that lament.

BIBLIOGRAPHY

A. Books

Avery, Thomas, and Avery Color Studios. *The Mystery Ship from 19 Fathoms.* AuTrain, Michigan: Avery Color Studios, 1974.

Ballard, E. G. *Captain Streeter, Pioneer.* Chicago: Emery Publishing Service, 1914.

Barry, James P. *Ships of the Great Lakes, 300 Years of Navigation.* Berkeley, California: Howell-North Books, 1973.

Berton, Pierre. *The Invasion of Canada, 1812-1813.* Toronto: McClelland and Stewart, 1980.

.... *Flames Across the Border, 1813-1814.* Toronto: McClelland and Stewart, 1981.

Boyer, Dwight. *Great Stories of the Great Lakes.* New York: Dodd, Mead & Company, 1966.

.............*True Tales of the Great Lakes.* New York: Dodd, Mead & Company, 1971.

.............*Strange Adventures of the Great Lakes.* New York: Dodd, Mead & Company, 1974.

Bowen, Dana Thomas. *Lore of the Lakes.* Daytona Beach, Florida: Privately published by Dana Thomas Bowen, 1940.

.............*Memories of the Lakes.* Daytona Beach, Florida: Privately published by Dana Thomas Bowen, 1946.

.............*Shipwrecks of the Lakes.* Daytona Beach, Florida: Privately published by Dana Thomas Bowen, 1952.

Burton, Patricia Owens. *Clarence Munroe Burton, Detroit's Historian.* Detroit, Michigan: Burton Abstract & Title Company, 1953.

Channing, Edward, and Marion Florence Lansing. *The Story of the Great Lakes.* New York: The MacMillan Company, 1909.

Chesnel, P. *History of Cavelier de La Salle.* New York, New York: G. P. Putnam's Sons, 1932.

Clary, James. *Ladies of the Lakes.* Lansing, Michigan: Michigan Department of Natural Resources, 1981.

Commemorative Biographical Record of the Count of Kent, Ontario. Toronto: J. H. Beers & Co., 1904.

Creviere, Paul J., Jr. *Wild Gales and Tattered Sails.* Wisconsin: Privately published by John Paul Creviere, Jr., 1997.

Curwood, James Oliver. *The Great Lakes and The Vessels That Plough Them: Their Owners, Their Sailors, and Their Cargoes, Together with A Brief History of Our Inland Seas.* New York: G. P. Putnam's Sons, 1909; 1967 James Pugliese reprint.

Cuthbertson, George. *Freshwater, A History and a Narrative of the Great Lakes.* New York: The MacMillan Company, 1931.

Dixon, Michael M. *When Detroit Rode the Waves.* Detroit, Michigan: Mervue Publications, 2001.

Duff, Steven. *The Wanderer's Storm-Song, The Travels of Etienne Dufour in the Service of the Sieur De LaSalle, 1678-1682.* Belleville, Ontario: Mika Publishing Company, 1988.

Folkes, Patrick. *Shipwrecks of Tobermory, 1828-1935.* Willowdale, Ontario: Published by Patrick Folkes, 1969.

.... *Shipwrecks of the Saugeen, 1828-1938.* Willowdale, Ontario: Published by Patrick Folkes, 1970.

Greenwood, John O. *Namesakes 1900-1909.* Cleveland, Ohio: Freshwater Press, Inc., 1987.

.... *Namesakes 1910-1919.* Cleveland, Ohio: Freshwater Press, Inc., 1986.

.... *Namesakes 1920-1929.* Cleveland, Ohio: Freshwater Press, Inc., 1984.

.... *Namesakes 1930-1955.* Cleveland, Ohio: Freshwater Press, Inc., 1978; rev. edition, 1995.

Hall, Captain Ernie, *Flotsam, Jetsam and Lagan.* Cambridge, Maryland: Cornell Maritime Press, Inc., 1965.

Hamil, Fred Coyne. *The Valley of the Lower Thames, 1640 to 1850.* Toronto: University of Toronto Press, 1951.

Harrah, Backward and Forward. Harrah, Oklahoma: Harrah Historical Society, 1999

Hatcher, Harlan. *The Great Lakes.* New York: Oxford University Press, 1944.

Havighurst, Walter. *The Long Ships Passing.* New York: The MacMillan Company, 1945.

Hennepin, Father Louis. *A New Discovery of a Vast Country in America, In Two Volumes.* Toronto, Ontario: Coles Publishing Company Limited, 1974 (Originally published by A. C. McClurg and Company, Chicago, 1903, reprinted from the second London issue of 1698).

Johnson, Curt, with R. Craig Sautter. *Wicked City Chicago: From Kenna to Capone.* Highland Park, IL: December Press, 1994.

Kohl, Cris. *The 100 Best Great Lakes Shipwrecks, Volume I.* West Chicago, Illinois: Seawolf Communications, Inc., 1998.

.... *The 100 Best Great Lakes Shipwrecks, Volume II.* West Chicago, Illinois: Seawolf Communications, Inc., 1998.

.... *Dive Ontario! The Guide to Shipwrecks and Scuba.* Chatham, Ontario: Published by Cris Kohl, 1990, revised 1995.

.... *Dive Ontario Two! More Ontario Shipwreck Stories.* Chatham, Ontario: Published by Cris Kohl, 1994.

.... *The Great Lakes Diving Guide.* West Chicago: Seawolf Communications, Inc., 2001.

.... *Shipwreck Tales: The St. Clair River (to 1900).* Chatham, Ontario: Published by Cris Kohl, 1987.

.... *Titanic, The Great Lakes Connections*. West Chicago, Illinois: Seawolf Communications, Inc., 2000

.... *Treacherous Waters: Kingston's Shipwrecks*. Chatham, Ontario: Published by Cris Kohl, 1997.

Lauriston, Victor. *Romantic Kent, The Story of a County, 1626-1952*. Chatham, Ontario: Corporation of the County of Kent, 1952.

Lydecker, Ryck. *Pigboat...the Story of the Whalebacks*. Superior, Wisconsin: Head of the Lakes Maritime Society, Ltd., 1981 (2nd edition).

MacLean, Harrison John. *The Fate of the Griffon*. Chicago: Sage Books/The Swallow Press, 1974.

Mayer, Harold M., and Richard C. Wade. *Chicago, Growth of a Metropolis*. Chicago and London: Chicago University Press, 1969.

McKenzie, Donald A. *More Notices from Ontario's Methodist Papers, 1858-1872*. 1993.

Millard, Joseph. *No Law But Their Own!* Evanston, Illinois: Regency Books, Inc., 1963.

Mills, James Cooke. *Our Inland Seas, Their Shipping & Commerce for Three Centuries*. Chicago: A. C. McClurg & Co., 1910.

Mansfield, J. B., ed. *History of the Great Lakes, Volumes I and II*, Chicago, IL: J. H. Beers & Company, 1899.

Metcalfe, Willis. *Canvas & Steam on Quinte Waters*. South Bay, Ontario: The South Marysburgh Marine Society, 1979.

.... *Marine Memories*. Picton, Ontario: The Picton Gazette, 1975.

.... *Memories of Yesteryear*. Picton, Ontario: The Picton Gazette, 1977.

Osler, E. B. *La Salle*. Don Mills, Ontario: Longmans Canada, Ltd., 1967.

Parkman, Francis. *La Salle and the Discovery of the Great West*. Williamstown, Massachusetts: Corner House Publishers, 1968 (reprint edition; originally published in 1897).

Quaife, Milo M. *Lake Michigan* (The American Lakes Series). Indianapolis and New York: Bobbs-Merrill Company, 1944.

Snider, C. H. J. *The Griffon*. Toronto: Rous & Mann Press Limited, 1956.

.... *Tarry Breeks & Velvet Garters, Sail on the Great Lakes of America, in War, Discovery, and the Fur Trade, under the Fleur-de-Lys* (First Book of Schooner Days). Toronto, Ontario: Ryerson Press, 1958.

Stabelfeldt, Kimm A. *Explore Great Lakes Shipwrecks, Volume I Covering Wrecks on Part of the Lower Lake Michigan*. Wauwatosa, Wisconsin: Stabelfeldt & Associates, Inc., 1992 (sixth edition, 1996).

.... *Explore Great Lakes Shipwrecks, Volume II Covering Wrecks on the Upper Part of Lake Michigan and Green Bay off the Coasts of Wisconsin and Michigan*. Wauwatosa, Wisconsin: Stabelfeldt & Associates, Inc., 1993 (fourth edition, 1996).

Sutherland, R. R. *County of Kent Gazetteer, and General Business Directory for 1864-5*. Ingersoll, C. W.: A. R. & John Sutherland, 1864.

Terrell, John Upton. *La Salle: The Life and Times of an Explorer*. New York, New York: Weybright and Talley, Inc., 1968.

Van der Linden, Rev. Peter J., ed, and the Marine Historical Society of Detroit. *Great Lakes Ships We Remember.* Cleveland, Ohio: Freshwater Press, Inc., 1979; revised 1984.

.... *Great Lakes Ships We Remember II.* Cleveland, Ohio: Freshwater Press, Inc., 1984.

.... *Great Lakes Ships We Remember III.* Cleveland, Ohio: Freshwater Press, Inc., 1994.

Wachter, Georgann and Michael. *Eric Wrecks West, A Guide to Shipwrecks of Western Lake Erie.* Avon Lake, Ohio: Corporate*Impact,* 2001 (second edition; originally published in 1997).

Weddle, Robert S. *The Wreck of the Belle, the Ruin of La Salle.* College Station: Texas A&M University Press, 2001.

Wiltering, John H. *McDougall's Dream, The American Whaleback.* Sturgeon Bay, Wisconsin: Lakeside Publishing Ltd., 1969.

Wolf, Julius F., Jr. *Lake Superior Shipwrecks.* Duluth, MN: Lake Superior Port Cities, Inc., 1990.

Woodford, Arthur M. *Charting the Inland Seas: A History of the U.S. Lake Survey.* Detroit District: U.S. Army Corps of Engineers, 1991.

B. Periodical Literature

"*Alvin Clark* Burns, The." *Diving Times.* Vol. 8, No. 4 (Fall, 1985).

Association for Great Lakes Maritime History Newsletter. "Sad saga of schooner *Alvin Clark* finally came to end this summer." Vol. XI, No. 4 (July/August, 1994), 1, 7.

Atkins, Kenneth S. "*Le Griffon*: A New View." *Inland Seas.* Vol. 46, No. 3 (Fall, 1990), 162-169.

"Australia and the *Success.*" *Inland Seas.* Vol 3, No. 2 (April, 1947), 106-112.

Baker, Wallace J., Sr. "On Manitoulin Island." *Inland Seas.* Vol. 3, No. 4 (October, 1947), 211-217.

Bery, Sterling. "The Day the *Tashmoo* Did Not Come." *Telescope.* Vol. 40, No. 4 (July-August, 1992), 92-95.

Bowen, Dana Thomas. "The Green Bay Mystery Schooner." *Inland Seas.* Vol. 25, No. 4 (Winter, 1969), 267-278, 308-309.

Bugbee, Gordon P. "The Coming of the *Tashmoo.*" *Telescope.* Vol. 27, No. 5 (September-October, 1978), 127-130.

.... "The *David Dows.*" *Telescope* Vol. 8, No. 8 (August, 1959), 3-7, 16.

.... "Stars on the River." *Steamboat Bill.* Vol. 58, No. 4 (Winter, 2001, Number 240), 256-303.

Burton, Clarence M. "LaSalle and the *Griffon.*" Historical paper delivered before the Society of Colonial Wars of the State of Michigan, January 26, 1902.

Calnan, Joe. "Moise Hillaret, The First Shipwright on the Great Lakes." *Inland Seas,* Vol. 58, No. 3 (Fall, 2002), 190-207.

Caravello, Joe. "The Raising of the *Alvin Clark*...and the Fall of Frank Hoffman. *Reader* (Chicago's Free Weekly). Vol. 8, No. 27 (April 6, 1979), 1, 28-31.

Chabek, Dan. "Quest of the *Griffon*, Cleveland divers search for ancient wreck." *Skin Diver* Magazine, Vol. 11, No. 12 (December, 1962), 10-11, 48.

Clary, James. "By Definition: Tashmoo." *Telescope*.Vol. 28, No. 4 (July-August, 1979), 94

"Convict Ship, *Success,* The." *Inland Seas*. Vol. 2, No. 4 (October, 1946), 276.

Dadisman, Quincy. "They Discovered Lake Michigan." *Wisconsin Regional* (September, 1980), 28-29.

Dickson, Kenneth. "The *David Dows* Revisited, Part I." *Telescope*. Vol. 34, No. 5 (Sept/Oct., 1985), 128-132.

.... "The *David Dows* Revisited, Part II." *Telescope*. Vol. 34, No. 6 (Nov./ Dec., 1985), 143-146.

.... "The Largest Schooner (1881) in the World Revisited." *Inland Seas*. Vol. 42, No. 1 (Spring, 1986), 2-11.

Drew, Richard C. "Lake Michigan's *David Dows*." *Skin Diver Magazine*. Vol. 38, No. 11 (November, 1989), 6, 88, 90, 91.

Engelbert, Peter. "Letters to the Editor." *Great Lakes In Depth,* Vol. 2, No. 4 (July-August, 1989), 3.

Fleming, Roy F. "The *Griffon* Again." *Inland Seas*, Vol. 2, No. 1 (January, 1946), 62. From articles by this author in the *Manitoulin Expositor*, September 13, 20, 1945.

.... "The Search for LaSalle's Brigantine *Le Griffon*," Parts I and II. *Inland Seas*, Vol. 8, No. 4 and Vol. 9, No. 1 (Winter, 1952 and Spring, 1953), 223-228, 258-259, 19-26, 38-39.

Gammage, Mark. "Discovery of the Schooner *Miztec*." *The Nor'Easter*. Vol. 9, No. 1 (January-February, 1984), 1-3.

Garrett, Wayne. "Rx for Stability: Add Sponsons." *Telescope*. Vol. 30, No. 2 (March-April, 1981), 38-40, 46-47.

Gerred, Janice H. "The *Myron* Meets November, 1919." *Inland Seas*. Vol. 41, No.1 (Spring, 1985), 9-10.

Gilbert, Jim and Lisa. "Waddell Meant Progress for Chatham." Regular column in *Chatham This Week*. January 6, 1993.

Great Lakes News, The. "Diver Will Hunt La Salle's Vessel." Vol. 20, No. 12 (September, 1935), 4.

.... "Yachtsman Seeking the *Griffon*." Vol. 22, No. 11 (August, 1937), 1.

.... "Ask Financial Aid to Raise La Salle's Ship." Vol. 24. No. 9 (June, 1939), 10.

.... "The *Griffon* Anniversary." Vol. 25, No. 12 (September, 1940), 13.

Hill, Lee. "Menominee's 'Mystery' Ship, Capsized by Violent Storm, Lay on Lake Bottom 105 Years; Now It's Yours to Explore." *Wisconsin Week-End*. Vol. 16, No. 21 (August 20, 1970), 1,3,4.

Johnston, Joseph E. "Schooner Alvin Clark." *Telescope*. (March, 1959), 3-5.

Johnson, Ken. "Strange Story of the Steamer *Myron*." *Diver Magazine*. Vol. 10, No. 6 (September, 1984), 20-21.

Kohl, Cris. "Battle for the *Atlantic*." *Diver Magazine*. Vol. 19, No. 3 (May, 1993), 36-37.

Kohl, Cris. "Beautiful, Tragic *Myron.*" *Diver Magazine.* Vol. 24, No. 8 (Dec., 1998), 25-27.

.... "Dead Captain's Secrets, The *(George A. Marsh).*" *Wreck Diving Magazine.* Premier Issue, February, 2004, 40-47.

.... "*George A. Marsh* Mystery, The." *Diver Magazine.* Vol. 24, Vol. 5 (July-August, 1998), 26-28.

.... "Great Wrecks! Great Lakes!" *Skin Diver Magazine.* Vol. 51, No. 6 (June, 2002), 52-55.

.... "The Steamer *Canisteo.*" *Diver Magazine.* Vol. 24, Vol. 6. (Sept., 1998), 26-28.

Langford, Chy. "Letter to the Editor." *Great Lakes In Depth*, Vol. 2, No. 3 (May-June, 1989). 3.

LaPointe, Paul. "Finding Your Own Wreck." *Dive Canada.* (Sept.-Oct., 1976), 7-8.

Lee, Robert E. "From the Ship's Bridge." *Detroit Historical Society Bulletin.* Vol. XXII, No. 1(Fall, 1965), 15.

.... "The Great Lakes' Only Five-Master." *Detroit Historical Society Bulletin*, Vol. XXVII, No. 7 (May-June, 1971), 18.

.... "'*Tashmoo,*' An Unsinkable Name." *Detroit Historical Society Bulletin.* Vol. XXIV, No. 2 (November, 1967), 12.

Mann, Al. "*Tashmoo's* Second Life in Canada." *Telescope.* Vol. 49, No. 2 (March-April, 2001), 32-35.

Marshall, O. H. "The Building and Voyage of the *Griffon* in 1679." Publications of the Buffalo Historical Society, Vol. 1 (August, 1870): 253-288.

McCutcheon, C. T., Jr. "*Alvin Clark:* An Unfinished Voyage." *Wooden Boat.* No. 52, 52-58.

Miller, John F. "*David Dows,* The." *Telescope.* Vol. 10, No. 3 (March, 1961), 43-45.

Murphy, Rowley. "Ghosts of the Great Lakes." *Inland Seas.* Vol 17, No. 3 (Fall, 1961), 195-201.

O'Brien, J. Michael. "*Tashmoo.*" *Telescope.* Vol. 14, No. 10 (October, 1965), 219-232.

Palmer, Richard F. "'*Success*' on the Lakes." *Telescope.* Vol. 35, No. 6 (November-December, 1986), 150-154.

Peterson, Howard. "The Rescue of the *Cort,* November 30, 1934." *Telescope.* Vol. 37, No. 2 (March-April, 1989), 40-42

Quimby, George I. "The Voyage of the *Griffin*: 1679." *Michigan History*, Vol. 49, No. 2 (June, 1965), 97-107.

Quinn, James L. "Time Capsule at 19 Fathoms." *Museum News.* (March, 1970), 14-19.

Ship-Shore News. Published by Upper Lakes Shipping, Ltd., (May, 1960), 6-7.

Snider, C. H. J. "Further Search for the *Griffon.*" *Ontario History*, Vol. XLVIII, No. 1 (Winter, 1956), 1-6.

.... "In Search of the *Griffon.*" *Ontario History.* Vol. XLIV, No. 1 (January, 1952).

Spectre, Peter H. "The *Alvin Clark:* The Challenge of the Challenge." *Wooden Boat.* No. 52, 59-68.

Swearingen, Richard. "Tonty and the *Griffon.*" *Soundings* (Journal of the Wisconsin Marine Historical Society), Vol. 18, No. 1 (1978), 1-4.

Tappenden, Richard P. "A Possible Solution to The Mystery of the *Griffin.*" *Inland Seas*, Vol. 2, No. 1 (January, 1946), 3-6, 40.

"*Tashmoo*...a Salute to a Lady." *Detroit Marine Historian.* Vol. 19, No. 10 (June, 1966), 1.

Tessendorf, K. C. "Captain Streeter's District of Lake Michigan." *Chicago History.* Vol. 5, No. 3 (Fall, 1976), 152-160.

Toronto Marine Historical Society. "*Minnedosa.*" *The Scanner.* (Vol. 5, No. 4 (Jan., 1973).

Triebe, Richard. "Queen of the Lakes." *Skin Diver Magazine.* Vol. 34, No. 2 (February, 1984), 106.

Ulrich, Barbara. "The *David Dows.*" *Historic Illinois.* Vol. 13, No. 5 (February, 1991), 2-5.

Warnes, Kathy. "Lake Erie's First and Last Great Official Steamer Race." *Inland Seas.* Vol. 48, No. 3 (Fall, 1992), 199-204.

Wilson, Louden. "How Now, *David Dow.*" *Telescope.* Vol. 10, No. 7 (July, 1961), 103-105.

Zillmer, A. T. "The *Erie-Tashmoo* Race." *Inland Seas.* Vol. 8, No. 1 (Spring, 1952), 41-48.

C. Newspapers

Various issues of the following newspapers were utilized:

Algoma (Wisconsin) *Record -Herald*
Alpena (Michigan) *News*
Bay City (Michigan) *Times Tribune*
Belleville (Ontario) *Intelligencer*
Border City (Windsor, Ontario) *Star*
Boston Daily Globe
Boston Herald
Boston Post
British Daily Whig (Kingston, Ontario)
Chatham (Ontario) *Daily News*
Chatham (Ontario) *Daily Planet*
Chatham (Ontario) *Journal*
Chatham (Ontario) *This Week*
Chicago American
Chicago Daily News
Chicago Evening Post
Chicago Free Weekly
Chicago Herald and Examiner
Chicago Inter-Ocean
Chicago Journal
Chicago Tribune
Cleveland Herald
Cleveland Leader

Cleveland News and Herald
Cleveland Plain Dealer
Daily Globe (Ironwood, Michigan)
Daily Oklahoman (Oklahoma City, OK)
Daily Ontario
Democrat Chronicle (Rochester, New York)
Detroit Free Press
Detroit News
Detroit Times
Door County (Wisconsin) *Advocate*
Duluth Evening Herald
Duluth Herald
Duluth News Tribune
Escanaba (Michigan) *Daily Press*
Flint (Michigan) *Journal*
Fond du Lac (Wisconsin) *Daily Reporter*
Grand Rapids Herald
Grand Rapids Press
Green Bay (Wisconsin) *Press Gazette*
Harrah (Oklahoma) *Herald*
Huron Signal (Goderich, Ontario)
Kingston (Ontario) *Whig-Standard*
Labor World (Duluth)

Lapeer (Michigan) *County Press*
London (Ontario) *Free Press*
Manitoulin (Ontario) *Expositor*
Manitoulin (Ontario) *Recorder*
Manitowoc (Wisconsin) *Citizen*
Manitowoc (Wisconsin) *Daily Herald*
Manitowoc (Wisconsin) *Herald-Times*
Manitowoc (Wisconsin) *Tribune*
Marinette (Michigan) *Eagle-Star*
Marquette (MI) *Daily Mining Journal*
Menominee (Michigan) *Herald-Leader*
Milwaukee Journal
Milwaukee Sentinel
Muskegon (Michigan) *Chronicle*
New York Times
New York Tribune
Oklahoma County News
Port Huron Daily Times

Port Huron Times Herald
Saginaw (Michigan) *News*
Sandusky (Ohio) *Register*
Sandusky (Ohio) *Register-Star-News*
Sanilac County (Michigan) *News*
Sarnia (Ontario) *Observer*
Sault Ste. Marie (Michigan) *Evening News*
Sheboygan Press
St. Clair County (Michigan) *Press*
Sturgeon Bay (Door County, WI) *Advocate*
Toledo Blade
Toledo News-Bee
Toronto Evening Telegram
Toronto Globe
Toronto Sun
Whig, The (Kingston, Ontario)
Windsor (Ontario) *Star*
Wisconsin State Journal

D. Miscellaneous

Blackwell, Karen, Branch Assistant, Goderich Public Library. Electronic communication on September 17, 2003.

Burton, Clarence M. "LaSalle and the *Griffon*." Historical Paper Delivered Before the Society of Colonial Wars of the State of Mich., 1902. Detroit: Winn & Hammond, 1903.

Chicago Maritime Society. "The *David Dows,* Map and Historical Profile, Centennial Edition." 1989.

Collections of archival materials available at: Center for Archival Collections, Bowling Green State University, Bowling Green, Ohio (formerly named the Institute for Great Lakes Research); Great Lakes Historical Society, Vermilion, Ohio; Cris Kohl Collection, Great Lakes Shipwrecks and Maritime History; Marine Historical Collection of the Milwaukee Public Library/Wisconsin Marine Historical Society, Milwaukee, Wisconsin; Rutherford B. Hayes Presidential Center, Fremont, Ohio.

Hall, Henry. Report on the Shipbuilding Industry of the United States. 1884.

Hundley, Paul F. "The Griffon Cove Wreck: A Case Study in Archaeological Reconstruction of Timber Hull Remains." Fremantle, Australia: Australian Institute for Maritime Archaeology (Special Publication No. 2), 1984.

Interviews/Communications with: Clive Cussler, Paul Ehorn, Dr. John Halsey, Richard Palmer, Linda Parrish, Doug Pettingill, Steve Radovan, John Steele, Dave Trotter.

Kohl, Cris. "The Importance of the Local Shipping Industry to Community Development in Chatham, Ontario, 1830-1850." Unpublished paper; 26 pages plus appendices; part of Master's degree course work, 1988.

Labadie, Pat. Letter to Cris Kohl, dated January 7, 2004.

Langford, Chy. Letter to Cris Kohl, dated April 23, 1989.

Maitland Cemetery (Goderich, Ont.). Detailed List of Grave Sites & Tombstone Inscriptions.

Marine Review, various issues.

Neave, Tanya, Curator, Chatham-Kent Museum. Letter to Cris Kohl dated Feb. 24, 2003.

Report of the Chief Signal Officer. 44th Congress, 2nd Session, Government Papers. Paper 22: "Recapitulation of disasters on the lakes from July 11, 1875 to June 30, 1876." Pages 372-375.

INDEX

Words in *italics* denote a ship's name.
A number in **bold** denotes a photograph or a drawing on that page.

ABOUT THE AUTHOR

Cris Kohl

PHOTO BY CINDY BURNHAM

CRIS KOHL is a rarity -- a professional Great Lakes Maritime Historian who also happens to be an accomplished scuba diver and a prize-winning land and underwater photographer. A diver for over 30 years, his specialty training includes Shipwreck Diving and Full Cave Diving certifications. He also has three university degrees in English and History, including a Master of Arts degree in History from the University of Windsor, Ontario. Cris Kohl is a popular presenter at major scuba shows and history conferences throughout North America.

Known for his "intense research" and "powerful narration," he has written over 250 magazine and newsletter articles. His work has been published in newspapers like the *Washington Post* and the *Toronto Globe and Mail*, and in magazines such as *Skin Diver, Discover Diving, Immersed, Wreck Diving, Sport Diver, Rodale's Scuba Diving* and Canada's *Diver* and *Cottage Life*, and maritime journals like *Inland Seas*.

He has edited and produced several maritime newsletters over the past 25 years: *Wreck Checker* (newsletter of the Underwater Archaeological Society of Chicago), *Great Lakes in Depth* (the newsletter of Save Ontario Shipwrecks, Windsor chapter), *Western Round-Up* (a newsletter of the Ontario Underwater Council for southwestern Ontario), and the Kent Divers Association newsletter, which won the top award in 1984 for best newsletter from among more than 50 Ontario scuba dive clubs participating.

Cris Kohl has taken part in many Great Lakes shipwreck searches, discoveries, identifications and surveys. He has appeared on numerous television programs, including on the History Channel, the Discovery Channel and Chicago's CBS-2. Currently President of the Underwater Archaeological Society of Chicago, Cris Kohl was inducted into the prestigious Boston Sea Rovers organization in 2004.

He has assembled extensive archives of Great Lakes maritime materials: over 8,000 archival photographs, more than 18,000 underwater images of over 500 Great Lakes shipwrecks which he himself photographed, thousands of books (including hundreds of signed first editions), and 28 filing cabinet drawers laden with research materials, including 5,000 individual file folders on Great Lakes shipwrecks.

He lives near Chicago with his wife, Joan Forsberg, who also has a History degree and researches, writes, edits books and scuba dives on shipwrecks.

Shipwreck Tales of the Great Lakes is Cris Kohl's tenth published book.

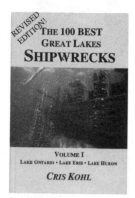
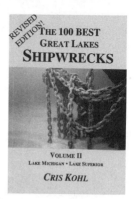

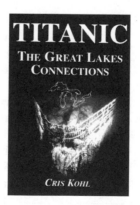
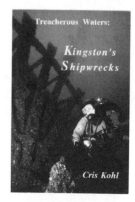